D1260906

Sexual Abuse by Health Professionals

A Personal Search for Meaning and Healing

The author of this book is a psychiatrist, and the survivor of sexual and emotional abuse by her first psychotherapist, also a psychiatrist. Penfold employs two voices in the writing of her book: the first, which starts each chapter, is that of the victim of abuse telling her own story; the second is that of the survivor and professional on her journey towards understanding the meaning of the abuse and how to heal from it. This voyage of discovery includes having a second, very different, experience of therapy; learning the stories of other survivors of abuse by health professionals; reading published accounts of such abuses; making her own story public to both professional and general audiences; becoming a member of a group dedicated to combating sexual abuse by therapists; talking to colleagues with experience in treating victims of abuse by health professionals; culling ideas from the literature; and herself treating patients who are survivors of abuse by health professionals.

Penfold's book is a powerful blend of the personal and the professional that penetrates the 'conspiracy of silence' that still holds sway and prevents victims from getting the compassion, understanding, support, and financial and legal aid that they deserve.

P. SUSAN PENFOLD is a professor in the Department of Psychiatry, University of British Columbia.

Sexual Abuse by Health Professionals

A Personal Search for Meaning and Healing

P. SUSAN PENFOLD

UNIVERSITY OF TORONTO PRESS
Toronto   Buffalo   London

© University of Toronto Press Incorporated 1998
Toronto Buffalo London
Printed in Canada

ISBN 0-8020-4269-4 (cloth)
ISBN 0-8020-8106-1 (paper)

Printed on acid-free paper

Canadian Cataloguing in Publication Data

Penfold, P. Susan
Sexual abuse by health professionals: a personal search for meaning
and healing

Includes bibliographical references.
ISBN 0-8020-4269-4 (bound) ISBN 0-8020-8106-1 (pbk.)

1. Penfold, P. Susan. 2. Sexually abused patients. 3. Medical personnel –
Sexual behavior. 4. Sexually abused patients – Canada – Biography.
5. Sexual abuse vicitims – Canada – Biography. I. Title.

RC560.S44P46 1998   3672.83'9 C97-932782-2

University of Toronto Press acknowledges the financial assistance to its
publishing program of the Canada Council for the Arts and the Ontario
Arts Council.

THE HIPPOCRATIC OATH

Into whatever houses I enter I will go into them for the benefit of the sick and will abstain from every voluntary act of mischief and corruption, and further from the seduction of females or males, of freemen and slaves.

Attributed to Greek physician Hippocrates, fourth century B.C.

We feel that when sexual seduction of patients can be firmly established by due legal process, regardless of whether the seduction was initiated by the patient or the therapist, the therapist should initially be sued for rape rather than for malpractice, i.e., the legal process should be criminal rather than civil. Few psychotherapists would be willing to appear in court on behalf of a colleague and testify that the sexually dysfunctional patient's facility for decision making could be considered normally objective when he or she accepts sexual submission after developing extreme emotional dependence on the therapist.

William Masters and Virginia Johnson,
'Principles of the New Sex Therapy,' 1976

Contents

ACKNOWLEDGMENTS   ix

Introduction   3

1 Vulnerability and Risk Factors   26

2 Initiation   45

3 Entrapment   64

4 Escape   88

5 After-effects   106

6 Healing   132

7 Breaking the Silence   153

8 Towards Less Abuse and More Healing   180

Epilogue   199

NOTES   201

REFERENCES   219

INDEX   229

Acknowledgments

The impetus for this book comes from victims of sexual abuse by health professionals. Their pain and suffering, their incredible courage, their struggles to transcend the terrible damage inflicted on them are largely invisible, hidden by the shame and stigma unfairly attached to victims rather than perpetrators. In chronicling my story, which reflects so many other untold stories, I hope to promote understanding and compassion for survivors of this and other kinds of abuses.

In addition to thanking the survivors who have shared their experiences with me, there are many others – friends, colleagues, and relatives – who have given advice, support, and encouragement. My women's group in the 1970s – Marie Campbell, Alison Griffith, Susie Innes, Ingrid Pacey, Joann Robertson, and Gillian Walker – heard my first disclosure about Dr A, and encouraged me to confront him. Author Lisa Hobbs-Birnie has repeatedly heard about my wish to understand, analyse, and write about my experiences in a constructive way. It was Lisa who suggested the use of two voices.

My therapist from 1984 to 1986 was Dr Naida Hyde. Her warmth, patience, and unflagging clear focus allowed me to understand how thoroughly I had been exploited by Dr A, and paved the way for this book. Credit for my decision to write a letter of complaint about Dr A is due to the Therapist Abuse Action Group (TAAG) network. The Canadian Health Alliance to Stop Therapist Exploitation Now (CHASTEN) in Toronto, in particular Temi Firsten, Cheryl Rowe, and Jeri Wine, have also been a source of inspiration and support.

I am grateful to the readers of the first draft of the manuscript – Lisa Hobbs-Birnie, Kate Parfitt, Mary Jane Frith, and an anonymous survivor. Harvey Armstrong and another reviewer for University of Toronto Press provided helpful feedback and suggestions. Gary Schoener and Laura Brown responded promptly to requests for information and help. Heather Jahrig contributed by collecting and recording some survivors' experiences. Margo Lane, librarian with the University of British Columbia Department of Psychiatry, helped with literature searches, and Mary Jane Frith and Francesca Wilson with word processing. Virgil Duff and the editorial staff of University of Toronto Press have aided with the publication process.

Finally, I would like to acknowledge my parents, Bertha and John Penfold, who always did what they thought was best for me and tolerated some difficult behaviour at times. Similarly, my children – Paul, Mary, and Robert – who are a constant source of love and support, also suffered some of the effects of Dr A's exploitation. My husband, Keith, is a steadfast provider of energy and optimism.

Sexual Abuse by Health Professionals

Introduction

On 20 September 1994 I found an unexpected message on my voice mail. It was from Pat, a lawyer with a state attorney general's department, who told me that Dr A's lawyers wanted to take a deposition from me. My heart began to pound. I felt nauseated and dizzy, replaying the message several times before I was able to grasp the content. I tried to return Pat's call, but could not reach her. For the rest of the afternoon, trying to focus on my work, I felt shaky and scared.

Over time I had come to recognize that my confrontation of Dr A in his office years earlier had done nothing to protect other women or to cause sanctions to be brought against him. In November 1991, urged on by several colleagues and a survivors' group, I had written to the Board of Medical Examiners in the state in which Dr A practises. A couple of months later, I was called by an investigator who said that there were two complaints and that she planned to conduct further investigations.

Later in 1992 I spoke to an attorney who said that both complaints were 'old' and unlikely to be pursued by the board, who, he said, were more interested in protecting the public from abuses revealed in more recent complaints. Dr A's response to the two allegations had been one of indignation; he said that he had helped us both a great deal, that we were ungrateful, that the allegations were fantasies. While the attorney commented that this was the usual response from accused physicians, I felt confused and hurt. Somehow I had always believed Dr A's comments, when I confronted him about the abuse, that I was special, the only patient he had ever had sex with. Yet he was a liar, and he was lying again when he denied the abuse. I had credited him with *enough integrity to admit his abuse of me if it ever came out. Was there nothing positive about this man, who had once been like a god to me?*

So, in the intervening two years, I had assumed that the matter had been dropped. As I heard more and more accounts of protracted court cases and inquiry processes, and of the array of strategies used by defence lawyers to discredit, shame, and humiliate complainants, I felt relieved that I had escaped such a potentially devastating experience. But then, listening to Pat's message, I felt frightened, scared of the inquiry process, and terrified of falling back into that spooky childhood world where I felt totally controlled by Dr A, felt that he was playing with me, tormenting me, as a cat would torment a mouse. Powerless, I felt like a puppet, and he pulled the strings.

Later that evening I talked with my daughter, who was supportive, and my husband, who agreed to accompany me to the discovery. I felt embarrassed, ashamed – 'What do they really think? How could I have become involved, how could I have allowed myself to be so duped and used? I was so blind, so needy. I kept going back for more, kept getting hurt again and again. I put up with his blame and rejections. I saw it as mutual, felt I loved him above everything, felt he cared about me, felt I was special, ignored all the clues, gave him unlimited power, idolized him, felt afraid to challenge him, complied, did what he told me to do. How could I have?' Feeling that they did not, could not, comprehend, and that I could never share some of the most painful and shameful feelings, I found myself struggling with the old feelings of wanting to put up walls, pull up the drawbridge, and distance myself from human contact, thinking that no one could understand the pain, the fears, the craziness of the six years that I was Dr A's patient.

In bed, waiting in vain for sleep, I saw scene after scene of those painful years. Remembering how desperately attached to him I felt, remembering how I felt like a tiny child needing a parent, recalling how I was so overcome with painful feelings that I was unable to talk to him, yet was sad and lost when I had to leave his office. Convinced that I had some serious mental problem, I felt that he, and only he, held the answer to my problems in his hands. He was my saviour, my rescuer, the only person who could possibly rescue someone like me from the stormy maelstrom of my convoluted emotional problems. Although I felt like a very small child, and had fantasies of being his infant daughter who brought him slippers and a pipe and clambered on his knee, Dr A repeatedly suggested that I was so constricted because I was holding back adult sexual feelings for him.

Astonished by this interpretation, because my feelings and fantasies seemed so childlike, I nonetheless accepted his convictions and actively tried to satisfy him by having sexual fantasies about him. During this time, however, I was bombarded by fragments of memories of being molested by my godfather, a doctor. Eventually, the relationship with Dr A became sexual, and somewhat later was defined as 'mutual,' although it was actually startlingly unequal. I was still travelling three hours each way to see him, the meetings were in his office, at his convenience, and, some of the time, I was still paying him! 'Mutual,' for him, appeared to mean that he was telling me about some of his difficulties with his wife and his job situation.

Although, during the first year, Dr A had appeared to be kind, warm, gentle, understanding, and supportive, his behaviour changed after the relationship became sexual. At times, appearing to regret the sexual involvement, he would blame me for being seductive and would become distant and disapproving. At other times, warm and supportive again, he would claim, 'You have found yourself through your love of me,' and, 'This relationship has helped you get over your fear of men.' A few sessions later he would castigate me for being a 'bottomless pit' and suggest that I needed to 'leave the nest.' I ricocheted between feeling special and cared for and feeling rejected because I was bad and seductive. Still feeling that my very life depended on seeing Dr A and finding the answer to my problems, I would beg and plead with him to continue to see me. If Dr A was negative, disapproving, and blaming, I felt terrible and found it hard to cope with my job and my life at home with my husband and young children. Sometimes, regretfully, I took out my anger towards Dr A on my husband.

Gradually, I became more able to compartmentalize what was happening to me with Dr A from my life in general. Increasingly, I enjoyed my family, and began to feel effective in my work. Intervals between visits lengthened to two or three months, and Dr A directed me to work on termination. Although I was coping more effectively, and weaning myself away from Dr A, I was at the same time paying a price. At some level, I felt that I was a failure at therapy, and that I was still far too attached to Dr A and reluctant to leave. But, determined to overcome those feelings, I pushed them away and spent several years unable to sleep without the help of Valium and often a nightcap as well. At the time, I was convinced that Dr A was a wonderful therapist who had helped me a great deal, but that I, still tending to be moody, tense, and anxious, had for some reason been unable to utilize the therapy properly.

As I lay in bed worrying about the prospect of the deposition process and inquiry hearing, I found myself returning to the state of mind where I took on all or much of the responsibility for what had happened. 'He wasn't so bad,' I told myself. 'He was trying, but he was out of his depth. He tried to help me, but he got caught up in my feelings about my godfather.' 'I was seductive; it really was all my fault.' 'But,' I argued, 'Why doesn't he admit it? Why did he tell me that I was the only patient he had ever had sex with? Why did he blame it on me, tell me I was so powerful and compelling, when there were others?'

Gradually I realized that I was trying to give myself some excuse to avoid the pain and humiliation of baring some of my most personal and distressing memories, being interrogated and shamed by lawyers, and, perhaps worst of all, seeing Dr A again. The next morning, I called Pat and agreed to make a deposition.

This book is written in two voices. Both are mine. One is the voice of a woman, sexually abused as a child, who was then sexually and emotionally abused while a psychiatric patient. The second is that of the woman psychiatrist who is trying to discover the meaning of her own abuse and how to heal from it. This voyage of discovery has included having another, and very different, experience of therapy; listening to the stories of other survivors of abuse by health professionals; telling my story to professional and public audiences; being a member of a group dedicated to combatting sexual abuse by therapists; reading books and articles; talking to colleagues who have treated victims of abuse by physicians and therapists; and having a few patients who are themselves survivors of abuse by health professionals.

In each chapter I give some details of my own experiences, then reflect on these as well as on the experiences of other victims. In some cases I use examples from already published accounts; otherwise, the descriptions are altered to protect the identity of people who continue to be muzzled by the conspiracy of silence that surrounds this topic, but who have, over the years, shared their experiences with me.[1] (When they first appear, pseudonyms are enclosed in quotation marks.) I conclude each chapter with a description of the books, articles, and studies from the professional literature that have helped me make sense of my experiences and the experiences of other survivors.

Sexual Exploitation of Patients by Health Professionals: The Problem

The first major survey of physicians' sexual involvement with patients was reported in 1973 by Sheldon Kardener and colleagues. They sent an anonymous questionnaire to a random sample of 1,000 male physicians – general practitioners, surgeons, internists, obstetrician-gynaecologists and psychiatrists – in California. Of the 460 physicians who responded, between 5 and 13 per cent reported that they had engaged in erotic behaviour with patients, and between 5 and 7.2 per cent had had sexual intercourse with patients. Although 87 per cent of the respondents deemed erotic practices inappropriate and never of benefit to patients, 13 per cent suggested that such behaviour could help patients, for instance, by illuminating areas of sexual blocking, helping resolve sexual maladjustments, making middle-aged women feel more desirable, and facilitating the process of therapy.[2] Several years later, a random sample of U.S. women physicians reported no sexual intercourse with patients, although half of them believed that non-erotic contact, such as a hug or hand holding, was sometimes appropriate. Two per cent of these women physicians believed that erotic touching could sometimes be helpful.[3]

A study of U.S. psychologists, using the same questionnaire, was reported in 1977. Sexual intercourse with patients was reported by 5.5 per cent of male and 0.6 per cent of female licensed psychologists with doctoral degrees. An additional 2.6 per cent of males and 0.3 per cent of females reported having sexual intercourse with patients within three months of the termination of therapy. About half of the respondents believed that non-erotic contact could be helpful, at least occasionally. Erotic contact with patients was described by 10.9 per cent of males and 1.9 per cent of female psychologists, who felt that benefits for the patient included treatment of sexual problems, promotion of personality growth, and the development of mutual positive regard.[4] Despite the publication of these articles in major journals, and a charge that sexual involvement with patients is a form of rape,[5] the professions paid little or no attention to these findings.

In the early 1980s a group of women psychiatrists, concerned about the extent of psychiatrist–patient sexual involvement and its detrimental impact on patients, designed a study and applied to the American Psychiatric Association for funding. Turned down by the APA and other sources of support for psychiatric research, they eventually managed to fund the project with private donations. In their nationwide survey of 1,442 U.S. psychiatrists, 7.1 per cent of the male and 3.1 per cent of the female respondents admitted sexual involvement with their own patients. Of those, 31 per cent admitted to sexual contact during treatment sessions or concurrent with therapy, and 69 per cent stated that sexual involvement began after termination. All the psychiatrists who had sexual contact with more than one patient were male, and 88 per cent of the involvement was between male psychiatrists and female patients. Male psychiatrist–male patient sexual involvement accounted for 7 per cent, female psychiatrist–male patient for 3.5 per cent, and female psychiatrist–female patient for 1.4 per cent.[6]

Most of the respondents who described sexual contact with patients acknowledged that they had become sexually involved with patients for their own sexual or emotional gratification. They also believed that the patients experienced the sexual involvement as caring or helpful. The researchers pointed out that these opinions contrasted sharply with the reports of psychiatrist respondents (1.6 per cent) who had been sexually involved with their own therapist. The majority of these psychiatrists rated this experience as exploitative and harmful.

In the same survey of psychiatrists, 65 per cent said they had treated patients who had been sexually involved with their previous therapists. Although they felt that 87 per cent of those patients had been harmed, the respondents reported the sexual abuse in only 8 per cent of the cases, citing reasons such as a desire to protect a colleague's reputation, patient confidentiality, and fear of retaliation by the accused psychiatrist. A distressing finding reported by the researchers was that offenders were more likely than non-offenders to have treated patients who had previously been sexually involved with therapists. This, the researchers postulated, suggested that therapists who sexually abuse their patients might then refer them to colleagues who are sympathetic or might even be offenders themselves, thus exposing the patients to the risk of further mistreatment.[7]

In a 1986 mail survey of U.S. psychologists in private practice, 9.4 per cent of males and 2.5 per cent of females acknowledged sexual contact with clients.[8] A survey of U.S. social workers conducted in 1984 indicated that 3.8 per cent of male social workers had had erotic contact with clients.[9] The abuse of hospitalized psychiatric patients by staff and the use of chronically mentally ill people for 'quickie' sex were felt to be extensive, but hard to document.[10]

With a few exceptions, professional concern about these findings has been minimal until recent years, when a mounting public outcry, court cases, documentaries, magazine articles, books written by survivors, and pressure from consumer groups have forced professional organizations and licensing bodies to form task forces and committees and to re-issue statements of professional ethics. At the same time, a 'backlash' can be discerned, which argues that patients' accounts of sexual contact are fabricated, that time-honoured patterns of practice are being disrupted, and that, in general, mountains are being made out of molehills. Canadian studies have been conducted in the 1990s. During the work of the Task Force on Sexual Abuse of Patients, commissioned by the College of Physicians and Surgeons of Ontario in 1991, a *Canada Health Monitor* study was requested. The *Canada Health Monitor* is a semi-annual national telephone survey addressing issues such as health status, service utilization, health promotion, and health policy. The survey of 549 Ontario women revealed that 7 per cent felt they had been subjected to inappropriate sexual comments about their body, underclothes, sexual performance, or choice of sexual partner, or had been watched dressing or undressing by their physician. Two per cent reported sexual touching, sexual contact, or sexual activity with their doctor. The results indicated that women were more likely to disclose such episodes if they were university graduates, were between 25 and 44 years of age, or were questioned by a female interviewer. For instance, among university-educated women, 15 per cent responded in the affirmative with respect to either or both of the categories described, with 12 per cent reporting inappropriate sexual comments or being watched, and 4 per cent disclosing sexual contact, sexual touching, or sexual activity with their physician.[11]

A survey of British Columbia physicians conducted by the Committee on Physician Sexual Misconduct of the BC College of Physicians and Surgeons achieved a response rate of more than 72 per cent. Sexual contact with a patient was reported by 3.5 per cent of respondents, and sexual involvement with an ex-patient was acknowledged by 7.3 per cent. A random sampling of 8,000 members of the public generated 2,456 responses. Of the respondents, 0.7 per cent reported sexual activity with a current physician, 0.3 per cent described sexual involvement with a former physician, 4.1 per cent believed they had been touched in a sexual manner, and 5.5 per cent had been upset by sexual remarks.[12]

A 1992 survey of members of the Society of Obstetricians and Gynaecologists of Canada also had a high response rate, of 78 per cent. Sexual involvement with a patient was reported by 3 per cent of male and 1 per cent of female respondents.[13]

Other health professionals lack the detailed incidence studies done among mental health professionals and physicians, but their literature documents similar concerns.[14] Although most of the major studies have been conducted in North America, similar concerns exist in other countries such as the United Kingdom and Australia.[15] The assumption that sexually exploitative health professionals are poorly trained, unskilled practitioners who have little understanding of their own personalities is belied by studies which demonstrate that offenders are more likely to have completed formal training and examinations and to have undergone personal training or psychoanalysis.[16] Neither do power, prestige, or prominence safeguard the professional. Describing abusive therapists, Pope comments, 'Unfortunately, therapists found to have sexually exploited their patients have served in capacities such as president of state professional associations, chair of state ethics committees, member of state licensing boards, university professor, prominent media psychologist, nationally known researcher, and so on.[17]

Special or minority populations may struggle with a variety of issues. For instance, health professionals living in very small, isolated communities argue that everyone in the community is a potential patient. They suggest that one brief contact, such as an assessment for a sprained ankle, should not put the patient out of bounds as a possible sexual partner. Despite concerns emanating, in particular, from more sparsely populated areas of British Columbia, the college committee recommended an absolute prohibition of sexual relationships between physicians and current patients. They recommended, further, that sexual relations between a physician and a former patient should be considered unethical if the patient had been in psychotherapy with the physician, was under 19 when the physician–patient relationship ended, or suffered from a disorder that could impair judgment or decision making.[18]

Although self-report surveys of health professionals indicate a fairly low incidence of female–female sexual contact, there are indications that this is a more widespread phenomenon. Schoener and associates at the Minneapolis Walk-In Counselling Center, pioneers in the study of sexual abuse by therapists, report that female–female sexual involvement comprises 20–25 per cent of their cases. A sizable number of these women professionals are not identified as lesbians or bisexual and 'are bewildered about how this has happened and what it means.'[19] Even though some of these exploitative women therapists are not lesbians, both Brown and Gartrell consider abuse by therapists to be a serious problem for the lesbian community.[20]

Sexual Exploitation of Patients by Health Professionals: The Process

A certain progression is evident in the accounts of many victims. The victim, who is seeking help for a disorder or problem, may have some vulnerability in addition to being in a patient or client role. The professional, too, may be going through a life crisis or emotional difficulty that seriously impairs his or her judgment.

The mystique and authority of the role of physician or therapist creates a situation in which the patient is likely to attribute special healing powers to the professional and will comply with directions, advice, and suggestions. Once the treatment begins, the health professional, particularly when counselling or therapy is taking place, comes to have a parentlike importance to the patient or client, who feels like a young child and readily complies with advice and suggestions. In relationships in which professionals begin to abdicate their responsibility to act only in the patient's best interests, they gradually begin to reframe or reshape the relationship in a way that allows them to meet their own, rather than the patient's, needs.

Whereas some clients or patients quickly perceive that they are being treated inappropriately and leave the scene, others get trapped and may stay in exploitative or abusive relationships for many years. For a time, entangled victims may feel wonderful, viewing themselves as special and feeling profoundly nurtured and cared for, but what is really happening is quite different. The professionals' manipulations, the mystique and power imbalance of the professional–patient relationship, and any vulnerability or fragility that victims bring combine to keep the victims in an emotionally crippling situation that undermines their mental health and stultifies their emotional growth. In addition, they are not working on the problems or difficulties that took them to the professional in the first place.

In many cases the relationships are ended by the professionals; in others the victims gradually realize that they are being duped and used. Often this happens when the victim realizes that he or she is not the only patient having a sexual relationship with the professional. Sometimes victims, as a result of life circumstances or interactions with others, realize that the relationship is damaging and that they must leave it. Terminating the relationship rarely ends the victims' problems. Often they are left with more difficulties and distress than they started with. The after-effects of sexual abuse by a professional can be extreme, and many victims suffer post-traumatic stress disorder. In addition to the emotional problems created by sexual abuse, many victims suffer crushing losses such as divorce, loss of custody of their children, loss of employment, and impaired physical health. A few have been driven to suicide, and some have needed psychiatric hospitalization.

Even when the victim has escaped from the abusive relationship, many other obstacles remain. Not least is the lack of community support. Unlike victims of childhood sexual abuse, these adult victims are mired in shame and blame. The public thinks that they should have known better and views them as merely having had affairs with the health professionals. The victims themselves often echo these sentiments and, deeply ashamed, are not able to share their humiliation with friends and relatives. Ironically, too, those who courageously come forward and make public complaints are sometimes assumed to be vindictive fortune-hunters who are besmirching the reputation of innocent professionals.

Victims of sexual abuse by professionals are usually left with massive difficulties with respect to trust, and are reluctant or unable to seek further health care or therapy. When they do seek therapy, to try to understand and heal from the damage done to them, yet another hurdle – that of finding an appropriate and knowledgable therapist – stands in their way. Healing from sexual abuse by a professional, an abuse that can be likened to rape of the soul as well as of the body, can take many years. Transcending the self-blame and shame is of utmost importance, and progress towards this goal can be accelerated by support from loved ones and contact with other victims.

These generalizations do not apply to all victims. Each of us is different. Already a professional with a career at the time of my abuse, able to continue my employment, already a mother of children, I am obviously far more fortunate than many victims whose chances of steady employment, reasonable finances, marriage, and children are jeopardized, if not thoroughly decimated, by their abuse.

I hope this book will answer some of the questions people have asked me over the past ten years, since I started to talk about my own abuse. These questions include:

'How could a woman like you allow it to happen?'
'Didn't you realize that there was something wrong?'

'Why didn't you just walk out?'
'Why did you go for such a long time?'
'Wasn't it just an affair, given that both of you were adults?'
'Weren't there a lot of helpful things about it?'
'Maybe you learned to trust men more?'
'When did you begin to realize that it was harming you?'
'How did you get out of the relationship?'
'How can you start to heal?'
'How can people disclose without ruining their career/marriage/relationship with their friends and children?'
'How can you trust another therapist?'
'How can you find another therapist?'
'Why did it take you so long to report it?'
'Does making a complaint to a licensing authority help?'
'Does a civil suit help?'
'What can we do to stop the abuse?'
'Why don't people believe victims?'
'Why don't the professionals themselves do more and care more about it?'
'Why do insurance companies continue to cover sexually abusive professionals?'

Although I am not silenced by a gag order, I have chosen not to name my abuser. Revenge is not my motive. What I hope to achieve is greater understanding, by professionals and the general public, of this widespread abuse, which is cloaked by the professions' conspiracy of silence and the victims' shame and self-blame. I have arbitrarily chosen the pseudonym 'Dr A' to distinguish my abuser from Carolyn Bates's 'Dr X,'[21] and have termed two other abusive therapists, who later enter my story, 'Dr Y' and 'Dr Z.'

Because the majority of abusive health professionals are men, and the majority of victims are women, I will, except where otherwise specified, refer to the health professional as 'he' and the victim or survivor as 'she.' The terms 'victim' and 'survivor' are used interchangeably. As I am a psychiatrist, and as much of the literature about sexual abuse by health professionals focuses on therapy and mental health professionals, this area will seem to receive unequal weight. I believe, however, that the damage done and the after-effects sustained are similar for victims of any type of health professional.

Recognition of the Psychological Effects of Trauma

Over the past hundred years, recognition and understanding of the impact of trauma on victims have waxed and waned. At times, focus on the individual, and diagnosis in medical or psychiatric terms, have thoroughly eclipsed or at least minimized the role of underlying trauma. Suggesting that society's response to atrocities is to banish them from consciousness, Herman believes that social or political impetus is necessary to keep alive the knowledge of trauma and its devastating effects.[22]

In late nineteenth-century France, a new bourgeois elite evolved with a commitment to replace religious concepts with more progressive scientific ideas. Although Charcot is usually credited as the originator of modern ideas about hysteria, he was preceded by Briquet,[23] who supplanted earlier beliefs that hysteria was a disease of the uterus and pinpointed its origin in emotional suffering. Working in the Salpêtrière, an asylum for the destitute and insane, Charcot studied loss of memory, convulsions, paralysis, and loss of sensation in a group of young women who had sought refuge there. He was able to demonstrate the emotional origin of these conditions, as they could be artificially induced and stopped by means of hypnosis.[24]

This view, that psychological trauma causes hysteria, was embraced by Freud, Breuer,[25] and Janet,[26] who discovered that hysterical symptoms could be alleviated by helping the patient recall the trauma and describe the intense feelings accompanying the memory. Initially Freud believed that hysteria was caused by childhood sexual abuse. But later, faced by the negative reactions of his contemporaries, he retracted his theory and attributed the scenes of seduction described by his analytic patients to internal fantasies.[27]

After this, psychoanalytic theory, which attributed psychological symptoms to inner drives and conflicts, held sway until the First World War. At first attributed to physical causes, 'shell shock' was later acknowledged by military psychiatrists to be a psychological condition resembling hysteria in women, caused by prolonged exposure to the violence and devastation of the battlefield. The conviction that men suffering from combat neurosis must be morally deficient[28] led to treatment strategies based on punishment, shaming, and threats. Humane treatment, based on the assumption that 'combat neurosis' was a genuine psychiatric condition, was advocated by more progressive physicians.

Between the world wars, medical interest in psychological trauma faded once more, although the back wards of veterans' hospitals contained many men with long-lasting psychiatric disabilities. Interest in combat neurosis was rapidly revived in the Second World War, when military physicians strove to normalize psychological reactions to combat, pointing out that 200 to 240 days in battle would break even the strongest soldier.[29] As with earlier work on hysteria, treatment strategies focused on recalling and reliving traumatic memories with the help of hypnosis or sodium amobarbital. Men were quickly returned to active duty, and the question of any ongoing ill effects was ignored. But some soldiers did suffer long-term effects, a 'traumatic neurosis' which, according to Kardiner, consisted of personality constriction, explosive outbursts, unusual dreams, preoccupation with combat trauma, and an exaggerated startle response.[30]

After the Vietnam war, massive political pressure from veterans' organizations led to increased recognition and study of the long-term psychological effects of combat exposure. Post-traumatic stress disorder (PTSD) became a formal diagnosis in 1980,[31] and psychological treatment programs for veterans were initiated. At the same time, it was recognized that the concept of PTSD had a much wider application. Starting in the early 1970s, the Women's Movement began to expose the widespread violence against women and children, and it became clear that the psychological effects of incest, child abuse, rape, and woman battering are similar to those seen in combat survivors.

With its symptoms of intrusive recollections, emotional numbing, and increased arousal, PTSD is caused by an extreme precipitating event or experience such as earthquake, fire, flood, severe motor vehicle accident, rape, violent assault, torture, terrorist attack, or incarceration in a concentration camp. The person's initial response is of intense fear, horror, or helplessness. In some cases, the onset of PTSD is immediate or shortly after the trauma. In others, it appears months or even years later.

Health professionals' responses to claims that pervasive violence, largely male violence, causes PTSD and other psychiatric disorders have been mixed. Ross attributes the majority of psychiatric disorders, including schizophrenia, to chronic childhood trauma.[32] Other writers and researchers, accenting the physical symptoms, identity problems, and amnesia that appear to stem from trauma, have suggested a 'dissociative spectrum' or 'traumatic spectrum' of disorders that includes PTSD, borderline personality disorder, dissociative disorders,[33] and, sometimes, somatization disorders. These replace the old concept of hysteria.[34] There is also a sizable body of literature alleging that all or most memories of childhood sexual abuse recovered during therapy are false, being manufactured by the therapist.[35] Clients of these 'poorly trained, overzealous or ideologically driven psychotherapists,'[36] claim Ofshe and Watters, may be led to believe that they were abused by a satanic cult or that they harbour multiple personalities.

Some Basic Definitions

Health Professional

A health professional is a person who has completed training at a university or college and has a licence to practice or is registered with a professional organization or licensing body. Health professionals include physicians, dentists, nurses, social workers, psychologists, physiotherapists, occupational therapists, chiropractors, naturopaths, massage therapists, nutritionists, and medical and dental technicians and assistants. They do not include people without formal training who may set themselves up as 'therapists' or 'counsellors' in the community.

Health professionals' organizations and licensing bodies have codes of ethics that forbid sexual exploitation of patients. The health professional–patient relationship is expected to be a fiduciary relationship.

Mental Health Professional

Mental health professionals are a subgroup of health professionals. The major professions are psychiatry, psychology, and social work, although there are other types of mental health professionals as well, such as licensed marriage and family counsellors, art therapists, and music therapists. Most of the studies and much of the literature that refers to sexual abuse of patients or clients focuses on mental health professionals. Sometimes pastoral counsellors and ministers are included, but this book will not deal with them.

Psychiatrists are physicians who have taken at least three or four years' additional training to develop 'sound clinical judgement and a high order of knowledge about the diagnosis, treatment and prevention of all psychiatric disorders and the common medical and neurological disorders which relate to the practice of psychiatry.'[37] They are able to prescribe medication and sign people into hospital, if needed, against their will.

Psychologists, whose work overlaps that of psychiatrists, have at least seven years of post-secondary education, with graduate degrees (Master's or PhD) in psychology. They 'provide services that may prevent the development of serious illnesses, or promote the building of attitudes and behaviour conducive to healthy lives, or contribute to renewed health for those troubled by psychological problems,' including psychotherapy, counselling, treatment of addictions, stress reduction, and pain reduction.[38]

Social workers, who may have undergraduate (BSW) or graduate (MSW, DSW) degrees are 'involved in direct practice, community development and administration in a wide range of health and social services' and are 'committed to provide professional services which: improve the problem-solving and coping capacities of people; help people better use resources in their environment; and effect changes in society towards the goal of social justice for all.'[39]

Fiduciary Relationship

A fiduciary relationship is one in which a person with particular knowledge and abilities accepts the trust and confidence of another to act in that person's best interests.[40]

Boundaries

The health professional–patient relationship is a fiduciary relationship. Each health profession has a set of professional standards, ethical codes, and administrative guidelines that dictate the boundaries within which the professional should practise.[41] Psychotherapists sometimes conceptualize boundaries as a therapeutic frame. This frame, thought of as an envelope or membrane surrounding the therapeutic role, defines, and holds constant, the elements of the therapeutic relationship. These characteristics include the office setting, the regular scheduling of appointments, the duration of the appointment, fee payment, and the dress and conduct of therapist and patient.[42]

Boundary Violations

A boundary violation occurs when the professional does something that is not customary in the health professional–patient relationship, and that may be contrary to the profession's standards of care or code of ethics.[43] Boundary violations include using the patient for business purposes, borrowing money from the patient, trying to develop a friendship with the patient, asking the patient for personal favours, giving or receiving substantial gifts, making sexual innuendos, and using the patient for sexual purposes.

Sexual Exploitation by Health Professionals

Many terms are used to describe this inappropriate and unethical behaviour. They include sexual abuse, sexual exploitation, sexual impropriety, sexual transgression, sexual violation, and sexual misconduct. The College of Physicians and Surgeons of Ontario has defined two levels, proposing different penalties for each level:

- Sexual impropriety: includes any behaviour such as expressions, gestures, or touching that is sexually demeaning to a patient or demonstrates a lack of respect for the person's privacy.
- Sexual violation: refers to sex between patient and physician, regardless of who initiates it, including but not limited to sexual intercourse, genital–genital contact, oral–genital contact, oral–anal contact, and genital–anal contact.[45]

Another important dimension is the length of time that the exploitative relationship lasts. The longer the relationship, the more likely it is to imply some kind of meaningful romantic relationship between the health professional and the patient. Thus, long-term sexual violation is likely to be the most damaging. But, on the other hand, a one-time sexual impropriety can be extremely distressing and upsetting to a patient and gravely shake or even totally eliminate her trust in helping professionals.

Psychotherapy

Often abbreviated to 'therapy,' originally called the 'talking cure,' psychotherapy embraces a variety of verbal treatment techniques. Psychotherapy provides support, understanding, new information, and new experiences that can produce learning, increase the range of possible behaviours available to the patient, alleviate symptoms, and alter unhealthy and maladaptive patterns of behaviour.[46]

Transference

Transference arises from a tendency to exclude new information, cling to what is familiar, and see the past in the present. Childhood experiences, which may be forgotten, are powerful influences on current attitudes and behaviour. But later life experiences can be important too, such as suffering a sexual assault or enjoying a rewarding relationship with a spouse. Describing the transference, Freud said, 'The patient produces before us with plastic clarity an important part of his life history, of which he could otherwise have given us only an unsatisfactory account.'[47] In other words, the patient re-enacts, with associated feelings, past relationships as if they were occurring in the present with the therapist.

The interaction between a health professional and a patient seeking help has some parallels with that between a parent and a child. The patient is in a trusting, vulnerable, childlike position, and the health professional is a parent-surrogate. In this situation, the patient displaces onto the health professional feelings that she had, as a child, about parents or other significant figures. For instance, if she was frightened of a parent figure, she may feel frightened of, or intimidated by, the professional. If she was sexually abused by a parent, she may develop sexual feelings for the professional or believe that the treatment situation will inevitably become sexualized.

In cases of therapist–patient sexual exploitation, malpractice charges are often based on allegations of distortion or mishandling of the patient's transference.[48] As the patient is in a childlike position, and the therapist or health professional is a parent-surrogate, a sexual relationship resembles incest.

Transference, this tendency to displace feelings about parents or other consequential relationships or experiences, occurs in other areas of the person's life as well, particularly in close relationships and with people who are in authority.

Countertransference

Countertransference refers to the feelings stirred up in the health professional by the patient. These emotions relate to the patient's attitude, appearance, personality, and behaviour, and are also influenced by the health professional's own past life experiences.

The professional's countertransference is increased by life stresses and unresolved emotional conflicts. Countertransference can lead to inappropriate over-involvement with patients, or unhelpful negative reactions. For instance, patients may remind health professionals of their own traumatic experiences as children, or of hated parents or ex-spouses. While all health professionals can benefit from recognizing how their personal issues impact on patient care, this is particularly important for those engaged in counselling.

Post-traumatic Stress Disorder

The diagnosis of post-traumatic stress disorders (PTSD) was first formulated in 1980 for the third edition of the American Psychiatric Association's *Diagnostic and Statistical Manual* (*DSM III*). Before this, as described earlier, with the exception of studies of battlefield trauma, the effect of severe trauma on people's lives was not well recognized and was often attributed to the person's internal conflicts. The current manual, *DSM IV*, is widely used throughout North America, Europe, and other parts of the world in health and mental health settings. The manual describes the 'diagnostic criteria' for PTSD. There are six criteria that must be present for a person to be diagnosed with PTSD. In brief:

1 The person is exposed to a severe trauma which is beyond the range of usual human experience, and the response involves intense helplessness, fear, or horror.
2 The person repeatedly re-experiences the trauma in the form of intrusive memories, flashbacks, dreams, or distress in response to reminders of the traumatic event.
3 The person has numbed emotions, constricts his or her activities, and avoids involvement with others and the outside world.
4 The person's nervous system is in a state of hyperarousal, shown by irritability, insomnia, agitation, or outbursts of rage.
5 Symptoms 2, 3, and 4 persist for more than one month.
6 The person is significantly distressed or impaired in occupational, social, or other important areas of his or her life.

The PTSD is deemed acute if present less than three months, and chronic if present three or more months. Delayed onset is specified if the condition begins more than six months after the traumatic event. Symptoms of PTSD are noted to fluctuate, with re-experiencing, avoidant, and hyperarousal aspects being predominant at different times.[49]

Personality Disorder

A personality disorder is a persistent pattern of thinking, attitudes, and behaviour that is rigid and inflexible, unchanging over time, markedly different from expectations derived from the person's culture, and leads to distress or impaired functioning.

Antisocial Personality Disorder

The person with antisocial personality disorder demonstrates an enduring pattern of disregard for and violation of others' rights, as shown by three or more of the following:

1 Repeated illegal acts
2 Repetitive lying, conning, use of aliases, or other forms of deceit
3 Inability to plan ahead or impulsiveness
4 Marked irritability or aggressiveness, with frequent fights or assaults
5 Thoughtless disregard for his or her own and others' safety
6 Repeated irresponsibility in work settings and with financial obligations
7 Lack of remorse[50]

Narcissistic Personality Disorder

The diagnosis of narcissistic personality disorder refers to an enduring pattern characterized by a constant need for admiration, a tendency to grandiosity, and a lack of empathy, as shown by five or more of the following:

1 Exaggerated sense of self-importance
2 Preoccupation with fantasies of unlimited power, beauty, brilliance, success, or ideal love
3 Belief that one is special or unique

4 Need for lavish admiration
5 Sense of entitlement to special favours or automatic compliance
6 Tendency to be exploitative, to take advantage of others
7 Failure to recognize or understand that others have feelings and needs
8 Envy of others, or belief that others are jealous of him or her
9 Arrogance and superciliousness[51]

Borderline Personality Disorder

To be diagnosed with borderline personality disorder (BPD), the person should demonstrate an extensive pattern of unstable relationships and emotional reactions, unclear identity, and striking impulsivity beginning in early adulthood, as shown by five or more of the following:

1 Frantic efforts to escape imagined or real abandonment
2 Intense and unstable relationships which alternate between extremes of devaluation and idealization
3 Markedly and perpetually erratic sense of self
4 Potentially self-destructive impulsiveness, for example, sex, substance abuse, reckless driving, spending, binge eating
5 Repeated suicidal threats or attempts, or self-mutilation
6 Repeated and intense mood changes
7 Constant feelings of emptiness
8 Extreme, inappropriate anger or problems controlling anger
9 Short-lived paranoia in times of stress, or severe dissociation[52]

Criticism of the concept of borderline personality disorder has suggested that it can be a 'wastebasket diagnosis,' one used in a sloppy and imprecise manner and usually applied to females, 'if the clinician is uncertain of the pathology or experiences negative feelings while interacting with her.'[53] The *DSM IV* cautions against using the diagnosis with adolescents and young adults who are subject to substance abuse and who may transiently appear to have BPD; unfortunately, it does not mention PTSD as a possible source of confusion.

In the 1970s, when I was seeing Dr A, the term 'borderline' was used in connection with similar symptoms, but the person was thought to be suffering from borderline schizophrenia rather than a personality disorder. Today, it is known that schizophrenia is a neurological disorder, but at that time it was assumed that the schizophrenic person was terribly damaged during early childhood, usually by a 'schizophrenogenic mother.'[54]

1. Vulnerability and Risk Factors

'How Could It Happen to an Intelligent Woman Like You?'

Because I had no conscious memory of my parents' behavior, I wasn't aware that with Dr Masserman, I was recreating a highly charged, interior motif from my childhood.

Barbara Noël[1]

The commander ... is demonstrating, to me, his mastery of the world. He's breaking the rules, under their noses, thumbing his nose at them, getting away with it. Perhaps he's reached that state of intoxication which power is said to inspire, the state in which you believe you are indispensable and can therefore do anything, absolutely anything you feel like, anything at all.

Margaret Atwood, The Handmaid's Tale[2]

When I was seeing Naida, my second therapist, we talked about my three layers of problems. The first involved my separations from my parents as an infant and young child; second was my sexual abuse by my godfather, in which my godmother colluded and occasionally participated; third was my abuse by Dr A. In therapy with Naida, and during my involvement with Dr A, I recalled fragments of memories from my early childhood, perhaps back to somewhere between two and three years of age. My mother was able to confirm these memories, with the exception, of course, of the memories of the abuse, by which she was shocked and horrified.

I was born in England in 1936 to a mother who had recently recovered from tuberculosis and had been advised to refrain from having children for several years. Her doctor, who later became my godfather, was married to a woman who was sterile as a result of tuberculosis of the ovary. They desperately wanted children. My godfather suggested that my mother should move into his house to have the baby, emphasizing that they already had a nurse there who was caring for a friend's child. After my birth, and for the next few years, a kind of tug of war went on, and I went back and forth between my parents and my godparents, who tried to convince my mother that they had more resources to care for me and that she needed to leave me with them while she regained her health and spent time with my father.

Early in my therapy with Dr A I had memories of being left by my mother at 'Normans,' my wealthy godparents' spacious house. I recalled feeling abandoned, terrified, panic-stricken, kicking the front door, and begging and pleading with her to take me with her. The visual image of the white front door and my mother disappearing was accompanied by a painful, sinking, tearing feeling just below my breastbone. This feeling, which I would feel also when I left Dr A's office, was accompanied by sensations of dizziness and unreality and an inability to concentrate. It would seem as if the world had changed, become dark, menacing, and hostile. I felt lost and alone, scared and helpless. I named the intense physical sensation 'the separation feeling.'

A few months later, I had memories of doorknobs turning while I lay alone in my crib or bed, as a small child, knowing that something very frightening was about to happen. So vivid was this memory, this visual image, that I sometimes felt that I could see doorknobs turning in real life – without anyone there. At the time I felt I must be losing my mind, must be very crazy. Then, devastating memory that I resisted and fought against, I recalled my godfather coming into the room, bending over me, and licking my genitals. There were also some very vague but scary memories of my godfather in a small dark room where cat baskets were kept, in the room where he had his X-ray machine, and in a train when I was about six.

After I was about four, visits with my godparents lessened in frequency and extent, and I have some happy memories from that time of long walks with my mother in rural Shropshire, a western part of England to which she and I were evacuated shortly after the beginning of the Second World War. My father, whose poor eyesight disqualified him from military service, was a volunteer firefighter. During the war, as a member of the Inland Revenue (Income Tax Department), he was transferred around England and Scotland

and was rarely home with the family. When I was almost five, however, the birth of my younger sister seemed to push me away from my mother again. My mother and newborn Sally were closeted away from me for several weeks because of concerns that the baby might catch whooping cough from me. For a while after Sally's birth, I had the idea that Sally was somehow older than I was and certainly closer to and more favoured by both my parents. My life, however, continued happily enough, and I developed a very close friendship with a girl named Iris, who was about eighteen months older. Iris, whom I idolized, took the lead in our play activities.

When I was nine, my younger and only brother was born. We moved, briefly to London, where I remember the VJ celebrations, and then to Wells, Norfolk, where both my godparents still lived. By this time my godfather had moved out to live with his ex-patient, Helen, and my godmother lived alone, still in Normans. This seemed like a tense and unhappy time for all of us. My sister, Sally, was ill, my mother was short of money, my godmother was unpredictable; sometimes welcoming my visits, other times telling me to go away. I don't remember having any contact with my godfather, except in his role as my sister's physician. At school I felt out of place, could not fit in, and ended up making friends with two ten-year-old boys with whom I would go swimming. This activity usually included mud slides and mud fights when we swam in a creek at low tide, or diving off the quay when the tide was high. I found myself ostracized by girls and considered a 'tomboy.' Missing Iris and Shropshire, I was often sad and lonely.

After about six months we moved to join my father, who had bought a small house in Cotton End, a village in Bedfordshire, where I spent the rest of my childhood and adolescence. The first winter there was very cold; the school ran out of coal, and classes were cancelled for several weeks. With three children, my father's small salary was stretched very thin, and the house had little heat that winter. My feet and legs, I remember, were covered with chilblains, which itched intensely when I finally got warm in bed.

When I was eleven, I passed the 'eleven plus' examination with very high marks. This was an examination that allowed children from lower-income families to gain entrance to schools that charged fees. So at age eleven I became one of the ten 'scholarship girls' to gain entrance that year to Bedford High School for Girls, a status that I was never really allowed to forget, as reminders came up frequently, when 'scholarship girls' were told to get their free books, free bus passes, and so on. In addition to my 'scholarship girl'

*status, I was a member of 'Country House.' The school population was divid-
ed into eight houses, four boarding houses where girls actually lived, and four
'day houses,' for girls who lived with their families and came to school on a
daily basis. 'Country girls' lived out of town and travelled to school by train
or bus. The 'country girls' proved ready to accept me as one of them, and
ignore my 'scholarship girl' status, so this was where I made all my close
friends.*

*After some years of minimal contact, and a year or two after we moved to
Cotton End, my godmother reached out again, and once more I became involved in a strange double life. My godmother invited me to spend summers
and some Easter holidays with her at Normans, and when I was fourteen my
godfather bought me a small sailboat. When at Normans, for three or four
weeks at Easter and five or six weeks in the summer, I had little or no contact with other children. Weekdays, at Auntie's (Godmother's) direction, I
would do housework, cooking, and gardening. At weekends I would go with
her to the sailing club where she functioned as a race official. I would either
help her or, when I got my own sailboat, participate in the races.*

*Even though Umpi (Godfather) had been living with Helen for some
years, he still had his office at Normans and would see patients there, and
make up medicines from the bottles that lined the shelves of the medicine
room. When he was not there I would sometimes wander through the red-
tiled waiting room or finger the large coloured bottles of medicine and jars of
ointment. Sometimes patients would call, and Auntie or I would direct them
to contact him at Helen's. Sometimes Umpi would come back in the afternoon
or evening and want to talk with me about sailing. He was convinced that I
could reach the Olympics if I tried hard enough. Usually his speech was
slurred, and he pushed his red-veined face close to mine as he drunkenly
tried to give me directions to 'watch the edge of the jib, as it begins to flutter.'
I felt uneasy, often scared, but beholden to him because, after all, he had
given me the boat.*

*Worst of all were the times when Godfather would come back drunk in
the middle of the night, and try to batter down the door of Auntie's bedroom.
By this time she would have got me into her room, and into her bed with
her, and I would lie still and terrified as he banged on the door or yelled and
crashed and broke things. Sometimes he would howl, in an eerie, wolflike
way. Auntie attributed this to the full moon.*

At the end of the holidays I went back to my family told them about the sailing, but nothing about the scary happenings. Why? It seemed at the time that going to Normans, strange and scary though that was, was preferable to staying at Cotton End, where there were lots of expectations for me as the eldest. In addition, another sister was born when I was thirteen. Sara, the only child who grew up with my father at home, was the apple of his eye. Mother, on the other hand, seemed quite resentful of Sara and gave much time and attention to my brother.

Between the ages of about ten and fourteen, I had a number of experiences of adult men coming on to me sexually. All these I kept to myself, feeling that I should know how to deal with them. When I was about ten, our new family doctor asked me to sit on his knee and give him a kiss. Our next door neighbour felt my breasts when the two families were walking in the woods and I had lagged behind to look at some flowers. My godmother's brother put his hand on my knee under the table, during lunch at a restaurant, on several occasions. When I was waiting in line for a bus, a man shoved his erection against my behind. When I was fourteen, I gave up being a Sunday school teacher after the vicar got me alone in a room and wanted me to sit on his knee. When I was alone in a carriage on a train, coming back from Norfolk, a man sitting opposite opened his fly and sat with his penis hanging out. I was paralyzed, terrified, did not know what to do. He got out at the next station. I wondered what was wrong with me, that all these things happened to me? Compared to other girls, I felt boyish, muscled, and unattractive.

By the time I was fifteen or sixteen, I was becoming uneasy with Auntie's possessive attitude and her attempts to alienate me from the rest of my family. At this time I was still planning on a career as a physical education teacher, and Auntie studied maps of possible locations that I could work and she could move in to live with me. Suddenly, I refused to go and stay with her. Nobody could understand it. How could I not want to go to Norfolk where I had my sailboat? Stubbornly I clung to my decision, but could not, would not, give my parents a reason. I could neither share with them the terrifying experiences of Umpi's drunken rages, nor tell them of Auntie's attempts to control me totally and to separate me from my parents and siblings. Distant though I often felt from them, I chose my family. It was shortly after this that I changed my career plans and decided to go to medical school. Previously a somewhat lackadaisical student, whose teachers had warned my mother, 'Your daughter won't even be able to get a job in Woolworth's if she goes on like this,' I began to apply myself and started to pull off the top marks needed for medical school entrance.

Once in medical school, I felt very grateful and privileged to be allowed into a 'man's world,' and accepted some harassment and discriminatory treatment without question. This attitude prevailed during my internship and training in psychiatry. With one exception, my supervisors were all men, and I deferred to their authority and knowledge.

During the second year of a psychiatry fellowship in the United States, Dr A was assigned to me as a supervisor, and he later became my therapist. During the course of therapy, I learned some details of his background.

Dr A was a middle-aged man from a traditional family background of businessman-father and homemaker-mother. As a younger son, he felt that his parents preferred his older brother and that he could never measure up to his brother's accomplishments. Dr A depicted his father as stern and distant, and he felt that his mother had been very controlling and infantilizing, trying to dictate his life. He described lifelong difficulties in expressing his feelings, and appeared to feel that his enjoyment of playing the recorder was not masculine. As a faculty member in a psychiatric department, he was seen by his juniors as authoritarian and by his seniors as rather ineffectual and unproductive. At the time of his involvement with me, he was realizing that he had not lived up to his own expectations and that it was very unlikely that he would succeed as an academic psychiatrist. At the same time, he described problems communicating with his wife, financial worries, and mixed feelings about having built and moved into a large, new house.

Dr A's view of women's place and role was very traditional. He told me that I should use 'feminine wiles' with my husband and never get angry with him; he also told me that he 'could not tell his most personal feelings to a woman.' He once suggested that I should get my husband to spank me. Sexually, he lacked skills, and seemed to have little or no interest in giving me any pleasure. He would penetrate, then rapidly ejaculate.

When I started therapy with Dr A, I accorded him tremendous power and believed that he had life-and-death control over my disturbed psyche; when he hypnotized me, my perception of his power markedly increased. Even when it came for me to move far from the city, I felt that I had to continue to see him. All his suggestions I incorporated, thinking that they were indubitably true. In a session just before I left, he told me, 'You feel like nothing without me.' And that was how I felt; I wandered on the beach, observing scum from the

waves settling on the sand, feeling that, without him, I was less than nothing,
less than a piece of sea scum. He had also commented on my intense anger
towards my mother, who was about to come from England to visit our family.
And angry I was, murderously angry, lying awake at night wanting to kill her.

Throughout my involvement with Dr A, I never questioned his right to
set the times of sessions, in his office, according to his needs, which for me in-
volved long hours of travel and time away from my family. I had trust in
him, blind faith; he was my doctor, my psychiatrist, who, I assumed, was
dedicated to my recovery. My role as a patient included telling him my most
intimate fantasies and secrets; giving him all the details of my dreams, even
if these seemed highly personal and embarrassing; reporting, without reserva-
tions, the minutiae of my day-to-day life with my family and my relation-
ship with my husband; talking about my feelings towards and perceptions of
Dr A, so that we could understand my transference towards him; working
hard to explore the issues, memories, and behaviours that he felt were impor-
tant.

Even when, after the sexual involvement had begun, part of me was clam-
ouring and telling me that it wasn't right, that Dr A wasn't helping me,
that he was merely repeating both my godfather's abuse and my mother's series
of abandonments, I bowed to his knowledge and authority and agreed that I
was being 'helped.'

We need to look at three major factors when we try to understand
how the situation of a person seeing a health professional for counselling or for treatment of a physical disorder, trusting that she
will obtain the care that she needs, can be radically transformed so
that the professional is able to use the patient for his own needs.
One or more of these factors may be present. The three factors are
(1) vulnerability on the part of the client or patient, (2) risk factors
on the part of the health professional, and (3) the special status
and role accorded to health professionals.

Vulnerability of the Client or Patient

Many victims describe difficulties in their families of origin, and
some have been sexually abused as children. Ellen Plasil depicts her

mother as abusive and describes her father as a passive man who molested her once and warned her never to tell anyone. Her abusive psychiatrist, Dr Lonnie Leonard, like her father, labelled Plasil's perceptions and memories as inaccurate. Like her abusive mother, Leonard controlled her by claiming to know and understand Plasil's inner thoughts and feelings better than she did. Recalling what her mother had taught her, Plasil writes, 'I was not sane, I was not good, and I was not worthy of being loved. Dr Leonard had only to nod at any one of these, and I, trusting him so, was reduced to the helplessness I had felt as the child first learning these lessons from my mother.' Approval, from Plasil's father, came from 'letting yourself be used and remaining loyal to the user ... willing to let the offender pretend that the offense was something else.'[3]

Referring to her sexual abuse by both parents, Barbara Noël states, 'Those of us who had low self-esteem or "shadow experiences" that would help keep us quiet were perfect targets.'[4] Noël was in therapy for eighteen and a half years with world-famous psychiatrist Dr Jules Masserman. During this time Masserman was often emotionally abusive and subjected Noël to at least two hundred sessions in which she was unconscious for several hours, deeply drugged with sodium amobarbital, a dangerous and addictive medication. While she was unconscious, he raped her.

Another woman, Carolyn Bates, learned that parental authority was absolute and that conflict must be avoided by appeasing authority figures. Her mother was very ill when she was a baby, and she was cared for by her grandmother. When she was fifteen, her father died of Lou Gehrig's disease. Bates was stunned, and her relationship with her grief-stricken mother became very conflicted.[5] The middle-aged Dr X, warm and supportive, was a parent figure to her, and she complied with all his directions.

A person's vulnerability may be greatly enhanced by current life crises or illness. One woman, seeing a specialist in orthopaedic medicine for the treatment of a back injury, had recently experienced the death of her mother and separation from her husband. In pain, feeling sad and lonely, she was initially excited and gratified when the specialist showed a sexual interest in her. Experiences like this are not restricted to women. A man, recovering from brain injury, went to a psychologist hoping for suggestions about how to regain his powers of concentration so he could return to his job. He was baffled and distressed when the psychologist exposed himself and suggested mutual masturbation.

There is some disagreement in the literature about the importance of client risk factors. Studying sexual involvement with therapists, Gary Schoener and his colleagues stress that characteristics of the therapist are the main predictors.[6] In an early paper on this topic, Michael Stone suggested that the patient at greatest risk is a pretty woman in her twenties or thirties.[7] He and other authors suggest that other 'risk factors' may well be rationalizations, as patients who are unattractive, elderly, or infirm are extremely unlikely to be sexually exploited. Richard Kluft, on the other hand, argues convincingly that a major risk factor is the vulnerability of the person who has been sexually abused as a child, particularly if the abuser was a parent. He describes this person as a 'sitting duck' who is likely to be revictimized by an exploitative therapist.[8] His theory is lent support by Mary Armsworth, who studied a group of adult incest survivors and found that 23 per cent reported sexual involvement with a person in a helping role.[9]

According to Judith Herman, author of *Trauma and Recovery*, people who have been abused as children are likely to have difficulty protecting themselves in intimate relationships. Herman writes that the survivor's 'desperate longing for nurturance and care makes it difficult to establish safe and appropriate boundaries with others. Her tendency to denigrate herself and to idealise those to whom she becomes attached further clouds her judgement. Her empathic attunement to the wishes of others and her automatic, often unconscious habits of obedience also make her vulnerable to anyone in a position of power or authority.'[10]

Women's socialization and low status in our society likely account for the preponderance of women victims. Women's sense of self, self-esteem, and moral development revolves around their sense of attachment and relationships to others.[11] Difficulty acknowledging and expressing anger is common for women, who tend to function as mediators and emotional organizers in families and other groups. Despite changes in society, women are still subordinate to men in many areas, and they tend to defer to men's power and authority. Women are more likely to go to health professionals and to believe that they have emotional problems,[12] and are more compliant with respect to professionals' suggestions, such as taking medication.[13]

Although I was a pretty woman in her thirties at the time of my abuse, it makes sense to me that there were other factors contributing to my inability to recognize that my dependency was being heightened, that I was being manipulated and taken advantage of, and that my needs were not paramount, as they should have been in a therapeutic relationship. My experiences of being shuttled back and forth as an infant and young child left me with a deep insecurity, a tremendous anxiety about being separated from parent figures. This came to the fore in my relationship with Dr A when, experiencing transference, I began to direct towards him my early anxieties about my mother leaving me. The part of me that was the tiny child wanted to cling to Dr A, wanted him to nurture me, wanted him to give me the constant and reliable parenting that I had missed. When Dr A rejected me or pushed me away, I tried even harder. As a young child, with a black-and-white view of cause and effect, I probably blamed mother's disappearances on my own behaviour and felt that if I just tried hard enough, and did not give up, things would eventually improve.

My family background had left me with much confusion about the role of physicians, which was not limited to the confusion resulting from the sexual abuse by my godfather, who was one. My godfather was my mother's physician, as well as my sister's. At the same time he was my godfather, and my mother's friend. My confusion was reinforced again by the family doctor who wanted me to sit on his knee. Where were the boundaries in these relationships?

My sexual abuse as a young child, and the many improprieties that I experienced later, interacted with my insecurities and left me with low self-esteem and a tendency to view relationships with men as inevitably sexual. My loyalty to the exploitative Umpi and Auntie, keeping secrets from my family, feeling that I and only I could solve my problems, all worked to influence my susceptibility to a relationship that seemed to promise something I had never had. Finally, my position as an oldest child who was expected to care for younger siblings, Auntie's use of me in summers to care for her and do all the household chores, and my socialization as a woman in our culture influenced how readily I accepted a role of caring for Dr A and listening to his troubles. At the time that the relationship between myself and Dr A came to be defined as therapy, I was nearing the end of my training as a psychiatrist, was several months pregnant, and would soon be moving back to Canada and assuming a part-time faculty position. My anxiety about all these changes was high, and I was especially concerned about my ability to combine the roles of wife, mother, and psychiatrist.

Health Professional Risk Factors

Like me, other victims also report that the professionals who abused them were going through life crises or changes. One victim, who felt that her family doctor was possibly unusually familiar during her first visit to him, reported that she left the community and then returned to find that 'in the meantime he had got divorced. After he had examined me he kissed me, and asked if he could visit me on his way home.' 'Josephine,' whose female psychologist had recently gone through a marriage breakdown, confided, 'She kept telling me that I was uptight about my body. So she suggested that we go to the nude swimming session at the YWCA together. Afterwards, she asked me back to her apartment.'

Perfunctory sex was a common experience with abusive professionals, as described by the nine women abused by therapists whom Phyllis Chesler studies in her *Women and Madness*. The professionals appeared to be interested only in their own sexual needs, and had no interest in the emotional or sexual gratification of their patients. One victim, describing her analyst's inept 'lovemaking,' told Chesler, 'Once I screamed, a really anguished howl, and he pushed me away, got up, dressed, and said, "don't you think you owe me an explanation ...?"'[14] One woman told me that her psychiatrist wanted her to fellate him, telling her that, because he was married, his principles would not allow him to have inter-course with her. 'Sylvia,' who became sexually involved with her family doctor, told me, 'There wasn't much to it, no foreplay or anything like that. I just took off my clothes and lay on the bed, he took off his clothes, put some kind of lubrication on his penis, climbed on top of me, took about three or four strokes, and it was all over. He got up, took his clothes with him to the bathroom, washed up, and when he came out he told me that he couldn't stay, he was expected at home, and he left.' When she next visited his office, she was lying in the examining room with her feet in the stirrups, and 'was really shocked when he came into the room stark naked. But I didn't have time to say anything because he just walked over to the bottom of the table and inserted himself in me. I didn't protest because I just didn't know how to.'

Some victims report unusually sadistic or bizarre forms of abuse. Christopher Hyde's account of the career of Dr Tyhurst describes victims' allegations that, in addition to sexual abuse, he subjected them to master–slave rituals, made victims wait on him and work in his garden, and flogged one victim.[15] An article about sadistic therapists describes how a patient told a therapist that, when she was twelve years old, her father would use his legs to force her knees apart so that he could have intercourse with her. During the next session, the doctor emulated her father's behav-iour, telling her that the abuse was 'treatment' and making threats to ensure that she told no one. In another case, a therapist, informed that the patient's father had beaten her with a broom-stick and molested her, broke a broomstick in half and pushed the frayed end into her vagina.[16]

Various attempts have been made to develop typologies of abusers and to delineate their supposed underlying motivations. Butler and Zelen, who interviewed twenty psychiatrists and psy-chologists who admitted to sexual intimacy with patients, reported that 80 per cent of those interviewed could not recall the events that led up to the sexual contact. At the time they felt vulnerable, needy, and lonely.[17]

Based on his clinical experience, Alan Stone proposed a typol-ogy of sexually abusive psychotherapists. Interestingly, he makes no mention of female psychotherapists. The six types of therapists are as follows:

1 The therapist who is middle-aged, depressed, and has problems in his own marriage. He usually gets involved with a younger female patient, to whom he tells his troubles. Sometimes the patient is led to believe that the therapist is contemplating divorcing his wife and marrying the patient.
2 The manipulative and sociopathic therapist who is exploiting his position and its opportunities with a goal of self-gratification.
3 The therapist who uses patients to satisfy perverse instincts. This group includes therapists who drug their patients into unconsciousness and then have sex with them. Unlike the other examples, this does not involve an exploitation of the transference, of the patient's view of the therapist as a parentlike figure.
4 The charming, expansive, grandiose therapist who wants to be loved by his female patients, particularly if they are young and attractive. He initiates hugging and kissing early in the therapy, and goes on from there.
5 The therapist who sees himself as 'sexually liberated' and believes that this includes sex with his patients.
6 The introverted and withdrawn therapist who is very uncomfortable with interpersonal intimacy. If a patient appears to be intensely sexually attracted to him, he succumbs. He may contend that the patient seduced him, but is likely to feel guilty and will probably confess.[18]

Another typology of sexually exploitative therapists, again with six categories, has been developed by Schoener and his associates at the Minnesota Walk-In Counselling Center. The clusters are as follows:

1 Naive and uninformed: This group includes trainees and poorly trained therapists who may lack knowledge of professional standards and the importance of boundaries.
2 Healthy or mildly neurotic: Sexual contact is minimal or comprises a single episode; remorse and requests for help are common.

3 Severely neurotic: This group have severe, long-standing emotional problems and focus on getting their personal needs met in the work setting. As intimacy grows in a therapeutic relationship, these therapists play seductive games, talk about themselves, and use touch excessively, and arrange business or social involvements outside counselling.

4 Character disorders with impulse control problems: These therapists have a variety of problems which may include legal difficulties; they have little or no appreciation of the effect of their impulsive and inappropriate behaviour on others, and tend to deny or minimize any harm they have caused.

5 Sociopathic or narcissistic character disorders: These therapists are adept in manipulating clients and professional colleagues; they are cool and calculating, able to cunningly seduce a variety of clients and cover their tracks.

6 Psychotic or borderline personality disorders: These therapists are more obviously mentally ill, with poor judgment and a tenuous grasp on reality.[19]

Peter Rutter, whose popular book examines the betrayal of women's trust by men in power, postulates that 'masculine woundedness is an elusive but absolutely crucial ingredient in the fatal conspiracy between men and women that leads to exploitative sex.' Our culture, he proposes, influences men to ignore or hide the wounded, defenceless aspects of their psyches. A fantasy of a sexual merger with a woman, representing the man's hidden and denied 'feminine' qualities, may appear to be a way to assuage the man's wounds. Other wounds experienced by men are loss of a sharing, intimate relationship with their father, and wounds received from mothers. Rutter notes, that 'In a curious kind of role reversal, a man in power can come to relate to his female protégée as he might have done with his mother.' But if he is angry towards his mother, he may use the relationship to avenge himself for the injuries that he feels his mother dealt to him.[20]

Other issues in male socialization doubtless underlie the fact that males predominate among the health professionals who abuse. Males in our culture feel entitled to have their needs met, usually by women, put their own needs first, and go after what they want. In their everyday lives, they may have little ability or opportunity to express their feelings and worries, so the chance to unburden to a sympathetic and compliant listener is appealing. In romantic and sexual encounters they usually take the initiative and, if needy, lonely, or deprived, might be inclined to mislead themselves about the ethics of the situation.

Another factor influencing abusive professionals is the failure of training programs, until very recently, to educate trainees about the universality of sexual feelings towards patients, and how these should be managed. Kenneth Pope and colleagues link this failure to psychoanalytic influences, which dictate that the therapist should be distant and impersonal. Thus, students who told their supervisors that they felt sexually attracted to patients were deemed abnormal and perhaps even unsuited to the field.[21]

Despite this attitude of moral righteousness, evidence suggests that in some training institutions, as in incestuous families, a hotbed of sexual harassment and exploitation seethes just below the surface. A 1979 study showed that 25 per cent of female psychology graduate students had been sexually involved with an educator. These women students were more likely to become sexually involved with their patients, showing a modelling effect.[22] In the past decade, more studies have examined training programs. In a national survey, 4.1 per cent of female psychiatric residents reported sexual involvement with an educator.[23] Abusive experiences in medical school are linked to an increased likelihood that students will behave abusively with patients.[24]

Unavoidable contact with, or identification with, patients may create problems, and enhance vulnerability, for health professionals who are gay or lesbian, belong to an ethnic or cultural minority group, or practise in isolated areas. For instance, health professionals who belong to close-knit lesbian communities will share their patients' struggles with discrimination and homophobia,[25] and may attend the same community functions. In such cases maintaining clear boundaries presents a major challenge. In lesbian communities, therapists often occupy a special position as 'perceived healers of the wounds of sexism, misogyny, and homophobia.'[26] Because of this special position, explains Brown, the lesbian therapist's power is magnified. But power is downplayed, or denied. 'The notion that a lesbian therapist is not particularly powerful because she, like her lesbian client, is oppressed in our culture is a dangerously seductive thought, and one very commonly used to rationalize the violation of boundaries by lesbian therapists who have become sexual, entered into business relationships, or otherwise behaved in a clearly unethical manner with their lesbian clients.'[27] Pressure on the lesbian therapist, from the patient, to relax rigid boundaries may be intense, as detailed in Heyward's *When Boundaries Betray Us*.[28]

When I have tried to understand Dr A's motivation, he has struck me as a combination of Stone's first and sixth types, possibly also fitting into Schoener's 'severely neurotic' category. He was middle-aged, seemed depressed at times, and talked of difficulties with his wife. Occasionally he said he loved me. He seemed introverted and uncomfortable with intimacy, and he misinterpreted my intense childlike attachment to him, believing that it was an erotic adult attraction. But Rutter's depiction of masculine woundedness, of the man who perceives himself to be wounded by his mother, seems particularly apt with respect to Dr A. On many occasions I felt that his emotional cruelty to me was related to his obvious anger towards his mother. In addition, he cultivated an intense hatred in me towards my own mother, so that I blamed her for feelings that were actually being generated by him in the course of therapy.

The Special Status and Role Accorded to Health Professionals

The survivors who talked to me in my office, in response to advertisements, in groups, and at conferences and presentations had trusted their doctor, dentist, chiropractor, psychologist, nurse, social worker, or other health professional and did not, could not, believe that they were being betrayed despite mounting indications that they were. One woman stressed, 'He was everything to me – sun, moon, stars, mother, father, confessor, everything.' They had faith that the professional was a person of honesty and integrity who had only the patient's best interests in mind. When the professional is able to cure or relieve the person's problems, the patient is even more likely to believe that the professional has special healing powers. One man described his family doctor, who later initiated a sexual relationship, 'She was like an earth mother, warm, kind and caring, and she cured my stomach problems. All the other doctors I saw couldn't figure out what was wrong.'

A telling example of understandable, but blind, faith is given by Barbara Noël, who was asked by Dr Masserman to bring her husband, Richard, with her to the psychiatrist's office. Dr Masserman presented the couple with a proposal to treat Noël's emotional difficulties with intravenous sodium amobarbital. This drug is dangerous and addicting, and it was totally unsuitable for the purpose of Noël's treatment. Pointing to a book on his desk, which he had written, Masserman inquired whether the couple wanted to take the material home to study. Lulled by the doctor's confident account of the safety of the procedure he was suggesting, they declined; neither did they make any other inquiries about the advisability of using Amytal. Noël states, 'I'm sure he was quite confident [the book] would remain on his desk when we walked out the door. We did just what he wanted us to do. But even in retrospect, I can understand why we trusted him. Why in the world would a former president of the Illinois Psychiatric Society, a former president of the Chicago Analytic Society, and a founder of the American Academy of Psychoanalysis steer us wrong?'[29]

It appears that Dr Masserman, like other famous people who exploit others, like Margaret Atwood's commander in *The Handmaid's Tale*,[30] may have considered himself entitled to use his patients for his own needs and may have felt supremely invulnerable to consequences. Or, like a modern-day Pygmalion, he may have believed that he had unique powers to mould and transform his patient. Patients, too, may view prominent health professionals with reverence and awe, and be convinced that treatment by such a person will cure their illness or solve their problems, that he or she has some special knowledge, skills, or curative power that is unavailable to lesser mortals. Because of their social programming as subordinates, women may be more readily impressed by men in positions of power. When Ellen Cole was a 25-year-old doctoral student with a three-week-old baby, her husband left her for his secretary, and Cole sought a therapist. 'I insisted on seeing not only a male, not only a psychiatrist, but the chair of the Department of Psychiatry at the State University's medical school. I was into the omniscience of male authority in a big way.'[31]

Out of a similar sense of awe and respect, members of a community, other professionals, and inquiry boards may be equally reluctant to confront well-known professionals and apply sanctions. Describing sexual abuse of patients in the lesbian community, Gartrell and Sanderson state, 'We are particularly reluctant to confront prominent women whose conduct has been exploitative. Placing such women above censure denies them the opportunity to receive constructive feedback ... Exempting our leaders from ethical conduct is sometimes excused by claims that their contribution will outweigh any damage they cause.'[32]

In her first session with Dr Lonnie Leonard, Ellen Plasil, who had moved her family in order to avail herself of an Objectivist therapist and who had heard about Leonard's charisma from friends, perceived the doctor to have special powers. When he asked her if she was close to tears, she felt, 'His question not only told me how perceptive he was, but his tone told me how compassionate, as well. His greatness seemed clearer to me now and my apprehension about the session disappeared.' She goes on to point out, in retrospect, that his seemingly insightful question was probably prompted by her previous description of being disowned by her mother or by the context of their meeting as doctor and patient. After several more sessions, in which he found out more about her background and difficulties, she believed, 'In revealing my past and finding his support and understanding, I felt my trust in Dr Leonard growing.'[33]

The relationship between health professional and patient is not just a business relationship. Its unique emotional and spiritual component helps explain the faith people have in their health professional. Marilyn Peterson, a social worker who has long been concerned about boundary violations in professional relationships, argues that 'Contemporary professionals are secular shamans who preserve, protect, and treat our minds, our bodies, our souls, and our relationships with each other.'[34] This 'secular anointment' includes power, privilege, superiority, autonomy, and esteem, and gives the professional authority to enter and explore vulnerable aspects of our bodies or minds. Conditioned as children to embrace the superiority and power of professionals, we readily admire their positions or titles, respect their knowledge, comply with their directions, and defer to their opinions. Because of our faith in professionals, we believe that they will take care of us, make a commitment to us, and have the ability to respond to our needs. This faith permits us to comply automatically and without hesitation.

Peterson describes the belief that professionals will put our needs before their own as an 'ethos of care' which 'requires a depth of care and commitment from professionals that raises the relationship to a sacred covenant of fidelity and obligation. Rooted in biblical and spiritual tradition, the covenant between us is currently expressed through professional codes and statements of purpose.'[35]

Why do we remain quiet and subservient when professionals behave inappropriately, offensively, or abusively? Why do we try to normalize conduct that we would otherwise deplore? Peterson links these tendencies to our fears of abandonment and our terror of the unknown, so that challenging the professional appears dangerous and could negatively affect his or her attitude towards us and concern for our welfare. 'Even when professionals disappoint us,' she says, 'we often continue to hope that our next encounter will be different. Since we are partially dependent creatures and cannot fully care for ourselves, we prefer to pay the cost of tolerating painful experiences rather than ending up alone.'[36]

I found Peterson's book very helpful in my journey towards understanding why I had trusted Dr A, why my faith in him had persisted despite obvious indications that he was using me as a sexual object and a scapegoat. Feeling that he knew best, I repeatedly allowed him to invalidate my perceptions and continued to think that my only hope lay in persevering with my conviction that I had a serious psychiatric disorder that he, and only he, could cure.

2. Initiation

'Why Didn't You Just Walk Out?'

I timidly stated that casual sex might not be as helpful to me as he had suggested. His response to my first attempt to stand up to him was his most disturbing suggestion to date. He wondered aloud if I was denying my sexual attraction for him.

Carolyn Bates[1]

Initially Dr A was my teacher and supervisor, as I was a trainee and he was a professor in a psychiatry training program in the United States. During my second and last year in this program, I had weekly meetings with him. During these hours I would tell Dr A about some of the patients and families that I was working with, and he would advise me about various treatment decisions and approaches. On several occasions he commented, seemingly envious, about my warmth, spontaneity, and ability to express my feelings. One of Dr A's responsibilities was to provide me with periodic evaluations, with feedback about my progress as a neophyte psychiatrist. About three months before the end of my training period, and three months before I was to return to Canada and a part-time faculty position, Dr A gave me my evaluation and indicated that he felt that my work was satisfactory but that I had some 'identity problems.' He based this opinion, he said, on his observation that although I was very serious, hard-working, and dedicated at work, he had observed me to be a 'party girl' in other settings, such as a recent staff party.

As he was a professor of psychiatry and my supervisor, I was distressed and concerned by his comments and readily agreed to his proposal that we should devote the last three months of my supervision time to therapy, focusing on my identity problems. At the time, I was several months pregnant with my second child and worried about leaving a familiar environment, returning to Canada, and trying to cope with the multiple roles of being a wife, mother, psychiatrist, and university teacher.

What happened next was scary and unexpected. As I spoke to Dr A about my family background and upbringing, I found myself falling into a boiling cauldron of emotions that I could neither control nor understand. In the sessions with Dr A I lost my usual ability to express myself and became increasingly inarticulate. Feeling both fearful of and dependent on Dr A, I had sudden bouts of weeping and felt increasingly hopeless, helpless, sad, and confused. Dreading our return to Canada, I became more and more convinced that Dr A held the answers to my problems, and the key to my unhappiness, in his grasp.

At home I withdrew from my husband and young son, and became sad and silent. My attempts to explain my need for therapy were met with puzzlement, if not incredulity, on my husband's part. He viewed me as a strong and competent woman, yet I felt like a helpless, hapless infant torn by powerful emotions and in thrall to a magical parentlike figure who held my fate in his hands. Clinging onto the last vestiges, it seemed, of my sanity as though I were scrabbling to retain fingerholds on a crumbling cliff, I was aware of a persuasive line of reasoning in my mind which argued that my departure from the city would mean an abandonment by Dr A. I would never see him again, and I would never recover from the terrible grief. So great was this irrational internal conviction that, at times, drowning in grief, I longed to die and thought out some complex suicide plans.

In the sessions, unable to express my feelings, unable to describe what was happening to me, I begged Dr A to help me come to grips with the forgotten memories and conflicts that must be churning in the innermost depths of my psyche. 'Do something, do anything, hypnotize me, help somehow,' I pleaded. During this time, I was continuing to function on a superficial level, at work and at home, organizing cooking, child care, and housework, packing and preparing to move.

In one of the sessions before I left, Dr A hypnotized me, and I was able to shed some tears and faintly recalled being left by my mother with my godparents. I was at the front door of Normans, frantically kicking and screaming, begging my mother to take me with her. By this time, Dr A had assumed gigantic importance in my life, and I felt that I would be unable to function without him. In the final session before I left, Dr A told me, 'You feel like nothing without me.' Amazed at his awareness of my inner turmoil, I agreed.

We arranged that I would travel back to see Dr A, as he felt that we could not leave something that had been started. While I was surprised, on one level, that he did not suggest that I transfer to a psychiatrist in Canada, I did not hesitate to agree because of the depth of my attachment to him, and my conviction that he alone held the key to my troubles – whatever they were.

On my return to Canada, I took up my part-time faculty position, and was expecting my child three months later. Still full of grief, pain, sadness, and longing, I mourned the supposed loss of Dr A; longing to be in a childlike role and to be cared for by him. Sometimes I felt so embroiled in my own pain and neediness that I feared that I would not be able to care for a new baby. After several weeks my mood began to improve, and I became clearer about the unrealistic nature of my thoughts and feelings. But then my mother's arrival from England provoked an onslaught of rage. I felt murderously angry about how she had repeatedly left me with my godparents when I was a young child. While I did my best to hide these emotions, which seemed impossible to explain, my mother realized that my attitude to her had radically changed. 'You looked at me with eyes full of hate,' she told me, years later. She, in turn, felt hurt and rejected.

On two occasions before the baby was born, I travelled to see Dr A. Both times I was unable to voice the intense emotions that I felt, said very little, and cried when I had to leave. At home the atmosphere was tense; I was withdrawn and preoccupied, eternally struggling to accomplish the most minor tasks, suffering horrible nightmares about death and loss. At times I was beset by flickering and frightening memories, of being alone in a room where firelight cast huge scary shadows on the walls, watching a doorknob turn and knowing that something horrible was going to happen.

Shortly after the birth of my daughter, the fog and confusion in my head began to disappear, and I felt as if I was emerging from a nightmare of several months' duration. Feeling very frightened by what had happened to me, I was convinced that I must be suffering from a grave psychiatric disability. About six weeks after my daughter was born, I resumed sessions with Dr A at two- to four-week intervals. He replied to letters that I wrote between sessions. Travelling was an ordeal, but I felt compelled to go. He was my lifeline, without him I would certainly drown. When I reached his office, however, I felt distant, mistrustful, fearful, and inarticulate. My greatest fear was that I would once more fall into that painful, nightmarish world in which I felt like a tiny, helpless infant. In a contradictory fashion, I believed both that Dr A had thrown me into that world and that he could rescue me from it.

As the months passed, I was gradually reassured that I could trust Dr A and that there was nothing to fear. Together, I hoped, we could understand and overcome my childhood pain. At times Dr A would hold my hand. This seemed to assuage the 'separation feeling' and ease the pain I felt on parting from him. I still felt constricted and inarticulate, and I could not understand Dr A's explanation of these feelings – that I was probably blocked because I was holding back adult sexual feelings about him.

After about six more months had gone by, I felt frustrated by my seeming lack of progress. Although I was more able to express myself, my dependency on Dr A was extreme. In my fantasies, I was his toddler daughter, climbing on his knee, bringing him his slippers, adoring him. During the two- to four-week intervals I missed him terribly, thought of him constantly, anticipated seeing him; only to find that the session sped quickly by, and I was once again faced with what seemed like a separation from him, with feelings of sadness, emptiness, and loss.

Repeatedly Dr A observed that he believed that my dependency had adult, sexual origins and was not based on father–daughter dimensions alone. Obediently, I wrote to him that I was trying to have sexual fantasies about him; none came, the best I could do was have a dream which suggested that he was having sexual thoughts about me! When I apologized for being a problem to him, Dr A termed me 'an attractive problem.' He began to give me advice on dress and hairstyle, to make me look 'more feminine and attractive.' Although I tried to comply with his directions, I felt hurt and rebuffed by his comments about my supposed adult sexual feelings for him. I tried anew to convey to him that my attachment was that of a tiny girl to a powerful father figure. Over these few months, he held me more closely, stroked my hair, touched my neck, and clasped me to him. He then suggested that we lie on the floor and hold each other. At the time, I gratefully accepted all this cuddling and stroking, feeling like a tiny child whose needs are being met by a nurturing parent. One day I was jolted from this belief by a comment from Dr A: 'Your femininity really reaches me.' Lying close to him on the floor, I realized that he had an erection.

It was during these few months that the images I was seeing of a doorknob turning became clearer. I remembered Umpi coming into the room, licking and nibbling at my genitals. Vague images of being with Umpi when I was six, on a train going to Scotland, included being alone with him in a carriage and being pushed down on a dark bottom bunk. It was after I told Dr A of this memory that he wanted to 'get off [his] pedestal' and lie with me on the floor. At home, my relationship with my husband had become tenuous. We did talk of having a third child, but I was very reluctant to have sex, as it inevitably brought up visions of my godfather abusing me. At times I felt extremely depressed and tried various antidepressant medications, to no avail.

On the other hand, my relationship with Dr A was becoming more and more intimate. He was starting to confide in me, telling me about his lifelong difficulties with expressing feelings. When I suddenly realized that he desired me, I was amazed and gratified, as I had always considered myself to be rather boyish and unattractive. I felt wonderful, sexy, alive.

Several months after this, Dr A left his office at the busy clinic and moved into a small private office. Here he had no secretary and was completely on his own. The outside door opened into a small waiting area and beyond this was an inner office. It was dark and quiet. It was here that, after more lying on the floor, holding and stroking, Dr A took off my clothes and penetrated me. By this time, I was several months pregnant with a third child.

From the time I felt his erection, I felt wildly desirous of Dr A and began to respond passionately to him. Once I covered his face with kisses, and he accused me of trying to tempt him. We discussed the 'mutuality' of our attraction and our wish to abandon moral scruples. Yet, as he started to undress me, I pushed him away, muttering that I was pregnant. He told me that I had a beautiful body, and that he found pregnant women very attractive. As he continued to undress me, I knew something was wrong, but did not resist further as I felt that I'd created the expectation, and now I had to go ahead with it.

Unless, like Barbara Noël, the victim is drugged and totally unaware that she is being abused by the unscrupulous health professional, various factors contributing to the outcome of sexual contact emerge. These factors can be identified both in the victim and in the abusive health professional, as well as in the situation itself, which may facilitate the emergence of an abusive relationship. Using victims' accounts and the professional literature, I will examine the following overlapping concepts: (1) reframing the relationship: grooming for sex, (2) boundary violations, and (3) Kenneth Pope's description of ten common scenarios that lead to sexual abuse by therapists. This will be followed by a consideration of situational factors, and finally, of special issues for victims of childhood abuse.

Reframing the Relationship: Grooming for Sex

I found that other survivors, especially therapy survivors, frequently experienced a similar kind of grooming for sex. The abusive professional would gradually reframe or reinterpret his patient's childlike dependency on a parental figure. In the course of this reinterpretation, the parent or parental figure would become a romantic or sexual partner. Carolyn Bates viewed psychologist Dr X as a parent figure, and initially he seemed warm, kind, and supportive. She became extremely dependent on him and reluctantly followed his directions to see a variety of men and not to hesitate to become sexually involved with them. She writes that when Dr X 'wondered aloud if I was denying my sexual attraction to him, I [reacted with] astonishment, followed by a sense of uneasiness and confusion ... I felt like a child around him, like a struggling, searching, hurting child.' Dr X told her that sexual intercourse had no more significance than a handshake and suggested that her reluctance to embrace polygamy and her refusal to accept her sexual attraction to him was a result of her insecurities. He held her for longer periods, and pulled her against his genitals. Eventually he told her to lie on the floor while he rubbed her stomach to relax her. He repeated this in the following session, then unzipped her pants and touched her genitals.[2]

Ellen Plasil's psychiatrist, Dr Leonard, presented himself as the ultimate well-adjusted man, and repeatedly suggested that a woman could not fail to be attracted to him. He arranged for Plasil to come to his apartment, where he also had his office, after working hours, ostensibly to watch a videotape. He appeared naked, foiled her attempt to leave, and insisted that she lie on his bed to recover from her anxiety. He told her that she was in no shape to leave, and later climbed into bed with her. While stressing that she could trust him, he coerced her into taking her clothes off by suggesting that she must be ashamed of her body. During the night, he demanded that she wrestle with him, pressed his erection against her, and fondled her breasts. In a subsequent session, Plasil told Dr Leonard that she felt confused and guilty about what had happened that night. He responded that she would understand when she was healthy.[3]

In her book *Betrayal*, Julie Roy describes Dr Hartogs' teasing her about having a 'bathtub party' and making frequent inquiries about her sexual fantasies about him. Later, he suggests that they have sex, claiming that this will remove her fear of men and cure her of being a lesbian. Initially she refuses, telling Dr Hartogs, 'I feel I would be destroyed. That in the end it would be bad for me.' Dr Hartogs insists that she needs to love him, so that she can learn to love men. Over the course of the next few months, he progresses from touching her, kissing her, and caressing her legs to inducing her to take her clothes off and lie on the couch. Eventually, as his last patient of the evening, she starts having intercourse with him.[4]

Another victim, Sylvia, described to me her first visit to her new family doctor. She informed me that the doctor seemed very professional until they went into the examining room, where 'he undressed me.' She stated, 'I knew that wasn't exactly right; every other time I'd had examinations I'd been left alone to undress. But he didn't say or do anything "wrong," he just undressed me … We didn't talk at all, but he stared straight into my eyes while he took my clothes off. He took my sweater, blouse, and bra off, and then asked me to get on the table, which I did.' After checking Sylvia's eyes, ears, throat, lungs, and heart, 'he had me sit up again while he took off my shoes and socks. Then he asked me to lie down again and he removed my pants and panties.' Saying that, apart from undressing her, he had done nothing unusual, Sylvia found herself 'thinking about how cute he was, how he'd stared me straight in the eyes, how gentle he was. I got more and more turned on at the thought, and I thought there must be some interest there too for him to have done that.'

Another woman, 'Jane,' saw her psychiatrist for three years, starting when she was a teenager, for weight problems. His sexual interest did not begin until she had lost much weight. He encouraged her to sit on his knee, like a little girl, and gave her a hug at the end of the session. Then, she said, 'His hands slipped, and I pushed him away. He said, "Its not wrong," and told me to make appointments after 4 p.m., when his secretary had left.'

'David' felt very upset about what had gone on with his family doctor when he was an adolescent, but did not know where the boundaries of acceptable practice lay. He felt that he had been used sexually, but was not sure that he was right. David, who grew up in eastern Canada, went to see his physician because he had frequent sore throats. The doctor remarked that David was now 'a grown-up man' and directed him to come back for a thorough check-up. David was instructed to bend over and lean against a wall, while the doctor did a rectal examination, and then he was asked about whether his penis was growing straight or curved. After David responded to some questions about masturbation, the doctor warned him that he could harm his penis if he didn't masturbate properly. He threatened to tell David's parents about the masturbation and told David to come back for further examinations and instruction. At his next visit the physician checked David's foreskin, got him to produce a sperm sample, and later asked him to have an erection. Then the doctor rubbed baby oil into David's penis, showing him how to masturbate 'correctly.'

Other victims did not experience a process of grooming for sex. 'Charlene's' initiation was much more abrupt. She was in a rural hospital, suffering from severe depression and physical symptoms, and she was on three different medications. During her first session with her psychiatrist, when she was telling him about being sexually abused by her grandfather, having an affair, and failing to enjoy sex with her husband, the psychiatrist reached over and fondled her thighs. Soon they were having intercourse on the floor in the hospital, with the doctor claiming that he could cure her sexual problems. Having read about her psychiatrist's impressive background and credentials in the local newspaper she felt 'In awe … that this famous psychiatrist wanted to have sex with me.'

Like me, the victims I interviewed were often aware, on some level, that entering into a sexual relationship with the health professional was a mistake. By this time, as I had, they felt responsible for orchestrating the situation, and complied. Recalling her abusive therapist, Jane said to me, 'He told me to come late the next session, and told me we would go to bed. I shouldn't have gone back, but I did … part of me knew I shouldn't go, but I still went. When I got there he showed me a drawerful of French safes. I didn't know what to do, so I just stood there. He came over and took off my clothes. And then we made love on the couch in his office.' Similarly, describing her sexual involvement with her family doctor, Sylvia said, 'I really didn't want to have sex with him. But I didn't know how to tell him that after coming on to him for a year. So I just went along with it.'

Most professionals appear to go down a 'slippery slope,' following a common sequence that involves a progression from last to first name, then personal 'chat' that intrudes on clinical work, then some touching, such as pats and hugs, then invitations to lunches, followed by dinners or other social events, and finally sexual intercourse.[5] Professionals often employ rationalizations to account for their behaviour. These include statements like, 'The patient responded favourably to my innuendoes,' and 'The attraction was mutual,'[6] or stated intentions such as helping patients to overcome their sexual inhibitions, feelings of inadequacy, fears of intimacy, rejection of femininity, or orgasmic difficulties.[7]

Although in the 1970s some health professionals maintained that erotic contact could be used to treat sexual problems, broaden experiences, enhance self-esteem, and develop mutual positive regard, very few clung to this belief in the 1980s. Only 2 per cent of a survey of U.S. psychiatrists thought that sexual contact in therapy could sometimes be appropriate. The reasons given included 'to enhance the patient's self-esteem' and 'to provide a restitutive emotional experience.'[8] Again, it is important to accent Marmor's observation that most erotic breaches of the relationship occur with an older male therapist and a physically attractive female patient, and almost never with a patient who is ugly, aged, or infirm. Marmor also stressed, 'I have yet to see a woman patient who became involved in an erotic relationship with a therapist who did not eventually wind up feeling exploited and betrayed by him.'[9]

Turning to my own experiences as a physically attractive female patient with an older male therapist, it seems obvious that Dr A started down the 'slippery slope' even before I had become his patient. In my therapy with Naida, she suggested that he was probably attracted to me when I was his supervisee, and was looking for some way to enhance, maintain, or gain more control in the relationship. Be that as it may, it was not until years later that his gradual initiation of the sexual involvement became clear to me. Before that time, I tended to shove the painful and humiliating experience into some deep, dark, shame-filled corner of my mind, thinking that the fault was mine, that I had seduced him. Yet when I went over it carefully with Naida, and read my notes and letters to Dr A, the progression, which he had engineered, was obvious.

Boundary Violations

In many instances some other kind of 'boundary violation' predates the sexual involvement. The professional does something that is not customary in a health professional–patient relationship, and may be contrary to the professional code of ethics. This initial infringement begins to erode the requirement that the professional should focus only on the care of the patient and the patient's needs. Boundary violations of other types, where there is no hint of sexual interest, may also be upsetting to patients and may compromise their relationship with, and trust in, the health professional. These include using the patient for business purposes, borrowing money from the patient, trying to develop a friendship with the patient, and asking the patient for personal favours.[10]

When Dr Masserman returned from his trips to conferences, for example, he brought Barbara Noël coins, records, trinkets, and other gifts. He invited her to go sailing in his yacht and to fly with him in his airplane. He persuaded her to accompany him and some other patients to a World Congress for Social Psychiatry in Paris. As president-elect of the association, Masserman induced Noël to be a hostess and translator for him at an event he was hosting.[11]

In the case of seven-year-old 'Don,' 'Dr Smith,' his dentist, ar-
·ranged a series of appointments to assess Don's crooked teeth.
Don's mother, who worked as a nurse in the same building, arranged for him to wait for her in Dr Smith's office after his appointments. Dr Smith assured her that Don would be no trouble; he
could work on his homework or talk to the receptionist. Don
would be better there, he advised, than in her own crowded and
busy setting. In addition to giving Don free toothbrushes and
toothpaste, Dr Smith started to buy him candy and comic books,
and later to take him out to lunch. He showered Don's mother
with praise about her well-mannered and well-brought-up son,
and she did not demur when he proposed to take Don on a ski
trip with his family.

After they swam nude together at the YWCA, Josephine's psychologist invited Josephine home for tea. As the two women talked,
Josephine told the psychologist that she had to move out of her
apartment. The psychologist responded that one of her adult children was vacating the basement suite in her home, and that Josephine could move in. After viewing the spacious accommodation,
much larger than she could afford under normal circumstances,
Josephine agreed.

Various pamphlets and lists have been produced for patients to
help them detect when boundary violations are occurring or may
occur. Warning signs of a possibility that the health professional
could become sexually exploitative include the following:

1 The health professional brings up his personal problems.
2 Sex is brought up out of context, and discussion of sex is emphasized in sessions. Sex may be put forward as *the* answer to the
  patient's problems.
3 Sessions are booked at odd hours or when there are no other
  staff in the office.
4 Sessions are arranged outside the office, or the patient is invited
  for a meal or other social occasion.
5 Forming a close personal relationship with the professional is
  presented as part of the treatment.
6 The professional directs the patient on how to behave and what

to do in everyday life. This may include directions about engaging in certain kinds of sexual behaviour.

7 The professional presents himself as the expert who has answers to every problem.

8 The patient is urged to become dependent on the professional and to separate herself from family and close friends.

9 The patient's assertive behaviour is criticized.

10 Touching, such as hand holding and hugging, is presented as a necessary or even central part of the treatment.

11 Alcohol or drugs, for use of the patient and professional, are made available during office visits.

12 Gifts are given to the patient.

13 Personal letters are written to the patient; unnecessary phone calls are made to the patient.

14 Fees, when applicable, are waived for treatment sessions.

15 The patient is directed to alter her physical appearance or dress to become more sexually attractive.

16 The patient is not getting help for the problem that took her to the professional in the first place.

17 The relationship feels uncomfortable, ambiguous, or confusing to the patient.

18 With survivors of sexual abuse, the professional seems to be titillated by details of the abuse.

Obviously, these are merely signs, and one or even several of these indicators do not necessarily mean that sexual exploitation is likely. They have to be taken in the context of the health professional's routine way of working and the patient's special needs. For example, physiotherapists, chiropractors, and massage therapists touch and manipulate the patient's body. Cognitive and behavioural therapists may be very directive about the patient's everyday life and behaviour. Narrative therapists sometimes write letters to patients. Physicians may make home visits in crisis situations, or see people at odd hours. If a patient is being abused, moving away from the abusive partner or family may be crucial.

Looking at boundary violations from the professional's perspective, Epstein and Simon developed an 'exploitation index' for therapists. They describe seven categories of exploitative behaviour:

1 Seeking a diversion from treatment: The therapist initiates social contact with patients.
2 Erotic: The therapist relishes romantic daydreams about patients.
3 Exhibitionistic: The therapist seeks out clientele who are famous or VIP.
4 Dependent: Talking about one's own difficulties.
5 Power seeking: Requesting personal favours from patients.
6 Greedy: Accepting large gifts.
7 Enabling: Failing to set limits because of apprehension about the patient's disappointment or anger.[12]

In my case, Dr A violated the boundaries of our relationship right from the beginning, when he stepped out of his role of supervisor and suggested that we use the final three months as therapy. Already he and I knew much more about each other than is usual in a physician–patient relationship and had mutual acquaintances and contacts. Already invested with the status of professor,[13] teacher, and mentor, he added the physician role. In addition, it is apparent that he made a number of other boundary violations, according to the above lists. He used excessive touching, he reinforced my dependency, he wrote personal letters, he gave me directions about dress and appearance, he saw me without fees initially, he criticized my assertive behaviour, and he recommended that I use 'feminine wiles' with my husband. He seemed to be aroused by the details of my abuse by Umpi.

Ten Common Scenarios That Lead to Sexual Abuse

Another way of understanding how abuse can be initiated by a professional is to examine the portrayals of therapist's characteristics or behaviour that lead to sexual exploitation. To paraphrase Pope and Bouhoutsos, these are:

1 Role trading: Patient and therapist exchange roles, and the therapist's needs come first.
2 Sex therapy: The therapist manipulates the patient into believing that sexual intimacy is a valid treatment technique.
3 As if ...: The therapist ignores the patient's transference and assumes that their intense and possibly erotic attachment is a sign that they are in love with the therapist.
4 Svengali: The therapist induces and takes advantage of an intense dependency on the part of the patient.
5 Drugs: These are used to facilitate the seduction.
6 Rape: Threats, intimidation, or physical force are used by the therapist.
7 True love: The therapist conceptualizes the relationship as a courtship or romance and tries to discount the formal professional nature of the relationship.
8 It just got out of hand: The therapist does not give sufficient attention, care, and respect to the emotional intimacy that develops in therapy.
9 Time out: The therapist considers that the principles and expectations of the therapeutic relationship cease to exist between scheduled sessions or outside the therapist's office.
10 Hold me: The therapist takes advantage of the patient's need for non-erotic physical contact and the possible confusion between this and erotic contact.[14]

Experiences may not fit neatly with these scenarios. Dr A's involvement with me shows aspects of 'role trading,' as he increasingly shared details of his personal life with me. 'Hold me' typifies the progression he promoted from hand holding to stroking and lying on the floor. Then there was a combination of 'as if' and 'true love,' as he repeatedly discounted my transference, my childlike devotion to an idealized parent figure, and reinterpreted it as love or lust. He abdicated his role and responsibilities as a physician and rationalized the relationship between us as a kind of mutual friendship that was sometimes a sexual or love relationship. There are some 'Svengali' dimensions, too, in that he appeared to enjoy my extreme dependence, even telling me, 'You feel like nothing without me,' and, 'You have found yourself through your love of me.'

Situational Factors

As implied in the long list of warning signs that suggest the possibility of the health professional's becoming sexually exploitative, the environment may play a part in facilitating the onset of the abusive relationship. In pointing this out I remove no responsibility from the professional, because, in most cases, the removal of possible constraints is planned by the professional.

Jane's psychiatrist told her to make a late appointment, after the secretary had left. Sylvia's family doctor, aware that her husband was on a late shift, invited himself to her home for a 'cup of tea.' 'Antoinette's' chiropractor always booked her as the last patient of the day; one session was almost four hours long. Ellen Plasil's abusive psychiatrist, Dr Leonard, had no secretary, ran his practice from his apartment, and had patients returning there in the evening to watch videotapes.

Dr A started touching, holding, stroking, and lying on the floor with me while his office was still in a busy clinic. Not until he moved to a small, dark, private office with no secretary did he progress further, to undressing and then penetrating me. I was surprised by his move, which seemed sudden. At the end of a session he announced that the next meeting would be in his new office. He must, however, have been planning the move for some months.

It has been suggested that the lower incidence of abuse of patients by social workers might be attributable to their work situations, often in busy public offices, agencies, or clinics. The lower incidence has also been ascribed to the more 'feminine' characteristics of men in social work, postulating that these men are more sensitive, caring, and responsible than men in psychiatry and psychology, and hence less likely to exploit patients.[15]

Special Issues for Victims of Child Abuse and Other Trauma

While this section applies particularly to therapist–patient relationships, it has some relevance as well to survivors' relationships with other health professionals and other persons whom they perceive to be in authority. As already remarked in the previous chapter, child sexual abuse victims, especially incest victims, are more vulnerable to sexual abuse by health professionals, and a special danger may exist early in a health professional–patient relationship when the survivor is disclosing details of the abuse. Health professionals may be sexually aroused by these accounts and more likely to violate their patient's trust.[16]

For example, 'Violet,' an extremely attractive woman in her early thirties, was in a rear-end collision, suffered whiplash, and was referred to a massage therapist. During the massage sessions, she became aware of very angry feelings towards her grandfather, and began to piece together some fragments of memory about his enticing her into his basement and inducing her to suck his penis and to allow him to touch her between the legs and insert his finger in her vagina. She was about six at the time. He gave her candy and warned her not to tell anyone, 'Or Granddaddy will be go to jail.' Violet adored her grandfather, so she told no one. Increasingly distraught about these memories, Violet confided in the massage therapist, who suggested that her family doctor could arrange a referral to a therapist.

Violet says that when she told her general practitioner about her memories, 'His eyes bugged out. He leaned forward in his chair. He started to breathe heavily. His eyes seemed to glaze over, and he wanted me to give the exact details of what my grandfather had done to me. He wanted me to tell him several times over. At one point he got out of his chair and came towards me, then changed his mind. I was quite scared. But nothing happened. He told me his secretary would make an appointment with a psychologist for me.'

After several months, Violet had her first appointment with the psychologist. He seemed warm and caring, and Violet told him about her stressful situation at work and as a single parent. In addition she was coping with pain from her neck injury. Because of the reception she had experienced from her family doctor, Violet delayed telling the psychologist about her sexual abuse. During this time, she became increasingly dependent on him and on his suggestions and advice. As her father had never been at home, and her husband had abruptly left her, Violet felt that her therapist was a special kind of parent that she had never had. She felt special, nurtured, and cared for.

Eventually Violet told her psychologist about her sexual abuse as a child, but by this time she felt that she was deeply in love with him, so she felt gratified when he held and stroked her, and readily acquiesced when he asked her to go away with him in his boat for the weekend.

It has been suggested that this tendency for professionals to abuse incest victims shortly after they disclose their abuse could be linked to a perception of the incest victim as having been 'publicly deflowered' and therefore no longer deserving of protection or respect.[17] Thus the health professional may view the incest victim as 'fair game,' and may excuse his seduction of her by telling himself that he cannot do her any further harm. The patient, trained as a child to stimulate and please men, may engage in a kind of ritualized seductive behaviour that arouses the professional and permits him to believe that she has an adult desire for sex with him. Because the victim has low self-esteem and may believe that no man will care for her without a sexual relationship, she may feel that sexual involvement with the professional is a necessary price to pay for his care.[18]

As a result of transference, of putting the therapist in the shoes of a childhood parent figure, the incest victim is likely to confuse sex with caring. Some patients become extremely sexually provocative and demanding, seemingly driven to re-enact their childhood abuse and to test the professional's ability to withstand seductive behaviour. 'Ruth,' sexually abused by her father from age two to fourteen, and the recipient of a 'home abortion,' was in a mental hospital as an adolescent. In her early adulthood, she was fortunate to find a psychiatrist who was skilled in treating abuse victims. Ruth remembers, 'I begged Dr C to have sex with me. He refused. I joined a therapy group and had sex with the psychologist who was the leader. Then I went back to Dr C. He was shocked and horrified, then I freaked out, and spent a month in hospital.'

She states that having sex with the group therapist was bad enough, but, 'If Dr C had done what I was demanding; if he had had sex with me, then that would have killed me.' If Dr C had acceded to her demands, this would have been a repetition of the incest. Ruth is now a skilled therapist and an exceptional advocate for abuse survivors.

People who have been traumatized as children and who may appear to be tough, competent adults, sometimes decompensate precipitately when they enter therapy. In his analysis of a series of incest victims who were subsequently abused by therapists, Richard Kluft notes that 'The process of therapy often triggered the abrupt emergence of acute and sometimes disabling symptomatology. One woman virtually decompensated when she began to experience flashbacks of her mother's genitalia coming closer to her face, and recalled being held down until she completed performing cunnilingus.'[19] Decompensation can also occur when former victims are faced with a major stress, illness, trauma, or developmental change. For instance, an adult whose child reaches the age that the survivor was when she was abused may find herself 'falling apart.' Survivors' tough suit of armour, their 'survivor skills,' may leave them, albeit temporarily, and they may suffer an array of symptoms which can include profound anxiety and depression, nightmares, flashbacks, emotional numbing, insomnia, difficulty concentrating, loss of interest in usual activities, feelings of alienation from others, anger or irritability, increased sensitivity to noises, suspiciousness, and physical symptoms such as nausea, fatigue, or choking. They may be suffering from delayed-onset post-traumatic stress disorder, an emotional reaction to severe trauma which sometimes does not manifest itself until years later.[20]

If the professional is not aware of this diagnosis, and does not impart this knowledge to the patient, then the sudden onslaught of feelings, nightmares, flashbacks, and so on, may convince both professional and patient that something disastrous must be wrong with the patient. This, in turn, may increase the patient's dependency on, and magical expectations of, the professional.

Yet another issue for the survivor of severe childhood trauma is the concept of 'traumatic transference,' described by Herman.

The experience of terror and helplessness has transformed the traumatized person's emotional responses to people in authority, so that his or her reactions to the health professional may have an extremely intense, life-or-death quality.[21] This fuels both the patient's initial reactions to a health professional and the development of a complicated, destructive, prolonged attachment to an abusing professional, which will be discussed more fully in the next chapter.

With victims of sexual abuse by therapists, therapy ends when the sexual relationship starts,[22] and the patient is left with more problems than she started with. The incest victim may be trapped in a prolonged destructive, even deadly, entanglement in which she repeatedly relives the betrayal and disappointment that she first experienced with her father or close relative. As several studies have shown, incest victims may be repeatedly victimized, by more than one professional. One person in Kluft's series was exploited by six therapists![23]

When I was Dr A's patient, the diagnosis of post-traumatic stress disorder was not in the diagnostic manual. It was known that battle victims broke down under extreme stress and that reactions were sometimes delayed. But this knowledge had not been extended to victims of other traumas. In those days, psychoanalytic theory was at the forefront, and it was recognized that relationships with parents shaped a child's life and that early traumatic experiences could be repressed and then unearthed in therapy later in life. Use of the patient's transference in the process of therapy was felt to be crucial.

Dr A may have been as disconcerted as I was by the emergence of my delayed-onset post-traumatic stress disorder, with its frightening intensity and suicidal impulses. Why, though, did he fail to refer me to a psychiatrist in my home city? In retrospect, it appears that his desire to continue as my therapist after my return to Canada outweighed any concerns he may have had about the effects of his physical distance and unavailability on my emotional decompensation.

3. Entrapment

'Why Did You Keep Going So Long?'

To know and not to know, to be conscious of complete truthfulness while telling carefully constructed lies, to hold simultaneously two opinions which cancelled out, knowing them both to be contradictory and believing both ... to forget whatever it is necessary to forget, then to draw it back into the memory again at the moment it was needed, and then promptly to forget it again, and above all to apply the same process to the process itself ... consciously to induce unconsciousness, and then once again to become unconscious of the act of hypnosis you have just performed.

'Doublethink,' in George Orwell's, *Nineteen Eighty-Four*[1]

This is the most difficult part to write about. As I sit staring at the piles of notes and letters, I find myself feeling at first numb, and then tearful, sad, ashamed, humiliated, guilty, angry, powerless, betrayed, duped, used, outraged, and disbelieving. 'How could I? ... how could I have been so stupid? ... how could I have betrayed my husband and family? ... why did I believe him? ... why didn't I listen to the inner voice that kept telling me it was wrong and just another seduction and betrayal, another incest? ... why was I so compliant? ... why did I keep making excuses for him? ... what was wrong with me? ... couldn't I have told someone else? ... how did he get me to keep it a secret? ... why couldn't I see that it was the sex, his use of me, and his blaming me for being so seductive, that was so upsetting? ... how come I kept letting him blame things on my problems, my mother, my marriage?' and, even more painfully, 'How could I have ever believed that he cared about me at all, even loved me a little?'

When, for the first time, Dr A initiated intercourse in his office, I felt warm, grateful, and nurtured. Dr A tried to reach his next patient and cancel the appointment so that we could have more time together. He was not able to reach her, so I had to leave. Suffused with warmth, feeling affirmed and cared for, no longer feeling fat and ugly, I left feeling very special. Before I left, Dr A asked me to ensure that the letters he had written to me would not be seen by my husband.

On arriving, a couple of weeks later, for the next session, which I had envisioned as a lengthy and romantic interlude, I found that Dr A was distant and controlling. Gone was my feeling of being special, unique, and cared for. I floundered, unable to find words, unable to convey the deep dismay I felt. I felt like a bad little girl who had transgressed, who had manipulated her father into a situation which he regretted. Eventually, towards the end of the session, Dr A announced that he wanted 'a little.' Without any attempt at foreplay, without any attention to my needs, he pulled off my underpants, thrust his penis into my dry vagina and relieved himself sexually. Soon after this he told me to go, as his next patient was expected. Feeling rejected, hurt, and angry, I burst into tears and was accused of being 'hysterical.' Physically sore, feeling rebuffed and used, I left the office. Driving fast and in angry confusion, I got lost several times and then was stopped by police for speeding. They noticed my pregnancy and let me off.

The next couple of sessions were equally confusing and painful. On the one hand, Dr A told me, 'You have found yourself through your love of me'; on the other, he chided me for my 'extreme dependency,' told me I needed to 'Get out of the nest,' and suggested cutting down the frequency of the sessions. He attributed the sexual involvement to my seductiveness, said he had reaffirmed his commitment to his wife, and that he did not want to take anything away from her. I felt terribly hurt, confused, and rejected; the 'separation feeling' was strong.

Some days later I started to bleed vaginally and was admitted to hospital for investigations and rest. No cause was found. In the back of my mind and the depths of my psyche I was convinced that it must be a retribution for my sexual involvement with Dr A. I felt like a whore, bad and seductive. As travel was forbidden, I did not see Dr A for four or five months, and struggled alone with feelings of depression, anger, guilt, loss, sadness, and *fears about my own extreme emotional instability. Again, I found it extremely difficult to meet the needs of my husband and two children, as well as to work part-time. As hard as I could, I tried to damp down, ignore, and push away my inner turmoil, and I wrote only a few formal and rather distant letters to Dr A during this time. In return I received several anxious-sounding letters from him, saying that he hoped that I was all right. He went on to say that he looked forward to seeing me as soon as I was able to travel.*

Following the birth of my third child, a healthy, easy, and cuddly child, I tried to put my relationship with Dr A in perspective. Was it therapy? Was it an affair? Surely he had merely re-enacted my childhood sexual abuse, stepping into my godfather's shoes? Then why did he blame me? Angrily I spoke to him on the telephone and told him that I was considering making a complaint to his licensing association. He accused me of 'betraying [his] trust ... visiting [my] problems on [him] ... acting out.' He suggested, 'Come down and see me, and we'll talk about it.' Sadly, his power over me reasserted itself, and I complied. He told me that he understood that I had a 'godfather transference' to him. Nevertheless, he insisted by saying, 'I am not your godfather, I am a totally different person, someone you love and trust. Your therapist. You are learning to trust men through your relationship with me.' We had intercourse again that very day in his office. Part of me felt cheap, used, and readily available, but I submerged these feelings. I told myself that Dr A was right: this was different, I was getting better, I was learning to love.

From this point on, the relationship came to be defined as 'mutual' or 'equal.' In retrospect, I am utterly amazed. How could I have believed it to be so? Dr A controlled the relationship completely. We met in his office, for a specified time, at his convenience. I did all the travelling. He refused to meet outside his office, ignoring my suggestion that this would be more comfortable and more appropriate. Self-righteously he stated, 'I couldn't deal with my feelings about having an affair.' What he viewed as equality appeared to encompass his confiding in me about his problems with his job and difficulties with his wife. Responding to these concerns, I was nurturing and supportive. Many of the letters that I wrote to him contain lengthy passages aimed at building his self-esteem, telling him from a student's perspective how much I appreciated him, telling him what a wonderful therapist he was, pointing out how his family relationships might have affected him, suggesting ways that he could handle the job situation, urging him to express his feelings more openly, and so on.

By the third year, I was continuing to see Dr A at intervals of two to four weeks, and occasionally more frequently. I continued to be obsessed and preoccupied with him. Feeling deeply in love with him, I spent many hours thinking about past sessions and indulging in romantic fantasies about the future. At times, Dr A would tell me that he, too, loved me 'a little bit.' Every few months he would initiate intercourse with me. The result was predictable. At the next session he would be controlling, self-righteous, and blaming, accusing me of having provoked him into a sexual response. Alternately feeling warm and cared for, and rebuffed, rejected, and belittled, I continued to accept the cyclical nature of our involvement. I was convinced that everything would fall into place and that it would all be all right in the end, if only I managed to keep hanging in.

Trying to deal with two diametrically opposite sets of feelings about Dr A, I wrote letters that increasingly reflected this duality. One set came to be defined as the 'angry part.' I assumed that the angry part was the primitive, angry, hurt child in me and that this part would gradually be overcome by the 'warm, caring woman part,' a part which would be eventually restored or repaired by therapy. For instance, a couple of weeks after a sexual episode, I wrote to Dr A, 'The angry, primitive part sneers derisively, "You abject failure, you stupid ass, you misguided idiot, why did you trust him? It wasn't a new experience, it just turned out the same old way, repeated horribly painful separations and seductions. Just the same as before, that's all that can happen. You may as well just claim you are cured and go sadly away, never trusting anyone again."'

In the same letter, I went on to voice the 'other part,' which 'struggles and struggles with the above conviction that is so strong and answers, "No, no, no, you can't make the relationship a vicious self-fulfilling prophecy. It wasn't that way, you can't distort such a wonderful experience along the lines of your pathology and past experiences."'

At times the 'angry part' would get loud and demanding, and Dr A would respond by reminding me, as in one letter, 'I think that I am giving to you as few other therapists would ... when you decided to become my patient and I accepted, we both made a commitment, for me to help you understand yourself, to build up a situation of trust and openness and human respect. I believe that I am doing everything to keep my side of the bargain.' In this letter he *also described me as tremendously angry, needy, and unpredictable, and suggested that I was distorting what he had said and done, and was 'attacking below the belt.' As a result of these responses, which typically placed all the blame for my chaotic feelings on me and my 'pathology' and defined the 'angry part' as bad and unacceptable, I would apologize for being such a problematic and difficult patient. I felt very grateful to him for putting up with my unpredictable moods and occasional tirades.*

Increasingly I came to view the 'angry part' as a dark, murderous, destructive, and vindictive part of myself which was primarily produced by my mother's repeated abandonments. I felt this part of myself should be restrained at all costs. If allowed to escape, the anger would be so immense that everyone would be consumed. One fantasy I had at that time involved my anger, liberated, which destroyed the whole world and left only a grey moonscape littered with twisted wreckage. Dreams of my children being attacked by ferocious animals and being maimed or killed paralleled these fantasies and were also considered, by Dr A, to be part of my destructive inner rage.

Sometimes Dr A's sexual involvement, subsequent withdrawal, defensiveness, and self-righteousness seemed unbearable. Six months after my third child was born, I was scheduled for a hysterectomy. Assailed by doubts and fears of being maimed or castrated, I felt reassured about my femininity and attractiveness when Dr A initiated sex a few weeks before the operation. The next time I saw him, a few days before the operation, he was rejecting, cold, and distant. The sex, he explained, had happened because he was feeling deprived because his wife was sick. He felt that intercourse with me had been a trivial incident, a lapse, but it had made him feel less tense around her. Aghast and terribly hurt, I became 'hysterical,' hit him once, and yelled at him that he was cruel and insensitive. This time he must have realized that he had gone too far, as he came to visit me in the hospital a few days later, bringing me a book entitled Friendship.

Following the operation I had another experience, which I now realize is normal and expected, but at the time served as further evidence of my grave psychiatric disorder. The operation, hysterectomy and repair, was extremely painful. It was so painful that I scarcely slept at all for the first few nights. On the third night I slept a few hours and dreamt of a fourth child; sweet faced and curly haired. Rudely shaken awake from this dream, I groggily beheld a young doctor who read me the pathology report on my uterus. Realizing that the fourth child was merely a dream, I burst into tears, to the consternation of the young doctor and the gynaecologist, who berated me for being 'neurotic' and prescribed Valium.

As the months went by I was still obsessed with thoughts of Dr A. At times I felt that he was playing a cat-and-mouse game with me, that I would never escape his clutches. I felt like a puppet. He jerked the strings, and I moved in whatever way he wanted. When I tried to discuss these feelings with Dr A, he attributed them to 'your deep distrust of men; something you are learning to overcome with me.' I tried hard to ignore the muttering of the 'angry part' and push away any criticisms of Dr A's behaviour. Sometimes this was very hard; and, shortly after another episode of sex followed by distance, withdrawal, and blaming, I penned, 'I have so many negative feelings about your past stupidities, irresponsibility, unpredictability. I am so angry about it, yet I feel "Please God let me forget it again. I don't want to think about it, I can't think negative feelings about you." I feel I can't face talking with you about it, can't even fantasize talking about it with you. I'm so pissed off with myself, I can't express myself about some areas when I see you, and I'm so damn compliant, subservient, and agreeable.'

Sometimes Dr A would go to a course or workshop, learn about a new technique, and try it out on me, sometimes with explosive or disastrous results. Once, during the fourth year, he had been to a Gestalt workshop and told me that he had decided to 'to call a spade a spade. The only reason you are coming here is because you love me.' He went on to emphasize that I did not need therapy any more. Later, in that same session, he told me that he was feeling sexually deprived as his wife was away, and we had intercourse. This consisted of a sudden climax for him, and no enjoyment for me. After this session, I wrote to him, taking all the responsibility on myself and trying to prevent his anticipated response of blaming me and becoming distant and judgmental. 'I am pissed off with myself for being so willing. I should have been a more objective and considerate friend and said No.' In this letter, I also told him that he had made a frontal attack on my feelings and, 'I felt confused, disorganized, and as usual so dominated and controlled by you that I completely deferred to your interpretation and that was the only way I could see it.' Falling into the role of his therapist, I went on to ask him if he had been attacking me because we had got emotionally close, and because he had talked of his feelings a great deal in the previous session.

On another occasion, he had wanted to try out a Gestalt technique, and had me visualize my godfather sitting in a chair and express my rage towards him by hitting him with a pillow. But as I began to get angry, Dr A and my godfather's image merged, and I began to hit Dr A! When I calmed down, I apologized profusely, and this was seen as one more piece of evidence of my unstable and aggressive nature.

More and more, however, I found myself able to compartmentalize the strange and unpredictable happenings in Dr A's office from the rest of my life. Often Dr A talked about himself, and I found that I was much more perceptive and able to recognize and respond to his moods and needs than I was to my own. Reminiscing about his childhood, he portrayed a stern and distant father and a mother who was powerful and controlling. As a second son, he felt constantly overshadowed by his elder brother, and felt that he was 'second best' to his parents.

During the fourth year I struggled against my dependency, against the ties that seemed to bind me to Dr A, against the wish that he would affirm me sexually – although this usually had disastrous results. I continued to hold the view that Dr A was helping me, and that, as a result, I was getting stronger and was more involved with my family and doing well in my job. He had, I felt, rescued me from a sticky morass of neuroses or from the intense and unpredictable emotions of the 'borderline personality.' Eternally grateful, I felt bound to do anything I could to help him in return.

As I grew stronger, my husband's recurrent depression and work difficulties came to the fore. When I tried to discuss my frustration with Dr A about my husband's passivity and his tendency to vent his anger on our eldest child, Dr A reconstructed my complaints within the framework of my supposed disorder. He accused me of 'masculine protest' and told me that I was a very angry woman who was extremely threatening to men. He told me to apologize to my husband, buy him presents, and use 'feminine wiles.' I tried to follow his directions.

In the last two to two and a half years that I travelled to see Dr A, the frequency of sessions declined, leaving one-, two- or even three-month intervals between sessions. My career was going well, and I moved from half to three-quarter time. Encouraged by a warm, perceptive, and understanding department head, I began to write articles. I was receiving much positive feedback from colleagues and professionals in the community. At the same time, Dr A's career seemed stagnant. Still trying to maintain some university involvement, he took on an administrative role, which he appeared to find tiring and stressful. He talked about being an underachiever, lacking motivation, and being unwilling to take risks.

Because our relationship had been defined as equal or mutual, it seemed natural that many of our sessions and much of my letter writing would focus on trying to help Dr A with his difficulties. In one letter, I wrote, 'Your description last time of how insecure you felt because someone else had possibly been offered your position obviously must be related to your low self-concept and the sibling relationship in your family where parent figures were critical and your brothers did better, were felt to have more ability, and were cited as examples. I am guessing a bit here, but I would be surprised if some of it isn't relevant. I hope you have accepted more realistic aspects of the situation, e.g., that someone who could work full-time would be more suitable.'

In the sessions, he often seemed tired, miserable, dispirited, and dejected. My role, it appeared, was now to humour him and to help him in return for all the wonderful therapy he had given me in the past. Sometimes his wishes were very hard to comply with. In one session, after I had shared with him my excitement about some very positive feedback about my work with a community agency, he told me that he wanted 'some contact' with me. He directed me to lie on my side on the floor, to be completely passive and 'non-erotic.' Compliant, but not expecting what was about to happen, I did as I was told. Dr A pulled off my underwear, unzipped the fly of his grey pinstriped trousers, penetrated me with his erect penis, and held himself motionless and silent. I began to feel sad, alienated, alone, and abandoned, and started to cry. Dr A ejaculated and withdrew, got up and motioned me back to my chair. When I tried to discuss what had happened, and how I felt, Dr A silenced me by blaming his 'sudden climax' on my 'sexy appearance' and claimed that he would have 'continued' if I had not started to cry. The next day after this session, I felt angry, scattered, and anxious and was in a car accident. It was the other driver's fault, but I could probably have avoided him if my concentration had been better.

It was after this disastrous session that I wrote to Dr A pleading for some clarification about our 'awfully one-sided' relationship. While apologizing for the unrealistic outpourings of the 'angry part,' I nonetheless asked him if his 'sudden climax' could be interpreted as '[his] hostile and sadistic reassertion of male supremacy?' I described all the work, and all the writing that I was doing, trying to sort out the 'equal relationship.' I chided him for putting no time or energy into disentangling the complications of our 'mutual' involvement and wrote, sarcastically, 'You write me occasional notes on your beautiful headed notepaper when you feel sorry for my separation anxiety. Notes which are a mixture of ambiguity and euphemism. Can't you call a spade a spade? You must have some fears of getting caught. If you feel that way, write on toilet paper and don't sign your name. I'd much rather have something honest and open to get hold of than "I won't go into details" and "You know what I mean."'

Sometime after this, Dr A admitted that he did not feel comfortable with an equal relationship, a friendship. He re-established himself as the therapist. He was the doctor, and I was the patient, and we were working on the termination of my therapy. Despite this clarification, our relationship drifted once more into a situation where I was hearing about his difficulties. For instance, I wrote to him saying, 'Last time you looked unhappy, unsure, preoccupied, and I felt a sort of maternal, protective wish to cuddle you like a little boy and tell you not to be afraid, that it was OK and that you could cope – that your expectations of yourself are always too high anyway. I wish I could do something to help you. However, I see now much more clearly that, as a mere patient, I can't and you wouldn't allow me to do anything to help. As you said also, "I wouldn't tell my private thoughts to a woman." On the other hand, you have told me quite a lot, periodically, so that, even though much is hypothetical, I have some idea of the kind of space you are in. Not as bad as mine, but not good either.'

During these months, related to long breaks between sessions, I was periodically aware of still feeling like a tiny child that was lost, abandoned, and alone. The 'separation feeling' was intense at times; I missed Dr A, and felt anguished and fearful. How could I ever separate from him, how could I ever do without him. He was so dear to me; I felt so attached to him, thought of him constantly. I grew thin, tense, unable to sleep, and became dependent on nightly Valium.

Having concluded that any anger towards Dr A was immature, irrational, and pathological, my anger towards my mother was rekindled, and I found myself seething with resentment towards her and entertaining murderous fantasies. I wrote a 'Hypothetical Letter,' which I thankfully never mailed, in which I wrote accusingly, 'You rejected me, you didn't care, you used me for your own needs, and then you said it was all my fault. And I believed you, said you were the best mother that existed and I was an ungrateful, mixed-up bitch. The only time that it looked like I could have any reasonable relationship with a parent figure you buggered that up too, you told me all those lies about father, you evil, nasty, self-centred bitch. You turned me against him *so that I whitewashed you and blackened him. So that I had even more angry feelings about men, bitterness and resentment, need to depreciate them, sabotage them, and put them down as you did to father. There are two men in my life [Dr A and my husband] who are warm and giving, and put up with a great deal from me, but you, my identification with you, and the terrible rage you left me with, prevent me from getting close and trusting them in the way I would like to.'* I went on to insist that *'You have made me feel that I am stupid, unworthy, unacceptable, a bad mother, a hopeless wife. You have made me depressed, anxious, insecure, fearful. You have made me some- one who will have a lifetime struggle with sensitivity, fears of my aggression, problems relating, and insecurity.'*

Because of my conviction, instilled by Dr A, that my mother was at the root of most of my problems, I withdrew from her for years, rarely wrote, forgot her birthday, did not want to visit England, diminished her role as grand- mother to my children, and rarely invited her to visit us. Distressed and un- comprehending, she turned to my siblings, who tried to suggest that I needed to change my attitude.

I left my last therapy session, some six and a half years after it had started, with an acute sense of failure. Dr A had told me how much I had helped him, how he had learned to trust and communicate more openly. Describing a recent brief affair that he had had with a young woman he had met at a con- ference, he said that his relationship with me had opened him up to the possi- bility of such experiences. Feeling hurt, abandoned, and misunderstood, I returned home to my family, still trying to convince myself that I had been through a wonderful psychotherapeutic experience. Actually, even though I was not as fragmented as I had been during the early years of therapy, I was left with many more problems than I had had before Dr A initiated 'therapy.' I was thin, tense, moody, felt inadequate and guilty, suffered from insomnia, found sex abhorrent at times, and was often critical and intolerant of my husband.

Other people who have been trapped for more than a few months in a sexually abusive relationship with a health professional have given similar accounts of feeling special; feeling isolated with their secret; hearing about the professional's problems and difficulties; being extremely dependent; feeling trapped, like a puppet, or 'under a spell'; and thinking that the professional, and only the professional, held the answer to their problems. In most cases the ex-patients described emotionally abusive or 'crazy-making' behaviour by the professional, while the professional attributed responsibility for his abusive behaviour to the patient. Looking back, most felt 'monumentally stupid' and angry about the amount of time they had wasted, and the detrimental effects the experience had had on their lives and the lives of those close to them.

All the written accounts that I am familiar with concern women, and all the people who told me about lengthy entanglements with health professionals were women. Men, and some women, were able to leave the abusive relationships promptly, realizing, as Jane reported, that 'I was mad. He shouldn't have done that. I felt betrayed. It was like having sex with my father. I never went back.' The fact that there are no reports of men trapped for lengthy periods in such relationships does not remove the possibility that some exist. It is possible that men, like boys who have been sexually abused, are much more reluctant to report the abuse, because it raises major concerns about their sexual identity and marked feelings of powerlessness. Or, in some cases, in line with our cultural expectation that men are the sexual aggressors, men may feel in control of a sexual relationship with a female health professional and deem this beneficial rather than a betrayal. Or perhaps they maintain a kind of ambiguity in their role, a non-patient status, as exemplified by the character of Tom Wingo in *The Prince of Tides*?[2] Nonetheless, this chapter will refer to women, and will focus on possible reasons why women get trapped in long-term destructive relationships with health professionals.

Trapped for five and a half years in a bizarre sexually and emotionally abusive relationship with Dr Leonard, Ellen Plasil found that his outlandish behaviour reinforced her confusion as she struggled to love him and comply with his prescription for perfect health. He was unpredictable. She never knew when he was going to invite her to his bedroom, and she struggled with the meaning of the relationship, asking him, 'We do not date, yet we do share a bed. We do not have intercourse, but I do fellate you. I do not take meals with you, yet I do take baths with you ... This is not therapy. You told me so once. But I need to know – what is this?'

After she tried to discuss this sexual relationship with another of Dr Leonard's patients, and with the doctor who referred her to Dr Leonard, Plasil became the object of Dr Leonard's fury. 'His eyes began to bulge as they slowly filled with rage. Then he broke the silence. "You're scum," I heard him say. "You're real scum."' She felt guilty, worthless, had suicidal thoughts, begged him to forgive her, and pleaded with him not to throw her out. Put on 'probation' by Dr Leonard, Plasil describes how the 'gradual suspension of my judgement, of my values, of my own sense of self, which had begun so early in my therapy, was all but complete. My life was now totally his to mold, alter and judge however he saw fit.'

Automatically obedient to his every whim, Plasil learned to detect his moods and wishes by reading his face, gestures, and tone of voice. She felt that he was her 'lifeline,' and he told her repeatedly that she could not get 'this kind of help anywhere else.' Increasingly numb, she experienced less and less anger at being used sexually.[3]

Barbara Noël, unknowingly addicted to Amytal, wanted to leave Dr Masserman after ten years of therapy. He insisted that she still had many unresolved problems, accused her of wasting her life on a younger man, and told her that she could return to therapy when she was ready to face reality. She returned, missing the Amytal, after a period of drinking heavily and smoking marijuana, and finding herself blocked in her song writing. Instead of being glad to see her, Dr Masserman was 'indifferent and detached, almost callous.' Because Dr Masserman seemed sarcastic, critical, and constantly angry at her, she left again, but soon returned seeking the Amytal. As she had been drinking very heavily, Masserman gave her Antabuse – a medication that creates a physical aversion to alcohol – as well as Amytal. Later, Noël discovered Amytal, a highly addictive drug, can trigger alcoholism, but at the time, 'I was too addicted and too bound to Dr Masserman to question his judgement.'

Whenever Noël met a man she liked, Dr Masserman would suggest that her judgment was wrong. He undermined her self-esteem and autonomy to the point that she felt cowed and defeated, suggesting that she give up her job, marry, and let her husband support her. In their discussions, 'The spotlight was almost always on him, on pleasing him, on keeping him from getting angry.' Later, she realized, 'Masserman had dosed me with emotional abuse and allowed me to stay suspended in a state of nongrowth, and when I was very, very good, he had given me an ultimate fogout, which he called Amytal.'[4]

During a year of monthly sexual encounters, Carolyn Bates's psychologist, Dr X, 'never seemed concerned that [she] was growing more closed and automaton-like as the months passed.' Although she was once aware of feeling special because he considered her attractive, she was more often confused and angry, feeling she had no choice. She felt guilty and ashamed about having premarital sex with a father figure, yet powerless to resist. Often Dr X talked about his personal issues, his anger towards his ex-wife, helplessness in the face of the upcoming divorce, and unhappiness about his relationships with his colleagues and his parents. Even though he was spending most of the time, each session, talking about his problems, he continued to charge her. Afraid to leave therapy, feeling that she could never get well on her own, she clung to the hope that he could give her answers, make sense of her confusion, and lift her depression.[5]

Like many other victims, Antoinette, entangled in a sexual relationship with her chiropractor for more than two years, said that the sex made her feel very special. The degree to which she felt special and worthwhile depended on the length of time they spent together after the treatment session ended, and how far 'things progressed physically.' Charlene spoke of getting affection and acknowledgment and admitted, 'I was delighted. This famous psychiatrist kept wanting me to go to bed with him. I felt really special, I thought he loved me.' While some victims had been directed explicitly by the professional to keep the relationship secret, all had the understanding that it must remain secret. The sense of specialness and secrecy was often accompanied by a conviction of being totally safe and secure with the professional, and many women spoke of the professional's office as being like a home, or even a sanctuary.

'Joyce' felt trapped in the relationship because her family doctor was giving her injections for migraines. He also cosigned a car loan for her. When she tried to leave the abusive relationship, he threatened to refuse to give her pills and to tell other doctors that she was an addict, so that they would not prescribe her any medication. Other women have described similar experiences when they tried to terminate the relationship, with health professionals telling them that they were far too sick or too emotionally disturbed to manage, and that they would never find such good treatment or therapy anywhere else.

Josephine moved into her psychologist's basement suite, and continued to go to her office for therapy. Sometimes the psychologist suggested that Josephine go home and prepare a meal, so that they could continue their discussion. Soon the women became sexually involved. The psychologist, declaring that she had found herself as a lesbian, began to 'come out' to friends and colleagues. Although enjoying an improved lifestyle, Josephine felt constricted and embarrassed. She could not discuss the relationship at work, withdrew from friends and family, and felt increasingly dependent on the psychologist.

Sylvia obviously had some mixed feelings about the sexual relationship with Ken, her general practitioner, but feared that if she ended the relationship, she 'would have nothing and nobody.' She says, 'The sex never varied. There was no talking and no foreplay ... My problems, personal and marital, were still there and still growing, and I was becoming more unhappy all the time. And though I truly felt totally used as far as our sexual relationship was, I didn't dare say anything about it because he was the only person I had contact with other than my daughter, husband and mother-in-law and I was terrified of losing my only friend in the world.'

Other women, often in the phase of feeling nurtured and special, were subjected to having their therapy suddenly and abruptly terminated. 'Anne' was told by her woman counsellor, with whom she had felt very dependent yet controlled, like a 'puppet on a string,' that the therapy was ended because Anne had lied to her about beginning to drink again. As Anne's counsellor was a prominent figure in their lesbian community, Anne saw her quite frequently at community gatherings. The counsellor deliberately avoided Anne, would not make eye contact, or would move as far away from her as possible. Anne noticed that the counsellor had a new partner, a woman who Anne realized was also one of the counsellor's patients. Anne felt doubly betrayed: first by the sexual relationship and then by the rejection.

It seems likely that these long-term relationships are most damaging, as they often seem to imply that a meaningful relationship is present or possible.[6] Why does a woman get trapped in such a destructive long-term relationship in which her interests and needs are being blatantly disregarded, her body used, her self-esteem undermined, her values sabotaged, and her emotions manipulated, trivialized, or ignored?

Research suggests that there may be many complicated and interrelated reasons why people are not able to leave abusive situations. These can be psychological, social, cultural, gender related, physiological, neurochemical, hormonal, or behavioural. Chapter 1 described some risk factors and vulnerabilities which may make health professionals or patients more likely to become involved in exploitative relationships. Added to this are the mystique and power, conveyed by the status and role of health professionals, that lead people to trust, and comply with their directions.

Various authors have tried to explain why people get caught up in abusive relationships. There is no single explanation. The thoughts and ideas of the various writers overlap, but all strike a chord for me when I try to understand what happened to me and to other victims who were similarly trapped and enslaved. The concepts that I review in this chapter are (1) Leonard Shengold's description of 'soul murder'; (2) traumatic bonding; (3) Peter Rutter's thoughts about 'sex in the forbidden zone'; (4) issues in female socialization; (5) Marilyn Peterson's description of the four factors operating during boundary violations; (6) attachment theory; and (7) Judith Herman's theory of 'traumatic transference.' All these can further aid our understanding of the complex interdigitated reasons why people, particularly women, stay in situations that are so destructive and inimical to personal growth. The last two concepts refer more specifically to people who have been traumatized as children.

Soul Murder

Expressing many of the ideas embraced by the notion of traumatic bonding, the term 'soul murder' was coined by psychoanalyst Leonard Shengold and applied to 'the deliberate attempt to eradicate or compromise the separate identity of another person. The victims of soul murder remain in large part possessed by another, their souls in bondage to someone else.' Saying that children are the usual victims, Shengold attributes soul murder to physical and mental torture, sexual abuse, and emotional deprivation. He suggests that 'a clinical situation analogous to that of a patient who has been seduced as a child is presented by one who has seduced or been seduced by a therapist ... [the analyst] will sense the distinct quality conferred by the actual experience and will feel its effect in the intensity of the patient's distrust, the corruptibility of the patient's superego, the depth of the expectation of repetition – and other resistances that affect the viability of future treatment.'

Soul murder elicits a combination of helplessness and rage, feelings that must be suppressed for the victim to survive. According to Shengold, 'Brainwashing makes it possible to suppress what has happened and the terrible feelings evoked by the erased or discounted experience. When it is necessary to retreat from the feelings, good feelings as well as bad ones are compromised, and the victim's deepest feelings are invested primarily in the soul murderer.'[7]

Traumatic Bonding

There are a number of situations in which people develop emotional ties to those who abuse them. Adults as well as children often make attachments to people who intermittently beat, threaten, or harass them. Hostages have become involved with their captors to the extent of having sex with them, putting up bail for them, and even wanting to marry them. Abused children often resist being removed from their abusive homes, and cling to their parents.[8]

Some authors have noted that, in abusive marriages, the batterer–victim relationship resembles the bond between captor and hostage or cult leader and follower. Major factors in the formation of this traumatic bond are captivity, isolation, and lack of outside support or influence.[9] Caught in a 'cycle of violence,' the victim is sustained by intermittent rewards, by positive interludes in which it seems that the batterer has reformed, become contrite, nurturing, and respectful. Wishing to believe that this is the reality of the relationship, thinking that by her behaviour or compliance she can enjoy this affirmative interaction on a permanent basis, she becomes even more firmly bound to the batterer. The repeated experience of reprieve followed by terror, 'especially within the isolated context of a love relationship, may result in a feeling of intense, almost worshipful dependence upon an all-powerful god-like authority. The victim may live in terror of his wrath, but she may also view him as the source of strength, guidance and life itself. The relationship may take on an extraordinary quality of specialness.'[10]

People who have been abused, neglected, or deprived as children are more vulnerable to traumatic bonding. Having accommodated to violence that may alternate with unpredictable affection, having experienced parents' failure to protect them, they feel devoid of control in relationships.[11] Stunted in their capacity for self-care, self-soothing, and empathic self-regard, they are unable to view themselves or their behaviour with compassion.[12] As adults, they may believe that they can erase the past by being perfect exemplary citizens, models of love and competency. When this fails, as it often does, they are likely to blame themselves.

In addition to these social, psychological, intergenerational, and behavioural components of traumatic bonding, it has been postulated that people can become addicted to their victimizer. The stress of the abusive interaction can liberate opiumlike substances, so that the person can become accustomed to feeling especially energized and 'high' after the abusive interaction has ceased. As well, people exposed to severe, ongoing trauma may experience a chronic state of increased arousal with changes in body chemistry. The person may experience this state of arousal as tension, agitation, anxiety, insomnia, weight loss, headaches, stomach problems, and other physical symptoms. It has been shown that this state of 'hyperarousal' interferes with the person's ability to make a clear-headed analysis of the situation and formulate ways to understand and deal with the trauma.[13]

These concepts of soul murder and traumatic bonding have direct application to the women who are enslaved by their health professional. They explain the otherwise paradoxical attachment, loyalty, and even worshipful reverence accorded to the abuser. Like a battered woman, the victim of sexual abuse by a professional experiences intermittent rewards which make her feel special and tie her even more firmly to him. Increasingly isolated from other relationships by the secrecy and 'doublethink' she has to maintain, she invests the professional with her deepest feelings and he may become her only source of strength and guidance. In addition, changes in body chemistry and 'hyperarousal' lead to a constant state of tension and fractured concentration, so that a careful, painstaking, objective examination of her situation is beyond the woman's capabilities.

In my case, as I was already a victim of childhood abuse, traumatic bonding to Dr A was promoted by the isolation, the secrecy, and Dr A's variable responses to me, sometimes warm and comforting, other times cold and distant. Looking back, I did experience states of 'hyperarousal,' often suffering from anxiety and severe insomnia, and was unable to make a rational assessment of the situation.

'Sex in the Forbidden Zone'

Writing from a Jungian perspective, cognizant of female socialization, Dr Peter Rutter has helped many women understand the dimensions of their betrayal and start to heal. He outlines three key factors in the 'masculine myth of the feminine' that facilitate abusive sexuality. Women's deference, expected in our culture, sets the stage. The second component involves the enormous nurturing, healing, and sexual powers that men believe women hold and can bestow on them. This archetype's opposite – the belief that women are vindictive and destructive – is the third factor which comes into play when men are disappointed. Thus men blame any pain, weakness, or reversal of fortune on women's dark powers.

Commenting that, on a superficial level, it may appear that a woman gets sexually involved in the 'forbidden zone' to preserve the 'enlivening specialness that she has come to feel,' Rutter postulates that she is actually influenced by danger and her powerlessness. Trying to preserve hope in the relationship, she reaches out to the wounded man who is exploiting her. Although the man has destroyed his ability to help her by consummating the relationship, this consummation reinforces the woman's perception of the man's wound. Now, as well as exploiting the woman's sexuality and spirit, he is misusing her compassion.

This compassion, rooted in women's instinctive and selfless response to babies, helps to explain why women allow themselves to be exploited for years. Rutter ascribes women's inability to leave abusive relationships to 'a conspiracy between their natural instinct to nurture, and a culturally accepted role that they have been taught to play and that men expect of them.'[14]

Female Socialization

Although there are class and cultural variations, most girls experience a series of expectations based on gender.[15] From the first, boys and girls are treated differently by parents. Commonly, two subcultures are evident in a family. Females are involved with child care, homemaking, and food preparation; males with cars, garages, outside chores, and sports. Boys are encouraged to assert themselves and stand up for their rights, and are directed towards activities, ideas, and things. Girls are encouraged to be sensitive to feelings, interested in people and relationships,[16] and compassionate and caring, and to avoid anger and confrontations. Preschool teachers and schoolteachers tend to reinforce these gendered expectations. In the family, in the media, in school, and in the community, children learn that men are usually more important than women, and that, although having a job or career may be tolerated, women's primary achievement is being a wife and mother.

Thus girls are programmed to believe that they will be happy and fulfilled by serving others, by devoting themselves to meeting the needs of husband and children or other deserving children or adults. In addition to providing for physical needs, the woman in a family is the emotional organizer, the mediator of feelings, whose job it is to dampen or absorb tensions, avoid confrontations, divert energies, and generally keep the family running smoothly.

With this background, a woman, any woman, is at risk for becoming entangled in an abusive relationship with a male professional. Socialized to defer to and serve men, and viewing herself as primarily responsible for mediating relationships, she can get stuck in a destructive relationship. Believing in the authority of the abuser's contention that she should stay and that she is being helped, basking in attention from a valued male, buying into his blaming of her for the vicissitudes of the relationship, thinking that if she tries hard enough all problems will be solved, she stays on and on. This is even more likely, of course, if the man is a prominent or famous member of the community.

My account of therapy with Dr A illuminates many elements of female socialization and 'sex in the forbidden zone' issues. Repeatedly I reached out to Dr A, the wounded healer, and he exploited my compassion as well as invading my body and soul. This role reversal, this focus on his needs, gained impetus after he had initiated sex and irreparably damaged the relationship. There are many examples of my deference to his power and authority; one of the most striking is when he made me lie motionless and submit to penetration by him. This seemed to follow an interaction where he may have felt that I was escaping from my subordination and threatening to equal or surpass him.

The stifling of my 'angry part,' which was, in fact the voice of sanity or reason, resulted from an agreement that the 'angry part' was primitive, immature, and pathological. As a woman, I felt uneasy with my anger, and Dr A obviously perceived it as a manifestation of my dark, destructive, and vindictive power. My perception of myself as potentially evil and destructive was enhanced by my fear that I was somehow like the drunken, raging Umpi, and it rested also on the self-image that most people who are abused as children carry. To preserve the idea that parents are good and trustworthy, abused children blame themselves and consider themselves to be bad, evil, vindictive, untrustworthy, and rotten.

The Characteristics of a Boundary Violation

In every account of a boundary violation, states Peterson, four issues surface: indulgence of professional privilege, role reversal, secrecy, and a double bind. These four characteristics interlock and set in train a series of relational changes that create a new system with a life force of its own.[17]

The professional's need and the client's vulnerability may combine to present an opportunity for the professional to exploit the relationship. A sense of entitlement allows the professional to intrude on the client and to shift the emphasis from helping the client to meeting the professional's needs. Often professionals rationalize their behaviour by claiming that they are still meeting the client's needs. For instance, women have been told that sex is therapy or, as in my case, that 'You have found yourself through love of me,' and 'You are learning not to hate men.'

When roles are reversed, the client becomes the caretaker and the professional can now look to the client to satisfy his or her needs. This, as Peterson points out, is 'twisting the ethos of care.' But the professional does not give up the control in the relationship and still defines the boundaries according to his own needs. This can be seen clearly in my situation. I was hearing all about Dr A's problems and difficulties, the relationship was defined as 'equal,' yet I did all the travelling, went to his office, fit in with his availability, and paid him or gave him gifts.

In a boundary violation, information is concealed from the client. The client is not aware of the professional's true motives or agenda. This gives the professional an unfair advantage in the relationship, potentially obscuring the client's reality and making a farce of the bond of trust. Once, when Dr A told me that I had to stop seeing him, I pleaded with him, saying that I had many more things to work out. At the time of the next session, he talked encouragingly of all the things we had to work on together. I asked him, 'How have I got back into favour?' Dr A replied, 'I've changed my mind.'

Secrets also produce three-person triangles, where two people are aware of the secret and one person is not. Professional and client share this conspiracy, and the person outside is likely to be damaged. In my case, my husband was the third person. He was deeply hurt and eventually permanently alienated by the secrecy.

Peterson suggests that clients are caught in conflicts of interest, or 'double binds,' during boundary violations. Attempts to resolve the situation appear very risky and expose the client to possible loss of the relationship or loss of attention to their needs. There is an implied threat to the double bind, so that clients feel blocked from taking action by fears of abandonment. At the same time, they lose their self-respect by failing to listen to the inner voice that is telling them that something is wrong. In this way, clients selectively blind themselves to the reality of their circumstances. This phenomenon is clearly evident in my account of gradually silencing my 'angry part's' accurate analysis of Dr A's exploitation of me, and turning its venom, instead, onto my mother.

Attachment Theory

Babies and young children develop attachments to their parents, siblings, and other family members. The quality of these attachments depends on a number of factors, including the consistency and availability of the main parent figure or figures, often called 'primary caretakers.' If, during the first three years, the child is exposed to repeated parental absences, emotional deprivation, or abuse, the child may develop an 'anxious attachment,' with clinging behaviour and fears of being separated from parents. This can lead to a lifelong tendency to cling to important others, be possessive, and fear abandonment. Relationships based on such characteristics are sometimes called 'symbiotic,' meaning that there is

a psychological fusion of the two people. The symbiotic relationship allows the person to avoid re-experiencing the vulnerabilities
and anxieties of childhood.[18]

This person is more likely to form a symbiotic relationship with
a health professional, to cling, to fear abandonment, and to be unable to leave the relationship even if it is damaging or exploitative.
As I have already described, I and many other victims suffered
dysfunctional childhoods, and our underlying propensity for forming symbiotic relationships may have been a further factor orchestrating our enslavement.

Traumatic Transference

Traumatic transference, introduced in the last chapter, refers to the
intense, life-or-death quality of the reaction of a survivor of childhood trauma to a person in authority. The survivor's emotional
responses have been deformed by experiences of terror and helplessness. She may cast the health professional in the role of
omnipotent rescuer, but, at the same time, mistrusting him, may
be prey to all kinds of doubts and suspicions and feel that she has
to try to control the professional's approach to treatment.

Judith Herman notes that 'The protracted relationship with the
perpetrator has altered the patient's relational style, so that she
not only fears repeated victimisation but also seems unable to
protect herself from it, or even appears to invite it. The dynamics
of dominance and submission are reenacted in all subsequent
relationships, including the therapy.' She goes on to point out that
'The reenactment of the relationship with the perpetrator is most
evident in the sexualised transference that sometimes emerges in
survivors of prolonged childhood sexual abuse. The patient may
assume that the only value she can possibly have in the eyes of
another, especially in the eyes of a powerful person, is as a sexual
object.'[19]

Mary Armsworth, who leads support groups for victims of therapists, describes how 'several women victimised by therapists
have stated they felt "robot-like" in their participation. They described the fact that particular cues, such as the lighting in the

therapist's office, a pipe that he was smoking, the color [of] the therapist's hair, or the way he laughed, seemed to trigger the client behaving in familiar sexualised or clinging ways ... It is very likely that the response with the therapist was parallel to their response to the incest as a child.'[20]

Doubtless this idealization of the professional, the wish for an omnipotent rescuer, the intense feelings bound up in the relationship, and the victim's impression that the survival of the treatment relationship is a life-and-death matter are all factors in the powerful entrapment of a childhood trauma victim with an abusive professional.

My feelings about Dr A were overwhelmingly intense, far beyond anything I had experienced before or since. I obsessed about him for hours at a time, and my letters were often carefully designed to placate him or stroke his ego. In his office, I felt particularly mesmerized by the way a lock of his hair fell over his brow. Not until years later did I come across a photograph of Umpi and saw that his hair was very similar.

4. Escape

'How Did You Get Out of It?'

Like an obedient automaton, I went to his office once a week. If he felt like it, we had sex. Then I saw a TV show about child sex abuse, and I began to realise what was happening to me. That was when I started to escape.

Survivor

Escape, relief from my bondage to Dr A, was a gradual process that started during the last two or three years of my involvement with him, and gathered momentum some months after my final session with him. My disclosure to my women's group and my confrontation with him in his office began to liberate the anger and dissolve the enormous shame and self-blame that accompanied the recognition of how badly I had been exploited. But, as I will describe in Chapters 5 and 6, the ripple effects of my abuse continued to cause distress and damage, and memories came back to haunt me, even years later.

As described in Chapter 3, I was working on 'termination' during the last couple of years of my therapy. This largely consisted of shutting down my feelings, silencing the 'angry part,' busying myself with work and family, and using Valium to sleep. Positive experiences, however, were building my self-esteem, and they must have played a part in my ability to separate, albeit reluctantly and unhappily, from Dr A. While team teaching, I realized that, compared with Dr A, my colleague and teaching partner was incredibly warm, open, and aware of his feelings, This colleague once commented on my attractiveness, and gave me several hugs, but, to my great relief, made no sexual innuendoes or propositions. My communication with my husband improved, he was less depressed, and I felt delighted with my three children. As I commented in a letter to Dr A, 'I love you, still, but I now realize that I love my family more.'

But, as described in the Chapter 3, I felt like a failure in therapy as I still struggled with the 'separation feeling,' my attachment to Dr A, and massive feelings of abandonment and loss. I felt that I had missed my chance, blown it, and now had to struggle on my own to get back to a semblance of emotional health.

Two months after my last session with Dr A, I had a brief affair with a physician whom I met at a retreat; about eight months later I wrote to Dr A in consternation, describing affairs with five men since I stopped seeing him, and expressing worries about being seductive and promiscuous. The sexual involvement with men other than my husband (and Dr A – but he had told me ours was not an affair!) was a novel and exciting experience. Yet, I was also aware of feeling bad, dirty, unworthy, and not in control of myself. In the letter to Dr A, I commented, 'It seems to me that my relationship with you as a patient ended kind of by default, or petered out, and left me with lots of unresolved feelings … Maybe that was the only way, in a practical sense, or I would have clung to you for ever.' I asked if I could come for a session, but got no reply.

Around this time I was sent by my boss to another week-long retreat, on the subject 'Human Dimensions in Medical Education.' One of the group leaders, Earl, seemed a powerful and charismatic man, and I became convinced that he had some answers for me. I thought he could help me with my feelings of inadequacy and my struggles with trust and intimacy. In one group session Earl confronted me about my dependency on men in authority and told me that he did not want to have that kind of power over me, that I had to take responsibility for myself.

Over the next few months, this interaction with Earl came frequently to mind, and I found myself re-examining Dr A's powerful hold over me for so many years. Feelings of anger and resentment towards him became stronger. I was aware that, for the preceding two or three years, a little voice in my head kept telling me, 'Its not quite right; how can you tell yourself that Dr A is a wonderful therapist and that you are all better, when in fact you are thin, tense, can't sleep, and are still all messed up about sex and relationships with men?' But for a long time I would not listen. Thinking of my last meeting with

Dr A, when he talked of learning to trust during his relationship with me, I realized that I had not learned this myself, and that I was engaged in a possibly destructive process of exploring relationships with men in order to see if I could ever trust anyone.

At the same time my relationship with my husband was improving, and eventually I overcame intense feelings of guilt, shame, and humiliation, and told him the truth about my 'therapy' with Dr A. Admitting that I felt really scared, I told him that I was still convinced, on some levels, that what Dr A told me was true. That it was all my fault, that I was seductive. Sharing with him that I felt like a filthy, rotten, dirty bitch, I emphasized the conviction that I deserved to be thrown out. Although I had so many negative feelings, at the same time I tried to convince my husband that it was not all bad, that I was grateful to Dr A for initiating the process of delving into my problems and helping me to overcome conflicts related to my mother.

My husband was incredulous, astounded, and terribly angry. He felt that the responsibility rested entirely with Dr A and insisted, 'That's abuse, even if you set it up because of your background. You were in a childlike dependent role with the psychiatrist as a parentlike authority figure. Two healthy adults take mutual responsibility for seduction, but in a treatment situation it's nothing but rape.'

His unqualified support, and his anger, helped me discover my own rage about my exploitation. We both wrote angry, confrontational letters to Dr A. Some passages from my letter follow:

'It boggles my mind how I could have let it happen, and put it in a positive light. It seems so sick, so crazy ... I was 100 per cent dependent on you, I had no one else to turn to ... I could do nothing but continue to travel to see you, counting the hours between the trips, driven by my past experiences to continue to relate to you in the only way I really knew. Caught in my dependency – that very deprived and vulnerable part of myself. A drowning woman clutching onto a straw.'

'You never took responsibility for your actions the way a doctor-therapist should. The patient has complete trust and is in a powerless situation. You are the helper, the doctor, and the authority figure, and the patient is going to accept what you tell her. But you told me that I initiated it, I was seductive ... you used me as a pawn, a puppet, as a scapegoat for your feelings about women.'

'Your moods dictated things, your needs, your relationship to your wife.

If you felt like it, you might give me the favour of your body. You denied the relationship. You said, "I couldn't handle my feelings about an affair." Well, what the fuck was it then? And what about my feelings? That never crossed your mind. I have a beautiful body and you used me, and told me you were doing me a favour.'

'I remember getting angry many times, even to the point of saying that I would inform the state medical association. I told you that you had more responsibility than me, but you could never accept this. I told you of the inequality of our equal relationship, which, incredibly, you could never see either. I did all the travelling, was a good little patient, paid you, gave you presents ... stayed in my subordinate role, praised you repeatedly for being a marvellous therapist. Is that equal? Is a pin equal to Mount Everest?'

My letter ended with the comment, 'I realize you have troubles and must be very insecure. So although I am terribly angry, I know that I won't be vindictive, I know that I won't try to get revenge. Although you deserve it.'

Again there was no answer to my letter. Feelings of rage, shame, and humiliation continued to seethe under the surface. I knew that I should seek out another therapist to help me work out the damage that I had experienced, but felt that I would be unable to trust anyone in that role. My relationship with my husband continued to improve. I felt very grateful to him for his wholehearted support and refusal to blame me for the relationship with Dr A and its negative effects on our marriage and children.

Like many other couples in the 1970s we had decided on an 'open marriage' – that it was all right for both of us to have affairs as long as we were honest about them with each other. He joined a men's group, and I joined a women's consciousness-raising and support group. Eventually I found the courage to share with my group some of the shameful details of my exploitation by Dr A. Their reactions were uniformly supportive, but their suggestions about how I might seek some emotional closure ranged from exhortations to 'beat the shit out of him,' sue him, or confront him to urgings that I try to forget about it.

After several abortive and angry phone calls with Dr A, in which I tried to convince him that he should meet me on my home ground, I decided to go and see him in his office. By this time two years had passed since I wrote the angry letter, and more than three since our final session. I was frustrated with how I still seemed to be obsessed with Dr A – in a different way than before – but still obsessed. I wanted him to know how much he had hurt me and humiliated me, and I wanted him to take responsibility for his actions. This had not happened during our phone calls, when he seemed to be blaming me and giving me responsibility, calling me 'powerful, seductive, and compelling.'

During the journey there I felt anxious, but resolved to be calm, reasonable, and assertive during the meeting. By the time I reached Dr A's office I was very tense and subdued. Dr A admitted that he too felt anxious. He told me that he would like to understand why I felt so humiliated. I described my vulnerability as a patient; how I felt used and exploited by him; how I felt stupid and guilty that the sexual involvement had gone on for such a long time and had created a barrier between me and my family. I talked about wanting to see him, to see what he was really like and how he felt about what had happened. I told him that I was still so caught up in my transference, in my feelings about him as an all-powerful parent figure, that I had no idea what he was really like. I wanted to try to understand what had happened and get things into perspective.

We discussed the phone calls, how we had both been defensive. I said that I thought he was seeing me as a crazy and seductive woman. He answered, 'Not at all, but it brought up a lot of feelings for me.' In response to my comment about being extraordinarily anxious, he marvelled that we were sitting talking – he would not have thought this possible. Saying that I wished it could have happened earlier, I told him that I had to be feeling really secure and 'together' before I could brave the fantasy about whether I would kill him or dissolve in a little puddle on the floor. Dr A seemed incredulous that I had felt so powerless.

I described reviewing my notes and copies of the letters I had sent him. During the first year I saw him as very understanding, warm, and supportive, so that, in reading this part, I wondered why I was being so critical, and asked myself why I was so angry. Then the situation changed. Feelings about my godfather came up, and somehow the relationship became sexual. It seemed that things were destructive from then on, more like an affair in some ways, a series of games and manipulations, with him being inconsistent and me feeling hurt and rejected.

He talked about his side, his original involvement with me as a student and then a patient. He admitted that he had needed me to get better and that he had been very worried about my extreme decompensation and suicidal threats while I was still a trainee. He had wanted to avoid putting me in hospital, but realized that he had not given me the licence to 'really go crazy,' to let the feelings out. During the time that he had been so concerned about me, he had withdrawn from his family and was having problems with his wife, and the whole thing seemed to turn into a vicious circle.

Later, as 'sex came to the fore,' he had felt pressured by me, had felt I was demanding and very powerful. He claimed he had never met anyone before or since with that kind of power. Refusing to accept this as some kind of criticism of my deviance or evidence that it was my fault, I pointed out that he had, for some reason, given me this power; actually, I did not have any power at all in the situation. Dr A then attributed his weakness, his 'inability to stand up to [me],' to the part of him that was a little boy of five, controlled by a mother who never wanted him to grow up. So he felt guilty, pressured, and inconsistent. The other important factor, he claimed, was his confusion about models of therapy at the time. He would go back and forth between the medical model and the Gestalt model, which, he felt, assigns equal responsibility to the client. So he would believe that he could show his feelings, whatever they were that week, rejecting or whatever, and I could take responsibility for mine. Then he would swing back to the more traditional model if I got upset! Admitting to rationalizing and intellectualizing, he said that he had given me more responsibility than I could handle. He did not take me very seriously as time went along, and I seemed to be coping with my job and my life.

He seemed surprised as I described the problems that I was left with – looking for sexualized, dependent relationships with men, putting men on a pedestal, not relating to women, not valuing women. I talked at length about how my support group had helped me to begin to sort out these problems.

According to Dr A, an equal relationship had evolved between us over time. Trying to refute this, I asked him in what way he considered it equal, when he set the hours at his convenience and I did all the travelling. Again I tried to impress on him how humiliated, how ashamed, and how exploited I felt. I described his control, and the 'double binds' he exerted. He had said, for example, that our relationship was not treatment, that we were equal; at the same time, he had insisted that it was not an affair and that he could not meet me outside the office. He had told me, 'I couldn't deal with my feelings about an affair.'

Dr A shifted in his seat, uncomfortably, and suggested that we had had a folie à deux.[1] *Still trying to reach behind his rigid perceptions and defensiveness, I talked about feeling angry, sad inside, and guilty about the barrier that there had been between me and my family. I stressed that I felt supremely guilty and stupid about having loved him for years. Dr A responded by saying that he had felt the same, preoccupied and estranged from his family to some extent.*

Again I described how the involvement had simply perpetuated my original difficulties and how I felt that I could never trust a therapist again, although I often thought I might need therapy. People suggested it to me when they heard about my experiences – did they really have a point, or was it just their response to something mind-boggling? I mentioned my propensity for getting into sexual relationships. Was this, I asked, just for fun, a need to prove myself, or a reaction to getting older? Dr A talked at length about his acceptance of getting old and of eventual death. He had given up being competitive, had let go his university position, and was interested in 'being.'

During this conversation I wondered if I was being conned. Part of me was thinking:

'Why did it happen to me?'
'He doesn't feel guilty enough.'
'He doesn't take enough responsibility.'
'He doesn't realize how awful it was for me.'
'He doesn't understand that I am giving him some kind of gift of forgiveness (which I really don't want to give, because I'm still so mad).'

On the other hand, I was aware of my strength, that I was not hopelessly helpless or murderously angry. At the end of our meeting Dr A stressed that I was the only patient that he had ever had sex with and that he had learned a painful lesson. He had talked it over with colleagues, and the subject had come up in group experiences. As I left I commented that I was glad that I had come, as I had been scared to return to the area in case I saw him, fearing that I would be murderously angry and be carried off screaming. Dr A acknowledged similar feelings.

At the end of the meeting, Dr A struck a discordant note in what had seemed like a reasonable and open discussion. He asked me if I wanted to resume therapy with him. Incredulous, I replied, 'No, no way!' Then I left, feeling drained and numb, wanting to get back home to my family.

At this point the reader may think that the problem was solved. I was receiving support from my husband and my women's group, feminism was providing a source of excitement, challenge, and validation, and I'd had the courage

*to confront Dr A and insist on his responsibility for my sexual abuse. Fond
hope. Various life events, my ongoing conflicts stemming from childhood sexual abuse and separations from parents, my failure to analyse many aspects
of my relationship with Dr A, and the ripple effects from his abuse of me com-
bined to undermine the sense of competence, confidence, and happiness that
I had begun to achieve.*

Like Chapter 3, this chapter applies mainly to victims of lengthy,
entangled, sexually exploitative relationships between health professional and patient. It is also relevant to survivors of relationships in which boundary violations of other types eventually lead
to molestation.

Other survivors have described a variety of experiences that
led to their gradual, or sudden, realization that they had been
duped and used, and their determination to escape from the influence of the abusive health professional. For many victims, this
happened when they discovered that the professional was abusing other patients. Covered in shame and humiliation, they were
forced to give up their notion that they were special, the only person with whom the professional had this kind of involvement.
Other victims began to realize, to their chagrin, that the professional had not addressed their initial problem, had misdiagnosed
them, or exposed them to hazardous methods of treatment. Some
victims did not engineer their own escapes, but were dismissed
by the health professional.

For Ellen Plasil, her discomfort about Dr Leonard's bizarre behaviour increased after he invited a group of patients to a party at
his apartment where he ferociously attacked one of the men. Later,
when she was in a rewarding and supportive relationship with a
man, she told Dr Leonard that she did not wish to have sex with
anyone except her lover. When she was told that another woman
patient described having sexual intercourse with Dr Leonard,
Plasil 'wondered why hearing his treatment of another woman was
so repulsive, when that same treatment of me had only evoked
self-doubts, guilt and anxiety. I wondered why his treatment of
her was so nauseating, but his treatment of me had become my

standard of mental health. I wondered why I thought she was victimised, but that I was sanctioned by the same behaviour. My body began to tremble, as I struggled in vain to control the eruption rumbling inside me.'[2]

Barbara Noël's confidence in Dr Masserman was first shaken when a dentist diagnosed her with tempero-mandibular joint dysfunction. She realized that many of the symptoms, such as headaches and dizziness, that Dr Masserman had dismissed as attention seeking, neurotic, or psychosomatic, were caused by this disorder. She was puzzled by Dr Masserman's seeming jealousy of other men in her life, and concerned when she once awoke from the Amytal to find her bra on her chest. She knew that she had folded it neatly, with her other clothes, on a chair. Dr Masserman's secretary sometimes frowned and shook her head when Noël was directed to make another appointment for the Amytal treatment. In spite of these and other clues, Noël, her self-esteem eroded by Dr Masserman's condescending and derogatory attitude, continued to see him for therapy sessions and Amytal treatments until the occasion on which she awoke prematurely to find him raping her.[3]

Carolyn Bates describes how she tried to extricate herself from the sexual relationship with Dr X by spacing out the sessions and by going off her birth control pills. Her awareness of his betrayal grew, and she realized that she was paying to provide him with sexual services. The final straw, however, that propelled her into leaving therapy, was his reaction when she called him, distraught, after her engagement had broken down. He invited her to his house, did not talk to her, but used her sexually in the usual 'brief, nonmutual, mechanical' fashion. As a result, she 'finally allowed [herself] to see the very cold and harsh truth of what was happening to [her],' and terminated therapy.[4]

Dr Hartogs lost interest when Julie Roy made demands on him. She began to realize that she had made false assumptions about the intimacy of their relationship when he returned from Holland without bringing her a gift. He forgot her birthday. After she found a stain on the sheet in his apartment, she told him that she did not want to see him any more. His later invitation to dinner and a movie excited her, because she hoped that he had realized the value of the relationship. But she found that he expected her to type some letters, and fell into a deep depression. Later, he refused to see her again, and would not recommend another therapist. 'How could he abandon her so abruptly? Did he not hold some shred of affection for her, after knowing her so intimately for more than a year? It was unbelievable, a man did not do this to a woman with whom he had been sexually close, much less to a patient whom he had urged into a sexual relationship on the grounds that it would make her "feel better" – whatever that had meant, she thought grimly.'[5]

Ken, Sylvia's general practitioner, sought an immediate end to the sexual component of their relationship when he was told by a patient, who was also a palm-reader and clairvoyant, that she knew he was having an affair outside his marriage and that the woman he was seeing had many personal problems. If Ken continued to see this woman, prophesied the clairvoyant, his wife would find out, she would divorce him, and he would lose everything. Sylvia told him she would do what he wanted, and said, 'Secretly, I was relieved. I felt bad in a way, because I valued the little bit of friendship and understanding we did have, but I was happy in the knowledge that the sexual part was over and it had been his decision, because I really think I would have let it go on for a lifetime if it'd been left up to me. Once it had started I just didn't know how to stop it, and he didn't want to stop it either, even though I'm sure he knew pretty well how I felt.'

When he was participating in a child sexual abuse prevention program, Don, by this time nine years old, wondered about his relationship with the dentist. Even after the series of dental visits during which Don had spent a lot of time in the office and the dentist had taken him to lunch and bought him comic books and candy, 'Dr Smith' had always been glad to see him. He had invited Don on several ski trips, which included Dr Smith's wife and two daughters, and had taken a special interest in teaching Don to ski. At first he had held Don between his knees as they went down the slope together. He seemed a very friendly person, thought Don, and there had never been any 'bad touching.' The very next week, Don was again invited on a ski trip. On the way to the ski resort, Dr Smith told Don that his wife and daughters were away, and that Don and he were to spend the weekend alone together. That night, Don awoke to find Dr Smith in his bed. Dr Smith stroked Don's hair and said that he had come to keep Don safe and make him feel good. Dr Smith's hands moved further down, touching Don's stomach, then brushing against his penis. Don knew exactly what was happening, yelled, jumped out of bed, and ran into the corridor screaming for help.

After Anne saw that her counsellor was romantically involved with another patient, she felt rejected and sad. Turning to friends for support, she learned that her counsellor had a reputation for getting sexually involved with women patients. Aghast, Anne asked, 'Why didn't you tell me?' Her friends offered some vague comments about what a wonderful therapist this woman was, and how she was a pillar of the lesbian community. Anne, however, became increasingly angry, realizing that she and other women were being exploited, and remembering with chagrin that she had believed herself to be so special, the only patient with whom the counsellor had become sexually involved.

Even though the professional–patient relationship has finished, the emotional entanglement, the profound influence of the abusive health professional on the survivor, is likely to persist. This influence merges with, or gives way to, the profound aftermath that many victims suffer. Survivors who spoke to me individually, or as part of a group, echoed this ongoing struggle to rid themselves of this now internalized abuser. They agonized about what the professional thought of them; they were torn between feelings of being 'special' and cared for and the growing certainty that they had been exploited. They cringed with shame, and fought back with disbelief against the image of the professional as someone who 'didn't give a shit about my needs.'

As can be seen in my account of my meeting with Dr A, victims desperately needed to believe that some of the treatment had been helpful and that, at least some of the time, the professional had focused on their needs as patients. Survivors who had reported the professional to a licensing authority or commenced a civil suit found, to their chagrin, that this had somehow rekindled their emotional bond to the professional and put their healing on hold.

Galvanized by her realization that Dr Masserman was raping her, Barbara Noël focused all her energies on trying to get a lawyer and beginning a civil suit against him. After she fled from his office and had begun to grapple with the enormity of his betrayal, she felt peculiar and disoriented. Attributing part of this to withdrawal from the Amytal, she realized, 'My whole world had been turned upside down. My trusted therapist was not at all who I thought he had been.'[6] With a more gradual and conflicted awakening, other victims, still psychologically bonded to their abusers, have been far less able to separate themselves and get on with their lives.

Three months after leaving Dr X, desperately needing help, Carolyn Bates began therapy with a minister. Although she found the therapy supportive and was eventually able to disclose her abuse, she had to terminate because she was financially strapped, still having to pay Dr X. Dr X had sued her through small claims court, and she had opted to pay the outstanding amount rather than face him in court. Later, after commencing a lawsuit, she ran into him at the airport. She writes, 'He greeted me in a kind and gentle manner ... told me how surprised he had been to see my name involved in litigation against him ... My face burned. I felt as I often had around him, like a child caught in the midst of committing a shameful act ... By the time I left the airport, I was certain I would drop the lawsuit.' Some months later, in therapy with Dr Hammond, a woman psychologist, she found herself struggling with her feelings about Dr X as a father figure and a trustworthy doctor whose career she might be ruining. It seemed like a betrayal of her long-dead father. Particularly difficult for her was her feeling that he had been most helpful to her in the early phases of therapy. She had a strong sense of loss. Beginning to see the parallels between Dr X and her boyfriend, Steve, she writes, 'Having invested so much of myself in pleasing others, I was at a loss what to do if I wasn't following Dr X's implicit suggestions or Steve's explicit demands. I didn't know who I wanted to be, much less what I wanted to do.'[7]

Ellen Plasil wrote, 'I wondered whether I could survive without his direction, his orders, his guidelines, his rules. I even wondered if I would miss seeing him every other week. I recalled, once again, his frequent reminder that no one could help me except him, and again, I wondered if it might not be true. Had I rid myself of a devil in control of my life, or the last hope for my salvation?' She was preoccupied about her last conversation with Dr Leonard, when he had admitted, 'I've suspected for a long time that what I have done to you has damaged you.' Realizing that he had knowingly harmed her was much harder to face than if he had been overinvolved, misguided, mistaken, or even demented. She cried as she recognized that '[she] had not mattered to him at all, not as a person, and certainly not as a patient.'[8]

After Sylvia's family doctor, Ken, stopped making sexual demands, he was no longer friendly and supportive and did not drop in for cups of tea. As she had no other friends, she felt lonely and abandoned. She did not have any contact with Ken for almost a year, although she was paying off a loan that he had given her. When she went in for a pap test, 'it was as if we'd never known each other outside a doctor–patient relationship.' A few months later, Sylvia left her husband and asked Ken for another loan so she could retain a lawyer to help her obtain custody of her daughter. Ken came to the house, had sex with her, then told her that his wife handled the finances and he could not lend her money. 'I felt like dirt, and I knew for sure he'd used me that time, but I didn't feel it was worth arguing about, so we just talked for a little while over a cup of tea and he went home.' Over the next few years they exchanged letters, then, when Sylvia, now visiting Ken's community, consulted him about an ear infection, Ken wanted her to spend some time with him.

In Don's case, when he rushed, screaming for help, out of Dr Smith's condominium at the ski resort, the police were called. Dr Smith explained that the child had been having a bad nightmare, and that he was just trying to comfort Don and settle him back to sleep. After interviews with the police and a psychologist, no one was sure what had happened. The psychologist thought that the material on preventing child sexual abuse might have stimulated Don, so that he misinterpreted Dr Smith's comforting behaviour.

Don was upset and confused, refused to continue to see Dr Smith as a dentist, and became irritable and cranky at home and with his schoolmates. About a year later, the family received a call from the police. There were some similar allegations about Dr Smith from another boy; the police wanted to interview Don again.

Involved in a secret but intense relationship with her psychologist, Josephine became moody and demanding, suffering frequent headaches. She was fired from her job, and stayed in bed most days watching television. She and the psychologist began to argue and blame each other. One day Josephine returned home to find her belongings on the front steps and the locks changed. Confused, penniless, without employment or a home, she entered a transition house for battered women, indicating to staff that she had been abused by a man. There she was withdrawn, secretive, and obsessed constantly about the psychologist, who, as an older woman with grown children, had seemed like a mother to Josephine. She blamed herself for her predicament, believing that her 'bad attitude' was responsible for all her problems.

Leaving Abusive Relationships

With the exception of a few details about how victims come to recognize that they are being abused, the professional literature is silent on the topic of how and why survivors of abuse by health professionals manage to leave the sticky, enmeshed relationships with their abusers. Escape, particularly in prolonged entrapments, is a relative term, a protracted phase that ebbs and flows and may continue for many years.

Descriptions of victimized people sometimes assume that they enter a state of 'learned helplessness,'[9] and, like 'sitting ducks,'[10] go through a series of abusive relationships in a vicious self-fulfilling prophecy of perpetual victimization. While some victims of abuse by health professionals commit suicide or succumb to intractable depression, alcoholism, or drug abuse, many others make an active choice to fight or try to escape. If we again draw parallels with research on battered wives and studies of hostages in captivity, some ideas emerge.

Far from the popular notion that the physically or emotionally abused woman stays on interminably in the abusive relationship, recent work shows that she moves through a process, eventually actively preparing herself to move out.[11] In the beginning phase of the abusive relationship, the woman, unable to discriminate between positive and negative relationships, focuses on her partner without any regard for her own needs. She believes that if she tries hard enough he will change and that she will still achieve the ideal family that she seeks. In the middle phase she remains subservient and self-effacing: she feels anxious, fearful, and powerless, and her self-esteem suffers, but she starts to realize that her partner will not change. In the final phase, realizing that the abuse will never stop, the woman starts to regain some control over her life, recognizes that the abuse is not her fault, and knows that she has to end the relationship. For some women, termination of the relationship ushers in a sense of freedom and liberation from emotional pain; others, unable to divorce themselves from the past, spend enormous amounts of time sifting through past scenarios trying to find out what went wrong with the relationship.[12]

Disputing portrayals of battered women and other chronically traumatized people as apathetic or defeated, Herman depicts an inner struggle that is much livelier and more complex. While the victim has not given up, she tends to be extremely vigilant and careful, knowing that any action can have potentially dire consequences. If captivity is prolonged, the enforced relationship with the captor comes to monopolize the victim's inner life, and continues, even after release, to engross the victim's attention. Although perhaps fearful that her former captor will hunt her down, or reimprison her, at the same time she may feel confused, empty, and worthless without him.[13]

Under extreme duress, writes Herman, captives can be broken. The person enters a state of 'robotization,' experiencing a shutdown of thoughts, feelings, judgment and initiative. Inner autonomy, moral principles, world-view, and a sense of connection with others are also lost.[14] Linda Lovelace, forced into pornography and prostitution, testified that 'The very thought of escape was terrifying. I had been degraded every possible way, stripped of all dignity, reduced to an animal and then to a vegetable. Whatever strength I had began to disappear. Simple survival took everything; making it all the way to tomorrow was a victory.'[15] In this state of psychological degradation, which is still reversible, victims may alternate between complete submission and more active resistance. People in extreme situations, such as Nazi extermination camps, sometimes reached a second stage; one of total surrender, losing the will to live.[16] Sometimes, on the verge of this surrender, captives reach a turning point and begin a fight for their lives. Patti Hearst, kept captive in a closet, describes growing steadily weaker, exhausted, drained, and tired. She wanted nothing more than to sleep, but realized that this could be fatal. Suddenly, aware of the danger, 'My mind ... was alive and alert to all this. I could see what was happening to me, as if I were outside myself ... A silent battle was waged there in the closet, and my mind won. Deliberately and clearly, I decided that I would not die, not of my own accord. I would fight with everything in my power to survive.'[17]

Although people who are being sexually exploited by health professionals are not living with them or being physically restrained in their offices, there do seem to be many parallels with battered women, hostages, captives, and cult followers, in the sense that these victims have experienced a kind of 'psychological captivity' with respect to the professional who is abusing them. The intense entanglement, merging of identity, isolation, secrecy, loss of self, suspension of values and moral principles, compliance, and subordination cement the person to the abuser and continue to bend his or her reality after escape. Yet survivors do resist, fight back, try to reclaim their identity, and look for other ways to build their self-esteem and thwart the professional's domination.

As seen in Bates's account, although she still clung to the therapy, she devised various strategies to reduce her availability for sexual exploitation. Noël left therapy several times, feeling confident that she was ready to cope on her own or wanting to escape from Dr Masserman's anger and derogatory comments, only to be forced to return by the strength of her addiction to the Amytal. In the fifth year of her involvement with Dr Leonard, Plasil describes an increasingly satisfying relationship with her son and a deepening involvement with two friends. Later, she was able to fall in love with Greg, her future husband. Although still subjugated to Dr Leonard, it appears that she was getting stronger, and was beginning to resist his enslavement of her. Thus, when she learned of allegations that he was having intercourse with another patient, she was able to recognize and disclose that she too had been exploited.[18]

In my case, I felt initially that my whole person was taken over by Dr A, who seemed many times larger than life. I felt fused to him, perhaps like a tiny parasite, and felt like nothing without him. When apart from him, I was suffused with intensely painful feelings of loss and abandonment and the 'separation feeling.' This strange sinking, pulling, gnawing sensation just below my breastbone was accompanied by dizziness, feelings of unreality, and the perception that I was being pulled into a scary, unpredictable childhood world full of images of flickering shadows and weird illusions.

As time went on, the sense that Dr A owned me, possessed me, that I was totally in thrall to him, lessened. But the 'separation feeling' could be rekindled by leaving his office, by lengthy intervals between sessions, by his comments that I needed 'to leave the nest,' and by his periodic rejection, blaming, and withdrawal. Although I was increasingly able to concentrate on my work and my family, I found myself thinking about Dr A in spare moments, usually with a stinging sense of loss and an intense longing to be close to him.

When I look over my notes and letters and recall the two to three years during which sessions were infrequent, it is obvious to me that I was trying to escape. It was not really a conscious process, as Dr A was the one who insisted that we were working towards termination, but I was growing personally and professionally, making friends, talking much more to others, and regaining my lively sense of humour. Reading books like *The Female Eunuch*,[19] I began to challenge Dr A about his traditional ideas, began to argue with his directives to use 'feminine wiles' and to refrain from getting angry at my husband. Although I disclaimed and apologized for the 'angry part,' it did become more active in my letters. The 'angry part' wrote explicitly about how the sex had been unhelpful or even destructive to me and how Dr A was inexplicably shirking responsibility. It accused Dr A of putting me in the position of merely re-enacting the relationships I had had as a child with my godfather and my mother, of repeated separations and seductions.

Although taking the lead in our *folie à deux* of terming the 'angry part' immature, primitive, and pathological, Dr A must have been bothered by these explicit comments and by my growing resistance to his beliefs about male–female relationships. In addition, he seemed threatened by my professional growth and status in my home community. It seems likely, then, that he was most relieved by the termination and not at all interested in replying to my letter requesting another session.

5. After-effects

'How Did You Cope with All That Stuff?'

Self

Frost rimmed icicle sadness
Cold mist enshrouding
Withered leaves, brown grass
Pained twisted branches
Bare bleak countryside
Dead dying landscape
No escape, desolation

> Poem from a poetry workshop I attended six years after my last
> session with Dr A, and about a year and a half after my husband left.

*After my confrontation with Dr A I felt relieved, but somehow dissatisfied.
Again, as with our final therapy session, I had a sense of failure. Certainly
Dr A had not denied the relationship, but it seemed too easy for him to attribute
responsibility to someone else – to me for being powerful and compelling, or
to his mother, who never let him grow up.*

*Over the next few years my husband's father died, and my husband grew
even more depressed and disillusioned about his work. Our learning-disabled
teenager was a source of much stress, and our 'open' marriage gave rise to
many tensions. While we did try to discuss these problems, on the whole I
tended to busy myself with my work, the children, my women's group, and*

*my growing interest in feminism, while my husband turned to the Human
Potential Movement.*

*Most of the time I pushed away thoughts of the now mind-boggling years
during which I'd been bound to Dr A. I just did not want to think about it,
and when it came up, in any context, I found myself actively trying to push
memories and thoughts away. With great dismay I read some professional articles about women who had been sexually abused by therapists. These women
were portrayed as unstable, impulsive, and angry, suffering from borderline
personality disorder, or, alternatively, as compulsively seductive man-haters
with a penchant for seducing professional men.*[1]

*Seeking a non-psychiatric view of what had happened, I turned to feminist
writings. Phyllis Chesler's portrayals of women sexually involved with their
therapists was no more reassuring. She depicted the women as 'all convention-
ally and frantically "attractive"; they were all economically limited and in-
tellectually insecure; they were both sexually fearful and sexually compulsive;
they were paralysed by real and feared loneliness and self-contempt; they all
blamed themselves for any "mistreatment" by men; they all confused econo-
mic and selfhood needs with romantic love; and they were slow to express any
anger.'*[2]

*Both these sets of images scared me, so I found myself trying to forget my
experiences with Dr A or, on the other hand, normalizing them, telling myself that most of the therapy was very positive and that the sexual part was a
minor aberration. I blamed myself for this, thinking that I had seductively
drawn Dr A into 'acting out my transference.' In effect, despite my earlier
anger and feelings of outrage, I took responsibility, as a patient, for creating a
situation in which Dr A would have no option but to behave towards me in
the way my godfather and mother had done.*

*Sometimes, when I was being more honest with myself, certain memories
would surface and I would feel guilty and ashamed about the length of time
I had stayed with Dr A, and the amount of time I had taken from my family.
Not just the travelling time, but also the amount of time I had spent thinking,
wondering, and fantasizing about Dr A. The memories, though, were rather
flat and factual, devoid of feeling and lacking intensity. On the few occasions
during those years that I talked about my experiences within my women's
group or with a friend, I was surprised that listeners often expressed amaze-
ment and suggested that I needed more therapy to help me get over the effects
of such a difficult experience. My responses usually included the belief that*

I'd had enough therapy, that most of what had happened with Dr A was very helpful and therapeutic, and I certainly did not need more therapy. Or I contended that I had managed to transcend the experience myself, with the help of my training, experience, and reading.

The suggestions that I may need more therapy did, in fact, strike a chord in me. Because I wanted to believe that my therapy with Dr A had been mainly positive, I told myself that I had made amazing changes, that I was now more warm, open, spontaneous, and so on. But my old friends did not support this notion. For instance, when I went back to England, my friends would exclaim, 'You're just the same as you always were. Open, warm, lively – we were afraid you might change when you became a psychiatrist!' So what was going on? Were they wrong? Or, had I in fact gone backwards with Dr A, and was now simply regaining lost ground? Maybe I did need some therapy? But I was scared, so scared that I did not want to think about it. Privately, to myself, I admitted that I could never trust a therapist again. And I was just too busy anyway, with a young family and a job that had now grown to a full-time commitment.

Occasionally, in the context of thinking about children sexually abused by parents, I did find myself thinking angrily about what had happened with Dr A. Someday, I thought, I will write about it to show colleagues how vulnerable adults, like defenceless children, can get caught up in these incestuous relationships and be mercilessly used. Rather than throwing them away, I carefully saved all the notes I'd made and the letters I'd written during the years that I was travelling to see Dr A.

In those years, my career was moving ahead by leaps and bounds, but my husband's was not so successful. Looking back, it seems as though I was replaying with him some of the issues I had raised, some of the arguments I'd made, with Dr A. In addition, I was influenced by the weekly discussions of the consciousness-raising group. No longer happy to be in a subordinate relationship in the marriage, no longer seeing my role as that of a Florence Nightingale who would selflessly minister to my husband's needs, no longer so tolerant of his depression, moodiness, and self-preoccupation, I began pushing for a more equal relationship and more sharing of responsibilities.

The outcome, in short, was more depression on his part. What happened next was a bombshell. When my husband met and fell in love with a young woman, he decided that I was the cause of all his difficulties. He left, contending that my 'affair' with Dr A had been a major factor in the demise of our

*marriage. This sentiment was reinforced by his group therapists and gurus,
Drs Y and Z. Before my husband left, Dr Y, a psychiatrist, had one session
with us together. When the subject of Dr A came up, Dr Y stated that I must
have been seductive and that he could understand why my husband felt so
angry about it. Aghast, I felt disastrously betrayed, as previously my husband had been so supportive and had insisted that I was not to blame. Unbeknownst to me, this was my second contact with a sexually abusive therapist.
Some years later, on the eve of an inquiry board hearing about their sexual
abuse of a woman patient, Drs Y and Z handed in their medical licences.*

*While I had been able, over the preceding years, to confide in a few people
about my disastrous experiences with Dr A, this stopped happening when
my husband left. My resolve to write and present papers about the topic of
sexual abuse of women patients by male therapists evaporated completely. The
departure of my husband led to a return of the 'separation feeling' and some
of the thoughts and feelings I had experienced with Dr A. I felt abandoned,
helpless, powerless, and terribly depressed. Blaming myself totally for my
husband's departure, I was preoccupied with thoughts about Dr A and what
he had told me. Dr A had been right. I should never have challenged my husband's authority, got angry at him, or tried to change his behaviour. It was
true, as Dr A had insisted, that I was an angry, destructive, powerful, nasty
woman, and I did not deserve to have a husband. I had been seductive with
Dr A, and with some other men, and driven away my husband. It was all my
fault, and now I had deprived my children of their father. Consumed with
shame, I longed to be able to vanish and imagined digging a hole in the garden,
climbing in, and staying there.*

*Gradually, the intense shame, grief, and sense of betrayal diminished. I
stopped blaming myself, and my more usual sense of optimism and enjoyment
of life returned. I spent four busy years as a single parent, devoting much
time to my three children and trying to keep limits on my professional com-
mitments. Then I decided to move into a blended family situation with my
future husband, Keith, with whom I am still living fifteen years later. The
difficulties and tensions of this situation, where we shared five children, were
heightened by increasing demands and frustrations at work. After about two
years, I realized that I was suffering from near exhaustion, with anxiety,
tension, insomnia, and constant fatigue. In England that Christmas, I was
stricken with such acute chest pain that a heart attack was initially suspected.*

On my return to Canada I went back to work, but continued to feel dizzy, jittery, and enormously fatigued. At first I assumed that I must be sick, that there was something wrong with my heart that had escaped detection. But test results were normal, and my doctor recommended another week off work. At the same time, intruding into my consciousness were almost constant memories about my relationship with Dr A and the conviction that I was bad, dirty, and worthless. Sometimes these memories were so vivid that I felt as though I were right there again, back in his office. I found myself feeling scared of the dark and of shadows, and inexplicably afraid of many men, particularly if they were older, physicians, or in any role of authority over me. By this time it was more than ten years since my last session with Dr A.

Feeling fragile, sensitive, jumpy, irritable, and weepy, I found it difficult to respond to my family. I felt totally drained, with nothing to give. Tending to withdraw from them, and from interactions with others, I felt no interest in or energy for my usual activities. Constantly tired, I found it hard to cope with day-to-day chores and responsibilities. I had terrible nightmares of death, destruction, and loss. Although constantly tired, I had difficulty falling asleep, or found myself waking very early in the morning. Sometimes I woke from a vivid nightmare and was unable to shake off the images, rerunning scenes in my head from bad dreams, such as one in which Dr A let tigers out of a cage to kill me and my children.

My intellect told me that I had to seek a therapist, but emotionally, I cringed. I had long ago decided that I would never trust a therapist again. But my condition got worse and worse. The nightmares became more vivid and sometimes included Dr A, who would be chasing me, accusing me, putting me in jail, taking away my children, or trying to kill me. Again I began to get chest pain, accompanied by rapid heart beat, sweating, dizziness, and fears that I was going to die. I realized that I was having panic attacks.

For at least six months after I started to see Naida, I struggled with similar feelings and constant fatigue. Afraid to stay away from work, with the feeling that once I stopped I would never be able to handle it again, I struggled to cope, to concentrate during the day. Previously able to compartmentalize my work, so that I was able to leave feelings and worries about patients and families at work and not take them home, I now found that I seemed exquisitely sensitive to everyone else's pain. I felt as if I had been flayed alive, that I had lost my skin, lost the protection that was a barrier between my nerve endings and the environment. Instead, I had no barrier, everything was right there, everything reached me immediately. I was so easily stimulated

*and overstimulated by all the nuances, all the innuendoes, all the glances
and facial expressions that people made that I longed to get home and go to
bed, to shut myself off from all input.*

*Worn down by this state of oversensitivity and by continued panic attacks,
I decided that I had to take some medication. As I had plenty of samples
available, I began to take a small dose of Xanax, which I continued for about
the next year. This stopped the panic attacks and dulled the pain to the point
that I was more able to handle work and family, because I was firmly determined
that I was not going to give in. Running and vigorous bike riding helped too.
I cut back my work demands as far as I was able.*

*At the same time, I had accepted the need for therapy, was seeing Naida,
and was already realizing that this would be a helpful and completely different experience, totally unlike the painful ordeal I had suffered through with
Dr A.*

*At the start of my therapy with Naida, I had several vivid images of where
I was and what had happened to me. In the most developed fantasy I was
running, and had been running for several years. At first, at a steady lope,
easily outdistancing the people who were behind me, I ran through flat and
pleasant countryside. But I did not look to either side of me, only kept on
running. The road narrowed and started going uphill; the sky darkened and
I began to run through a rocky gorge. The path got narrower and narrower,
my breathing more and more laboured, and I felt that the rock was about to
crush me. I knew that I could go no farther and that I had to take a stand and
face my pursuers. When I turned to face them, they seemed to fall back a
little, and I was struck by how ineffectual they seemed and wondered why I
had been running away from them for so long.*

*The three front runners of this posse were Dr A, Umpi, and my ex-husband.
Dr A was first, wearing his white doctor's coat, darting from side to side,
pursuing me doggedly. Umpi, red faced and puffing in a crumpled white suit,
was second. My ex-husband, appearing formal in suit and glasses, looked very
disapproving. Also in the throng that pursued me were my various bosses,
my ex-lovers, and my parents. My parents, however, seemed more intent on
trying to get me to stop running and to help me.*

Some victims have described similar experiences, commonly going
through a long period when they submerged all or most of their

feelings and thoughts about the abuse. Then, related to stresses or life changes, they found themselves suddenly bombarded by a variety of symptoms including severe anxiety, guilt, shame, panic attacks, nightmares, depression, plummeting self-esteem, various physical symptoms, poor concentration, feelings of alienation and numbness, loss of energy and interest, and vivid memories or 'flashbacks' of the abuse.

On leaving the transition house, Josephine faced the laborious task of putting her life together again. She found an apartment, obtained a job, and resumed visits with friends and relatives, but told no one about her relationship with the psychologist. She gave up drinking as she was distressed by the thoughts, memories, and feelings that sometimes emerged. Bothered by nagging doubts, by confusion about whether she was heterosexual or lesbian, she resolved to remain celibate and thus avoided worrying about it. Eight years passed. She had several promotions at work, but she still suffered periodically with inexplicable mood swings and feelings of numbness or emptiness. Her brother introduced her to a friend. Josephine felt attracted to this man, and they started dating. The first time they had intercourse, Josephine broke into copious tears, remembering scene after scene of her exploitation by the psychologist and, in particular, her final rejection. She felt anxious, guilty, and ashamed, unable to share what she was experiencing with her man friend.

Others have experienced more immediate effects, developing during the abuse or shortly after termination. Severe depression, eating disorders, alcoholism, and drug abuse were among the problems suffered. Charlene described 'toxic shame,' severe depression, and alcoholism. Antoinette began to lose weight during the time that she was being sexually exploited by her chiropractor. After she had disclosed the abuse to her family doctor and been encouraged to stop seeing the chiropractor, Antoinette lost even more weight and was eventually hospitalized with anorexia. During this period her marriage broke up, and her career was irreparably damaged. Looking back over that extremely painful time, she says, 'Everything was out of control. I couldn't concentrate, couldn't sleep, couldn't think, couldn't plan. My emotions were all over the place. My husband was leaving, my career was shattered. It seemed like the only thing I could control was my eating.'

Like me, some survivors went through a period when they felt that some of their treatment had been helpful, but most, in the end, viewed the relationship with the health professional as destructive. Some still had very mixed feelings. Sylvia explained, 'I really don't know if I was used or not, or who seduced who. He did a lot for me, and I appreciate that very much, but deep down I really think he saw my vulnerability and took advantage of it.' Asked how the sexual involvement with the family physician had affected her life, Sylvia said, 'This is hard to explain. In the long run, I think it was good for me. It kind of forced me to settle my problems. My self-esteem, as far as Ken is concerned, is somewhere around the slug area. I feel like an object. But it pushed me to better things with myself and with other people ... I don't know why I can't project that growth to him, it's like with him alone I'm frozen mentally to when I was twenty.'

For many victims, their abusive experience with a health professional set in train a series of terrible losses or traumatic events. These included loss of employment or destruction of career; marital breakup; deterioration in relationships with children, other relatives, and friends; loss of custody of children; disastrous remarriages or abusive relationships; financial problems; poverty; loss of homes or other accommodation; and loss of physical or mental health, to the point of hospitalization in some cases.[3] Younger victims felt that they had lost their innocence or youth; some felt that impaired trust had sabotaged their ability to enter into intimate relationships, and had consequently deprived them of the opportunity to have children. In the same way that a rock dropped into a pond causes ever-widening concentric ripples, so an abusive experience with a health professional can affect every aspect of the victim's lifestyle, relationships, health, and well-being.

Moving beyond the individual victim, these ripples involve many others as 'secondary victims.' In a chapter devoted to this issue, Schoener and colleagues explain, 'Devastating as the effects of sexual exploitation may be on the client-victim, the impact is not limited to him or her alone. Those persons close to the client (spouse, children, parents, friends, etc.) may also be, and often are, affected variously. The same holds true for the spouse, family, friends, colleagues, and clients of the therapist-perpetrator.'[4] Even though they themselves have not been abused, other patients of a health professional exposed as an abuser may be thrown into turmoil, doubting the validity of their own treatment and their judgment of the professional's character. A mental health professional who had undergone therapy with a psychiatrist and later found out that the psychiatrist had sexually abused several patients told me, 'I have so many mixed feelings about [my therapy]. At the time, it seemed to help me, but now I wonder if my therapy meant anything. If he was so irresponsible sexually, perhaps he didn't take my problems seriously either? ... After I'd been seeing him a couple of years, I found myself using some of his gestures, sayings, and techniques with my patients. Now I really worry about that and feel I have to monitor myself carefully in case I've picked up some very negative things from him ... Then, I'm kind of ashamed about this thought, I find myself thinking why didn't he come on to me as well, wasn't I as attractive as his other patients?'

The undermining of public trust in the health professions and the impact of sexual abuse of patients on health professionals and their institutions and governing bodies will be dealt with in Chapter 7. There, we will see that health professionals as a group often respond like the parents and other relatives in a family in which incest is disclosed. Although there may be an initial response of outrage, it is all too often lost in attempts to deny, distort, minimize, trivialize, and obscure the victim's complaints, protect the offender, and ostracize the victim.

While every victim's experience is unique, an understanding of the effects of sexual abuse by a health professional can flow from examining three overlapping frameworks that address the effects of trauma or, more specifically, of sexual abuse by a therapist. These are (1) the diagnosis of post-traumatic stress disorder; (2) the 'three levels of victimization,' proposed by Aphrodite Matsakis; and (3) the 'therapist–patient sex syndrome,' described by Kenneth Pope. Although much of the literature and many of the examples given relate to therapist abuse, we must recognize that the effect of sexual exploitation by other types of health professionals can be just as destructive. A study conducted by Feldman-Summers and Jones demonstrates that the extent of damage done was similar whether the sexual contact was with a therapist or some other health care practitioner. The study showed that the impact of sexual contact was more damaging when (1) the health professional was married; (2) the person had already suffered sexual victimization; or (3) the victim already had emotional problems before starting the exploitative treatment.[5]

Post-traumatic Stress Disorder

Post-traumatic stress disorder, described in the basic definitions section of the Introduction (see pages 17–25), is a normal reaction to an abnormal amount of stress. Given enough stress, anyone can get PTSD. For example, during the Second World War, some soldiers with exemplary records of mental health and family stability developed PTSD after prolonged combat exposure. It was concluded that 200 to 240 days in combat would break even the strongest soldier.[6] Many studies showed that the best protection against the development of PTSD in wartime was the presence of support from close buddies. This kind of support is often absent for the child or adult who is sexually abused.

The person with PTSD often alternates between an intrusive phase of re-experiencing the trauma and a phase of numbing and avoidance, when the person tries to bury the memories. A person with 'delayed-onset' PTSD may be symptom-free for months or years. Some see this as a very prolonged phase of numbing and avoidance. The person is propelled out of the symptom-free phase and into the intrusive phase by life changes or stresses, or by 'triggers' or reminders of the original trauma.

Although use of the diagnosis has been criticized and seen as a way to pathologize the person and medicalize a normal response to a traumatic event, I have found in my practice that survivors welcome being told that such an entity exists. They find it comforting to know that their frightening perceptions and unpredictable emotions are totally normal, in view of the disastrous and intrusive nature of the ordeal they have suffered.

Looking back, I realize that I have suffered at least three episodes of delayed-onset PTSD. One occurred when I first started therapy with Dr A, and the second was when I was remembering my sexual abuse by my godfather. I continued to have some symptoms of PTSD, on and off, over the whole time that I saw Dr A as a patient. I was often tense and irritable, I lost weight, had nightmares, and suffered terrible insomnia, often staying awake until 3 or 4 a.m. The third episode came much later, and was even more florid; it was precipitated by increasing stress at work and the demands and difficulties of a blended family.

Three Levels of Victimization

In her well-written and useful handbook for trauma survivors, *I Can't Get Over It*, Aphrodite Matsakis delineates three levels of victimization.[7] These concepts aid our understanding of the trauma and its ripple effects and lay some of the groundwork for the next two chapters, in which the complicated, often difficult, long-term processes of healing and disclosure will be described.

The *first level of victimization* involves the actual trauma, which shocks the body and emotions and diminishes or destroys victims' beliefs in their own invulnerability, and in the notion of a just, orderly, and predictable world. Feelings of helplessness, powerlessness, and anger or rage are often accompanied by a desire to withdraw from others and a return to more childlike emotions.

The *second level of victimization*, extremely pertinent to survivors of abuse by a health professional, comprises the 'secondary wounding' to which victims are subjected by those around them or by systems or institutions that they approach for help. Critical or negative responses make victims feel ashamed of having been traumatized, ashamed of how they reacted to the trauma, and even ashamed or apologetic about asking for help. Victims may be blamed for the event, stigmatized for their reaction to the trauma, or subjected to denial, disbelief, or discounting of the traumatic event that they are describing.

Such reactions are frequently experienced by victims of sexual abuse by health professionals. This secondary wounding can be so intense that the victim is effectively shamed and silenced. One victim disclosed his experience of abuse to another psychiatrist, who 'leaned forward, gripped the edge of her chair. Her eyes bugged out. She said that Dr B would never do anything like that. She said [he] must be making a mistake. She didn't suggest another appointment and [he] didn't make one.' As a result he felt confused, was afraid to consult other health professionals, and began to doubt his own perceptions. He wondered if he had somehow caused the abuse, blamed himself for overreacting, and no longer thought about reporting Dr B to the licensing board.

Similarly, Jane, needing further help with her eating disorder and wanting to talk about her abuse by her psychiatrist, eventually found the courage to visit another psychiatrist. Her story was met with disbelief; she felt rebuffed and betrayed by yet another father figure. Several years later, after watching the movie *Betrayal*, which describes Julie Roy's sexual abuse by Dr Hartogs, she realized that she had many unresolved feelings and wondered about trying again. Jane's reluctance to face another demeaning barrage of disbelief was finally overcome when she developed some unusual symptoms and was referred to a psychiatrist as part of the evaluation. 'This time it was a good experience. He believed me, gave me support. I grew a lot.'

One respondent in the Canadian Mental Health Association's study of sexual abuse of women by mental health professionals reported the following: 'Earlier a lawyer said: "It happens so often it's considered acceptable practically. Can't you consider it a compliment?" My psychiatrist said: "What do you expect? We're all humans." The police were rough – treated me as if I were the guilty one.' Another respondent to the study said, 'I was told no one would believe anything I said because I was on a psychiatric ward.'[8]

Charlene told her second psychiatrist about the abuse by her first doctor. He responded, 'We doctors have our code of ethics.' There was no further discussion, and he gave her no advice, so Charlene did not know whether he believed her or not and, if he did, whether he considered the abuse to be damaging. He insisted on focusing on her life as a child, attributing all her difficulties to this period.

One woman reported to her general practitioner that the neurologist she'd seen had stimulated her clitoris while telling her that he was testing her nervous system. The GP said that he'd never heard of this before, but that it was presumably a new method of practice.

Joyce, trapped and sexually exploited by the family doctor, who was giving her migraine pills, went to another family physician in her small community. He advised her to terminate her 'affair' with her doctor and to continue to see him as a patient, because 'he knows your family, he's known you for a long time, and he has all your records.' Feeling hurt and ashamed, Joyce tried to comply with his directions.

In hospital, feeling severely depressed and suicidal, 'James' began to trust a warm and friendly student nurse. He told her about his sexual involvement with a physiotherapist who had treated him after he'd hurt his back in an accident at work. It had seemed wonderful at first, but then the therapist grew cold and distant and cut down the frequency of his treatment sessions. One day, while waiting for a treatment, James heard the familiar sound of a bolt being drawn back from the door, and realized that the physiotherapist was now involved with another patient. Concerned about James's story, the student nurse told her supervisor, who confided in the psychiatrist in charge. On the following day, James was interviewed behind a two-way mirror with medical students observing the interview. His dose of medication was increased, and the student nurse was reassigned. Years later, on obtaining his medical record, James learned that the physiotherapist had been contacted and had indignantly denied James's allegations. The psychiatrist assumed that James was 'delusional' and suffering from 'homosexual panic.'

Many people, unaware of the dynamics that make sexual involvement between a health professional and a patient similar to incest, cannot understand how an adult could allow herself to become involved in such a situation, unless she enjoyed it or initiated the seduction. Such victim blaming, which I experienced with Dr Y, is common.

'Mary-Lou's' counsellor suggested that Mary-Lou confide in her husband, 'Bob,' and tell him about the sexual exploitation by her obstetrician that had started shortly after the birth of their third child. Both Mary-Lou and the counsellor hoped that this would help Bob understand Mary-Lou's panic attacks, moodiness, anger, and dislike of sex. Planning it carefully, so that the children were in bed, the house was quiet, and no interruptions were expected, Mary-Lou had hoped that Bob would listen supportively. But when Bob, who – unbeknownst to Mary-Lou, had been laid off that day – heard about 'Dr Jones,' he erupted with pain and rage, accusing her of having had an affair behind his back and of being a slut and a whore. He packed, left the house, and went to live with his widowed mother. After this he steadfastly refused to go for a counselling session with Mary-Lou and her counsellor, and petitioned for custody of the children, claiming that Mary-Lou was an unfit mother. Mary-Lou, devastated, became very upset and self-blaming. To support herself and the children, she had to resume work as a legal secretary. As a result of the stress of this position, her long daily bus ride into work, her difficulties finding day-care and after school-care for her children, her husband's contemptuous attitude and continual belittling of her to the children, she became very depressed, made a suicide attempt, and was put in hospital.

Even when the abuse is believed, reactions to victims may be stigmatizing. Victims may be met with condescension or ridicule or may be assumed to have severe emotional or personality disorders rather than PTSD. The diagnosis 'borderline personality disorder' and the label 'hysteric' are often used in a pejorative sense in relation to patients, usually women, who are perceived to be difficult, angry, moody, argumentative, and sexually active.[9] As will be discussed in the next two chapters, victims of sexual abuse by health professionals are sometimes assumed to be looking for attention or sympathy or to be out for financial gain. In one U.S. trial of a physician accused of molesting a woman patient over a period of twelve years, a psychiatrist appeared for the defence and maintained that the victim had not suffered any ill effects as a result of the 'sexual relationship.' Even though the victim's fortunes had taken a radical downturn during and after the period of abuse, the psychiatrist attributed all of her emotional distress, her marriage breakdown, the loss of her job, and her financial difficulties to her early childhood, marital choice, and personality difficulties.

The *third level of victimization* occurs when the person takes on a lifelong identity of being a victim, and the traumatic event and its after-effects come to dominate her life. Feeling permanently scarred, hopeless, helpless, betrayed, and degraded, the person develops poor self-esteem and a negative attitude that may serve to further alienate her from relatives and friends, disrupt relationships, and damage job or career prospects.

Matsakis believes that 'victim thinking' can be traced to one of the following four common patterns of thinking that emerge during the actual trauma, during the secondary wounding experience, or as a result of PTSD:

1 The person cannot tolerate mistakes in herself or others.
2 Personal difficulties are denied.
3 Black-and-white thinking prevails.
4 Survival tactics are continued.[10]

Because of the severe damage often sustained by people who are sexually abused by health professionals and the frequency of secondary wounding experiences, these people are at risk for the development of the third level of victimization. Immersed in a desire for revenge or compensation, lacking community and family support, unable or unwilling to get therapeutic help, still struggling with PTSD symptoms, they may be unable to transcend the victim identity and unable to get on with their lives.

In my case, as a psychiatrist with a job and some status in the community, I was less likely to be met with secondary wounding attitudes, or to be hurt by them if I was. But when Dr Y, himself a sexual predator, reinterpreted my behaviour as 'seductive' and effectively allowed my ex-husband to change his attitude and blame me, this seemed like another cruel stroke of fate, and it is a clear example of secondary wounding or revictimization. At that point I reinternalized the blame, decided that my transgression had caused the breakup of our marriage, and once again judged myself as sick, bad, crazy, and seductive.

The Therapist–Patient Sex Syndrome

Psychologist Kenneth Pope, author of a number of articles and books in this area, proposed this group of ten common reactions to sexual exploitation by therapists as an assessment tool, a guide for interventions, and a help to jurors or other laypersons who find victim's behaviour impossible to understand. Pope emphasizes that this is not an inevitable pattern, that every patient is unique, and that some may have few or even none of these reactions to sexual exploitation.[11] The ten common reactions are described below.

1. Guilt

Feelings of guilt are almost universal among sexually abused people, including young children. Various hypotheses have been developed about why guilt feelings in these situations are so strong. Often the perpetrator deliberately induces guilt in the victim, hoping to silence her. In some cases, guilt feelings seem to serve a purpose for victims. For example, they may give the victim a sense of being in control, and thus of being able to avoid the situation on another occasion. In children, and in adults who have regressed to a childlike mode of thinking, guilt feelings may have developmental origins. Young children are 'egocentric,' see themselves as the centre of their world, and sometimes believe that they have the capacity to control what goes on around them.

Research into separation and divorce has shown that children between four and seven years of age are more likely than older children to blame themselves for the family breakdown, a fact that is usually attributed to the young child's immature thinking. It seems likely, then, that a similar process is operating in children who are abused and in adults who are in a treatment situation that has parent–child dimensions.

Because of their socialization to care for others, to mediate in relationships, and to maintain attachment bonds, women are more likely to feel guilty about reporting the health professional and 'betraying' the intimacy of the relationship. Antoinette and several other victims described their qualms in this situation. When the chiropractor realized that Antoinette might report him to the professional organization, he came to her house and made a special effort to persuade her not to report him, saying that he was already in financial difficulty. Although she went ahead with her complaint, Antoinette felt 'like a squealer.'

It seems likely that abusive health professionals are aware of the tendency of victims to feel guilty, and are ready to capitalize on it. As described in Chapter 3, Dr A, faced with the possibility that I might report him, accused me of 'betraying my trust ... visiting your problems on me ... acting out.'

2. Decreased Ability to Trust

Betrayal of the deep, profound, childlike trust that the patient accords the professional is likely to damage the patient's trust in other professionals and may become generalized to all relationships and shake the person's previous trust in the world as a just, stable, and predictable place. Fears of intimacy may reduce or eliminate a young person's chance of making a happy marriage and having children.

As a result of the abuse, some victims, it seems, develop a kind of 'trust hierarchy.' If they were abused by a male family doctor, they may be able to seek out and attend a woman physician. In many cases, however, they may decide to avoid physicians altogether and seek alternative health care or decide to have no health care at all. I have heard of several tragic situations in which people who had been abused by health professionals felt so wounded and mistrustful that they were unable to seek any further health care. Ignoring symptoms of illness, or trying to treat themselves with folk remedies, they eventually collapsed and were taken to hospital with now terminal or untreatable conditions. A woman in the Manitoba study said, 'I have to be at the point of death before I would make a medical appointment. This reluctance to seek medical attention could endanger my life.'[12]

Distrusting men and male institutions, Anne had carefully chosen a lesbian feminist therapist. Exploited by this counsellor, and rejected in favour of another patient, Anne felt hopeless. Now she trusted no one, of either sex.

In my case, abused by a male psychiatrist, I eventually settled for a woman psychologist. But, like many other victims, I was desperately afraid that something would go horribly wrong, not necessarily in a sexual sense, if I went to another therapist.

Referred for a psychiatric opinion because of very unusual symptoms, Jane was very reluctant to attend, thinking, 'I would rather have had a tumour!'

3. Ambivalence

Mixed feelings about the abuser are evident in many victims' accounts. As shown repeatedly in my own account, there was much fluctuation between two extremes. At one extreme, the abusive health professional is viewed as a predator to be escaped from, expunged from one's life and, perhaps, brought to justice. At the other, the abuse is denied or minimized, and the professional is once again extolled as the wonderful, magical parent figure that made one feel so special.

Don's emotional swings felt to him like being at the end of the pendulum of the antique clock that stood in the hallway of his home, or like being on a teeter-totter. Recalling with fear and disgust how the dentist got into his bed and started to stroke his stomach and then his penis, Don wished he could punch Dr Smith or beat him with a baseball bat. 'What a pervert,' he thought angrily. Later in the day, he found himself wondering if he had, as the psychologist suggested, made a mistake. Dr Smith had been so kind, taking him to lunch, taking him skiing, paying for lift tickets and lessons. Maybe Don was wrong, maybe he was dreaming, maybe he had got Dr Smith in trouble with the police for no reason.

More resolved ambivalence is seen in Sylvia's account of how she felt about Ken and in her ideas about how he viewed her. She seems aware of her own vacillations, saying, 'It's taken me eleven years to sort it all out in my head ... in the beginning he seemed to see so far inside me and understand me so well. But that must be something I'm trying to see into it because whenever he sees me he thinks I'm an object that will lie down on command.'

For many years, I clung to the notion that I was somehow special to Dr A; he had assured me that I was the only patient he had ever had sex with, and I believed it. As described in my account, I liked to think that part of the therapy had been helpful, and that the sexual involvement was but a minor aberration. At other times, however, I castigated him for being inadequate, irresponsible, manipulative, and abusive.

4. Emptiness and Isolation

Many patients are left with pronounced feelings of emptiness, hollowness, or numbness after the abusive experience. This can be related to a number of factors, including the following: the constrictive phase of PTSD; feelings of loss of the self, resulting from such a massive betrayal of trust; the loss of the idealized health professional who was seen as a nurturing parent figure; strategies or techniques that were used by the abusive professional to enhance the patient's dependency; loss of the orders, directions, and requirements made by the professional; the secrecy, isolation, and withdrawal engendered by the abusive relationship, which may leave the patient bereft of support from friends and relatives; feelings of shame and self-blame, which operate as obstacles to disclosing the abuse.

As a result of this experience of inner deadness, survivors sometimes feel that they do not belong to the human race, that they are permanently set apart and alienated, that they can never connect up with other people. About six years after my final session with Dr A, I wrote the poem that is reproduced at the beginning of this chapter. The instructor at the poetry workshop asked us to describe a landscape that conveyed a sense of ourselves. Reading it again, the poem reminds me of how I sometimes felt dead and numb inside. As described in Chapter 6, I later told Naida about feeling like a suit of armour with nothing but air inside – apparently strong, but actually hollow.

During and after my therapy with Dr A, I had many feelings of alienation, desolation, and aloneness, sometimes imagining being alone for ever on a grey and devastated moonscape. Doubtless these feelings were caused by my extreme attachment to him; the loss of my idealized perfect father figure; the loss of some aspects of myself that had merged with him during the period when he suggested, 'You feel like nothing without me'; and feelings of being different from others because of the secrecy of the involvement and the shame and guilt that I felt. Feelings of being stigmatized and unlike others, because of my sexual abuse as a child, were also involved.

5. Emotional Lability

Emotional lability refers to sudden changes of emotion, without any apparent reason. The person feels she is not in control of her emotions and may find herself crying at a happy moment or feeling angry during a seemingly neutral event. Bursting into tears during a movie or TV program is common, with the person having no idea what she is crying about. While everyone experiences small swings of emotion (which may be larger in the temperamentally intense), the abuse victim may feel as if she is on an emotional roller-coaster, as may her relatives and friends as well.

Supported by her friends, and encouraged that her new man friend was warm and understanding – even when he learned of her abuse – Josephine began therapy. For several months she experienced extreme, and often seemingly inexplicable, mood swings. She believed that they were a result of having held in her feelings for such a long time.

As with the other manifestations of the therapist–patient sex syndrome, emotional lability has several different roots. As the traumatized person moves between the phases of PTSD, she may vacillate between intense reactions and numbness. As well, her ability to recognize, express, and control her emotions has been damaged by her subordination to the authority of the abusive health professional, her adoption of his values and attitudes, and the suppression and denial of her own feelings. As a result, her emotional reactions may seem alien and disconnected from both outer events and inner processes.

6. Suppressed Anger

Sexual violation causes intense anger and rage. But victims of sexual abuse by health professionals have usually been so coerced and manipulated by the professional that they have denied, ignored, or pushed away their anger. After the exploitative therapy or treatment ends, it may take months or even years before the survivor can recognize and feel the anger. Once this anger erupts into awareness, it can be extremely intense, and potentially very frightening. Barbara Noël found that 'More often than not [she] was on the edge of boiling over with rage, and [she] walked around barely contained.'[13]

As a result of Julie Roy's realization that she was enraged with Dr Hartogs, she stayed up all night 'crying, mute. She thought, when you're so angry that you are afraid that you may destroy yourself and everyone around you, you can only sit in terror, immobilise your arms, your legs, your tongue, so that you won't betray your rage. There were no words to describe her fury at being exploited sexually, her even greater fury at being abandoned. Dr Hartogs had taken away what little identity she had, reducing her to a messy pulp ... Instead of helping her he had used her – and then deserted her ... And because she thought of him as the substitute for her mother and father, the sexual relationship was like an incestuous affair ... All she knew was that she had been betrayed.'[14]

Although being intensely, even murderously, angry is a normal response to sexual violation, women have particular difficulty with the acknowledgment and expression of anger. Because of women's socialization, the anger is seen as unfeminine and destructive to relationships.[15]

My 'angry part,' which was deemed primitive, non-feminine, and immature by Dr A and was gradually tamed, ignored, and excluded by us both, is a classic example of suppressed anger. Although the 'angry part' was never entirely suppressed and did return periodically and sometimes explosively, the full force of my anger towards Dr A did not surface until I realized the enormity of my betrayal by him.

7. Sexual Confusion

Like children who have been sexually abused, people who have been sexually exploited by health professionals may be left with a great deal of confusion about their sexual relationships with other people. Some are left with the perception that sexuality is bad, destructive, and dangerous, and they tend to lead celibate lives. Others, seemingly programmed by their sexual involvement with the health professional, appear driven to re-enact their abuse with others. This is also influenced by the victims' low self-esteem, and possibly by a pervasive sense that no one would want to have a relationship with them if they were not sexually available.

Julie Roy describes how 'Once in a while, maybe every six months, she would feel the urge to have a glass of wine at dinner, then go out and pick up a strange man and spend the night with him at a hotel or motel. She wanted to be with men who didn't ask a lot of questions, who, like herself, were interested in being with someone just for the night ... She had a dim awareness that her escapades, seldom though they occurred, showed how little she cared what she did with her life.'[16]

When I have spoken to groups about the affairs and one-night stands I engaged in shortly after I ended therapy with Dr A, many women survivors have echoed my sentiments, some stressing that they felt extremely ashamed of that period of their lives. Many judged themselves very harshly, in some cases referring to themselves as 'promiscuous.' In the light of survivors' intense concern and enormous shame over this common reaction, the term 'sexual confusion' does not adequately convey the dissolving of moral scruples, the alienation from one's previous principles and conscience, the internalization of some of the abuser's sentiments about sexuality, and the reckless or even out-of-control pursuit of sexual liaisons that can follow sexual abuse by a health professional.

8. Increased Suicidal Risk

Studies have shown that about 14 per cent of people who are sexually involved with a therapist will make at least one suicide attempt, and about 1 per cent will succeed in taking their own lives.[17] People struggling with the after-effects of being sexually exploited by health professionals are likely to be grieving the betrayal, the lost relationship with the professional, and other losses which may have taken place during or after the therapy, including loss of self-esteem and self-respect, and loss of relationships, family, friends, job, career, health, and so on.

Sometimes the wish to die comes suddenly and impulsively, as described by Evelyn Walker: 'I do not remember clearly planning anything. I just went straight to the medicine cabinet when I got home, and I lined up all the bottles of pills I had accumulated ... then I emptied them into my hand and swallowed them a handful at a time.

After I had done it, I had the most marvellous feeling. Maybe it was the peace of mind I had originally sought through therapy. Whatever the source, I lay on my bed and felt light, peaceful, calm.'[18]

Suicide attempts may, on the other hand, be the outcome of a gradual downward spiral. After she stopped seeing her sexually abusive psychiatrist, Charlene experienced the breakup of her marriage and started drinking. She had another, disastrous, relationship and began to feel really hopeless. She felt extremely ashamed and hated herself for what had happened with the psychiatrist. No longer wanting to live, she made several suicide attempts and underwent several hospitalizations.

9. Role Reversal and Boundary Disturbance

As discussed in Chapter 3, Peterson considers role reversal to be

one of the four cardinal issues in the process of boundary violation. A sense of entitlement allows the professional to intrude on
the client and change the emphasis from helping the client to
meeting the professional's needs.[19] The end result, after the exploitative relationship has ceased, is that the abused person may
continue to focus on meeting others' needs while ignoring his or
her own.

This tendency is likely to be reinforced by the low self-esteem
and sense of unworthiness and even badness that many victims
are left with. Women, who have already been socialized to put others
first and to submerge themselves in the care of men and children,
may be pushed towards extremely self-sacrificing and self-abne-
gating behaviour.

The breach of personal boundaries suffered with the professional may make the person more vulnerable to other non-sexual
opportunists. One man was swindled by a door-to-door salesman.
He told me 'That would never have happened before. I don't
know what was wrong with me. Why would I let myself be taken
in like that?'

10. Cognitive Dysfunction

People who have been severely traumatized often have difficulty
maintaining attention and concentrating. Capturing the essence
of the 'intrusive' phase of post-traumatic stress disorder, cognitive
dysfunction refers to intrusive thoughts, flashbacks, nightmares,
and unwanted images that can be so vivid, they seem to be occurring in the present. Some people who have been sexually abused
by health professionals are continually tormented by such intrusive, unbidden cognitions. They may be unable to work, parent, or
carry on a social life.

Barbara Noël writes, 'I was a wreck. As each day and night went
by, I couldn't shake the pictures in my mind. I barely slept. Just
when I'd find a comfortable place in my pillow, I'd sit up again,
seeing Dr Masserman's bare buttocks gleaming in the light of the
examining room. I'd hear the jingle of coins as he pulled up his
pants, and I'd break out in a sweat, gasping for breath.'[20]

Like me, most survivors experience a relatively brief phase or phases of intense flashbacks, nightmares, and intrusive thoughts, to the point that they feel unable to cope with their everyday lives. A few, those terribly wounded by cruel and sadistic health professionals, may have to face a much longer struggle in their attempt to free themselves of this continual bombardment, a perpetual reminder of their excruciating and humiliating victimization.

Shame: A Central Emotion

Based on my own experiences and those of many survivors, it is clear that understanding the role of shame is crucial, although it is given little attention in the professional literature. Sometimes shame appears to be lumped together with guilt, thus making an unhelpful conglomeration of two issues that should be considered separately. Looking at dictionary definitions, guilt refers to an action or omission, a 'failure of duty, delinquency, offence, crime, or sin,' or the feeling of culpability for such an act or omission. Shame, on the other hand, is defined as 'a painful emotion arising from consciousness of something dishonouring, ridiculous or indecorous in one's own conduct or circumstances, or of being in a situation which offends one's modesty or decency' (*Shorter Oxford English Dictionary*, 3rd ed.).

While someone who has been sexually exploited by a health professional may blame herself and feel that it is her fault, the definition of shame appears perfectly apt for the victim's perception that she has been used, duped, fooled, and taken in, and that she has acted indecorously and been made to look ridiculous.

Barbara Noël thought, 'Was this what I deserved? Was I some worthless piece of ass? Was this the only purpose I could serve for men, including Dr Masserman? ... I pictured him standing there, smiling at his admirers and laughing to himself: I screw this woman, but she doesn't know it. She's too empty and stupid to know what's happening to her ... If anyone deserved Fool of the Year Award, I did. I screamed and cried about my own stupidity.'[21]

Carolyn Bates mentions shame on many occasions; she states,

'It was tremendously difficult for me to let go of my anger at having played the fool. Compassion for myself came slowly and stubbornly.'[22]

The issue of shame will appear repeatedly in the next two chapters, as it is a massive obstacle to healing, and to breaking the silence.

6. Healing

'Is It Possible to Have a Happy Life?'

Self – 1984

Sadness like a lump in my chest
Badness a conviction in my heart
Madness a label for my head

I am a cold frozen snow queen
Detached, mistrustful, aloof, alone
I am a malicious, destructive enemy
Angry, bitter, cold, ruthless
I am a maniacal, bloodthirsty madwoman
Demented, howling, devious, frantic

I am a little girl who felt unwanted
I am a tiny child who was abused
Pain, intimidation, fear, abandonment
Doorknobs turning. Don't, don't!
Mother leaving. Don't, don't leave me!

Nevertheless I grew up somehow
Looking for a family
Warmth, stability, nurturing, caring
Something was missing, it didn't quite work.
Entrusting myself to [Dr A] I opened my soul

Only to find darkness, destructiveness, pain
Craziness, misery, seductiveness, loss
Dependency, nothingness, rage
My sickness, badness
Hopeless case.

This poem was written during the early part of my therapy with Naida.

*Healing, for me, seems to have spread over many years and is intertwined
with the subject of the following chapter, 'Breaking the Silence.' The journey
commenced, I think, when I began to give voice to the 'angry part' and then
started to read books that called into question my compliance, my reliance on
male authority, my respect of male power, and my focus on meeting others'
needs while neglecting my own. It gained momentum when I disclosed to, and
was given support by, my husband and the women's groups I had joined. It
was given impetus by my experience with Earl, in the Human Dimension of
Medical Education Group, when he pointed out that I was giving far too
much power to males in authority. Around the same time, this idea was reinforced by my boss, who expressed much confidence in my abilities.*

*As described in Chapter 5, I went backwards, lost my sense of anger and
righteous indignation about my abuse by Dr A, and was once again mired in
shame and self-blame after the session with Dr Y and my husband's departure
from the family. After this, I regained my composure once again and was able
to get on with my life reasonably well and happily until, worn down by a
variety of stresses, I was overcome by constant fatigue, then developed chest pain
followed by flashbacks, nightmares, fears, and constant thoughts about Dr A.*

*A few months before the onset of these disturbing symptons, I had attended
a lecture given by Naida, about the treatment of adult survivors of child
sexual abuse. Her quiet confidence, warmth, and calmness impressed me, and
when she started to talk about how she conducted therapy with adult survivors,
I found myself thinking, 'I'd like some of that.' Since my abuse by Dr A, I had
periodically contemplated going for more therapy, but always found a reason
why I could not. The reasons were various: I did not need it; I had figured it
all out for myself; only part of the therapy had been abusive, and I had got a
lot of good things out of it; I could not go for therapy in a community where
I was well known; I could not trust another therapist – something dreadful*

was sure to happen; I might behave 'badly,' as I had with Dr A – hitting him, running from the office, getting angry at him, acting 'hysterical,' being very difficult and demanding; I might become seductive with another therapist, and he might be unable to resist my transference.

When I felt so terrible that I could barely get out of bed, overcome by fatigue, panic attacks, and flashbacks and seemingly unable to get out of it on my own, I knew that I needed help, and was finally forced to confront all my excuses and fears. Thinking back to Naida's lecture, and aware of her reputation in the community as an excellent therapist, I knew that I wanted to see her. But, could I get up the courage to call her? And if I did, what was I going to do if she turned me down? Eventually I called her, telling her that I thought I was suffering from stress and the after-effects of therapist abuse. On the telephone, she sounded warm and concerned and agreed to see me as soon as possible.

For the first few sessions I was extremely tense and anxious and extraordinarily vigilant, until I gradually realized that my fears were unfounded, that this experience would not repeat the indignities, isolation, or inculcation of intense dependency that I had suffered with Dr A. Neither would I act in a 'hysterical' or 'borderline' fashion. Naida made it clear that there were very distinct, firm boundaries to our relationship. She 'absolutely would not' come on to me sexually, and said that she would never be able to relate to me socially, as a friend.

Talking non-stop, my thoughts racing and the words falling over each other, I spent the first session telling Naida how awful I felt, but that I didn't understand it. Describing my abuse by Dr A, I told her about the early sessions when feelings about separations from my mother emerged, followed by memories about my godfather. I had feelings of guilt and shame towards my parents for having isolated the family from them after becoming so murderously angry towards my mother. I went on to tell Naida about the mounting stresses at work, my ex-husband's departure from the family, being blamed by Dr Y and another therapist my ex-husband was involved with. Naida commented, 'So many open wounds.'

By the time the session ended I felt dizzy, tense, and anxious. Having realized that the session would be very hard for me, I had arranged to meet a friend afterwards, and we went for a long walk in the rain. She was very supportive when I told her of my extreme anxiety about going to a therapist and my fears of some kind of disastrous outcome.

During the second session with Naida I felt almost impossibly tense and anxious, scared, and tearful. Asking 'Why can't I cope with work?,' I told her that I didn't know what to do. I was afraid of falling apart completely and disappearing like a puddle on the floor. For years, I said, I have felt like a suit of armour with nothing inside. I give the appearance of strength, but if you open the visor of the suit and look in, there's nothing but air. Discussing my fear, I recalled feeling very scared with Dr A. At the end of this session, Naida wondered whether I should go back to work, but I insisted that I needed to try it, that I must be able to cope.

By the third session, I was somewhat less scared and anxious. Discussing Dr A's having initiated a change in the relationship from teacher–student to doctor–patient, Naida felt that this action was abusive in itself, and that it showed that he had boundary problems. She asked me questions that I had never contemplated before. 'What did Dr A put into the relationship that made it so intense? ... Was it his needs? ... What did he want from you as a student?' Puzzling over these questions, I realized that I had always assumed that he had initiated the relationship because he realized that I had a problem and needed treatment.

During these early sessions, when I was still feeling so fragmented, confused, and muzzy and had trouble putting my feelings into words, my emotions seemed to be much more clearly conveyed by vivid fantasies. In the last chapter I described the fantasy in which I was running from pursuers, primarily Dr A, Umpi, and my ex-husband. In another fantasy I was behind bars, shut in, boxed in, limited, and constricted. I felt like a madwoman in Bedlam.

In another fantasy I was in a pit, which was well made, with vertical dirt sides. My three persecutors had pushed me down there. Dr A and Umpi turned away, rubbing their hands, with self-satisfied smirks on their faces. My ex-husband seemed to have mixed feelings, and peered down the hole before he left. I was about twelve feet down, clinging to a tree root to prevent myself from falling farther. Looking up, I could see the starry sky, but I knew that I couldn't get out.

In my journal, where I recorded these images, I wrote, 'How come I don't think of myself as a victim when this is a central theme of all my fantasies? I prefer to see myself as in control, but also sick, evil, immoral, and destructive.' In these early sessions with Naida, I often felt detached and constricted, aware of no emotions as I talked of Dr A. I maintained that my pathology had been a major cause of the relationship's going awry and that I had some responsibility in the seduction. This went on until mild-mannered Naida stood up and shouted at me, 'Sue, you were a VICTIM! You must realize that. We can't get anywhere if you keep blaming yourself.' This was a turning point. At a meeting of women psychiatrists and psychiatric residents I was able to disclose my abuse by Dr A, although I felt embarrassed and ashamed, wondering what they would think of me. When I told Naida about this she commented that I must feel less shame than before. Even by this point, I was unable to feel any anger towards Dr A. Naida suggested that shame was blocking my feelings.

Gradually, I began to feel safe and trusting in sessions with Naida, although my anxiety about a 'repeat performance' took strange forms. For instance, remembering how I had become so intensely attached to Dr A and how I would try to make an indelible imprint in my memory of how he looked, I decided not to wear my glasses to my sessions with Naida so that I would be able to see only a fuzzy image of her! Naida viewed my involvement with Dr A as 'a horror story,' and I gradually began to realize that his exploitation of me had gone well beyond the sexual realm. I recalled how he seemed to be attracted to me as a student and how he had commented enviously on my spontaneity. It became clear that Dr A relished my 'breakdown,' which tied me to him as a seemingly special and powerful therapist; basked in my dependency; and used me to work out his feelings about mothers – both putting me in his mother's shoes and focusing my rage and despair on my mother. My insecurity, vulnerability, need for affirmation, and childhood suffering made me vulnerable to victimization, and led me to take responsibility for my own exploitation, letting Dr A off scot-free and ensuring that I would be grateful for whatever he did.

It was both shocking and liberating to realize how much I had been programmed by Dr A. What else could account, for instance, for the otherwise inexplicable and uncharacteristic 'promiscuous behaviour,' that started immediately after my final session with Dr A, and for which I now judged myself so harshly? Naida suggested that I might have been 'addicted' to Dr A; a suggestion that began to make sense to me only recently, since I started writing this book. At the time, I felt that 'addiction' was an excessive or even pejorative term for what had happened.

When I was riding to work on my bicycle one morning about six months after I had started therapy with Naida, I had a fantasy about Naida and me doing a huge jigsaw puzzle together. It was my life, and it had 4,400 pieces.

I could see that some of the bottom-right-hand corner was completed, but on looking more closely I realized that it was done wrong. Pieces were jammed in, some even upside down, with the cardboard side showing. Naida and I had to redo this section, which seemed related to Dr A. I felt helplessly overwhelmed by the size of the project, but then noticed with surprise that quite a large section – some two to three hundred pieces – was already done in the centre. It was in warm colours: orange, red, gold, and dark yellow. I realized that the centre had always been there, but had come perilously close to disappearing a few months previously. Naida had helped me add a few pieces to the centre, but there was still an enormous amount left to do.

Not long after this came another turning point. I was involved with some colleagues and lawyers in a discussion about a young woman psychologist's case against a man who had been her teacher and then sexually exploited her as her therapist. The male psychologist's lawyers were contending that the relationship was merely an affair and that the young woman should have known better because of her education, her status as a psychologist in training, and her previous sexual experience. My colleagues pointed out that sexual involvement during therapy is harmful to any patient; that becoming a patient means abandoning one's adult monitoring system, trusting, regressing, becoming dependent; and that in this case the young woman was in double jeopardy, because a professor–student dimension was added to the therapist–patient interaction.

It was, of course, exactly what had happened to me. I felt enraged on behalf of the young woman psychologist, and in my journal I wondered why I wasn't exploding with anger on my own behalf. I wrote,

> *Why does it all seem somehow unreal, detached? I have viewed things upside down, sideways, and backwards. Somehow I am sick, bad, and devious, and Dr A was responding to my overwhelming need and its manifestations. A feeling of having always been different, a dark side, devious. A witch, bitch, and a whore.*
>
> *But what evidence is there for this? I was OK as a kid and a young adult. Had friends. A bit prone to periods of loss of confidence, moodiness. Afraid of being exploited by men.*
>
> *It could be that what I viewed as my unique craziness was, as I have written so often (but never entirely believed), my reactions to a crazy-making situation. And struggling with the guilt, and role conflicts of*

being a doctor, wife, and mother. And Dr A caught me in my second pregnancy, just before moving and starting a new job.

It was shortly after this that Naida and I started to discuss my early childhood. Bringing up my godfather filled me with terror. Terror about the memories, and fear. I wrote in my journal, 'It's so scary. After I grew to trust Dr A, all that sex stuff came up, and I felt so upset, crazy. And then the abuse started.' In the session, I said to Naida, 'I can't understand it. You're so neutral, and I'm so well behaved. Yet with Dr A all hell broke lose!'

As time went on, I had some more, although still *fragmented*, memories of my godfather abusing me. Sometimes my godmother observed, sometimes she joined in. We talked about how it had been for me when my mother, unawares, left me with this abusive couple. I felt abandoned, unprotected, very angry at my mother. Most of the time now we were working on these issues with parents and godparents, making occasional connections with my vulnerability to Dr A and how entangled I had become.

In the second year of my therapy with Naida, feeling much better and having regained some energy, I looked for a respite from the constant demands and stresses of my clinical work. A position as Chair of Women's Studies was advertised at Simon Fraser University, and I applied and was selected for the post. During this year, when community involvement was part of my job, I began to talk openly to groups of women about my abuse by Dr A, as well as my other concerns about the power and control exerted by psychiatry.

After about two years of therapy, I stopped seeing Naida, feeling that I had resolved most of my issues, although I felt that there was something else, something quite elusive, that I would need to deal with in time. This second experience of therapy was so different from the first that I was left feeling immensely saddened that this had not happened the first time. If Dr A had been a better therapist; if he had not used me for his own needs; if he had not encouraged my dependency; if he had not kept telling me it was my problem, that I was sick, disordered, angry, and so on; if he had not sexually exploited me, what would my life be like now?

After my therapy ended, there were many things going on in my life: my work, outdoor activities, and time with Keith, my friends, and my grown children. Ending my year at Simon Fraser University, I went back to my position with the University of British Columbia and the children's hospital, where I work with severely damaged children and their families, and teach medical students and psychiatric residents. Thoughts of Dr A became sporadic, usually set off by some kind of trigger or reminder.

As I will describe more fully in the next chapter, I decided that I wanted to use my experience to help other people who had been sexually exploited by health professionals. Realizing that a central issue is shame, which plays a major role in silencing victims, I resolved to talk openly about my experiences, hoping that this would reassure victims who felt mired in shame and embarrassment. I hoped that they would feel, 'If it could happen to her, then I shouldn't feel so bad about it happening to me.'

As my experiences became known, I was contacted by a group of women, the Therapist Abuse Action Group (TAAG), who were having monthly meetings. Getting to know these women, from diverse backgrounds, all of whom had been abused by physicians, has been inspiring. All of them have fought massive obstacles, including shame, self-blame, PTSD, poor physical health, loss of partners, damaged careers, loss of jobs, poverty, financial problems, and lack of support from professionals, relatives, and friends. Yet all of them have wanted to contribute in some way to reporting, education, or prevention of sexual abuse by health professionals. Going to the TAAG meetings mobilized my feelings of rage on behalf of the women who had been so needlessly exploited, with such damaging consequences. More anger erupted one evening when I was in the middle of writing a requested paper about sexual abuse by therapists. Suddenly, I found myself consumed with rage, grabbed a carving knife, and, for just a moment, was ready to jump in my car and drive to Dr A's city, locate him, and kill him!

Sometimes I wonder how long one goes on healing, how long it takes. Will I always have these flashes of anger? Or could writing this book get it finally out of my system? Does my intense reaction to the prospect of having to go to a discovery and then a hearing mean that I am still in some way enslaved to Dr A, or could possibly become enslaved again to someone else?

Although sometimes, briefly, I have viewed myself as permanently scarred or damaged, most of the time I don't feel that way at all. One can see conflict and difficulties in various lights – the old saying goes, you can see the glass as half empty or half full. Could I perhaps, despite all the pain and anguish, have become a more complex, more interesting person, who has much to contribute? If I hadn't been abused by Umpi, then I probably would not have grown up with the conviction that I could rely only on myself and that I had to care for myself. This conviction, together with memories of Umpi as a *doctor, led me to go to medical school. So, if none of this had happened, might I have ended up a bored housewife in England rather than a professor of psychiatry in Canada? Who knows?*

If Dr A had not abused me, I might have had a more illustrious and traditional career. But again, who knows?

Healing is a process, not a one-time occurrence. It often stretches over years, progressing in fits and starts that may include periods of seemingly going backwards. Some survivors have likened the process to a kind of spiral, where the same issue is periodically revisited, but from a different perspective or stage of maturity. Studies have shown neurochemical changes in PTSD, and suggested that a person's nervous system may remain more vulnerable and more easily aroused, so that later stresses can cause a return of the PTSD symptoms. These symptoms can appear in the form of hyperarousal with irritability, insomnia, and agitation, or they can manifest themselves as emotional constriction, detachment, and numbing.

Sandra Butler, author and leader of workshops on 'Healing the Healers,' has identified three main phases of healing from sexual abuse. In the 'victim' phase the person is being traumatized, but may not recognize her victim status. Next, while beginning to reclaim control of her life, feel the feelings, and transcend shame and self-blame, she is a 'survivor.' As a result of her healing, she may decide to become a 'warrior,' and devote time and energy to helping other victims or planning educational and preventative strategies.

Healing should not be equated with going for therapy or professional help, because there are many aspects of a person's life, experiences, and relationships that can give the survivor the sense of safety, support, recognition, acceptance, understanding, and empowerment that she needs. Many clients of the Walk-In Counselling Center in Minneapolis who have been sexually abused by therapists have stated that group therapy, discussions with other victims, or filing a complaint or lawsuit have been more important in their healing than one-to-one therapy.[1]

Healing from sexual abuse by health professionals will be explored from several perspectives. Survivors' descriptions of their own healing process will be followed by a look at self-help approaches, using Matsakis's book as an example. Next I will give a brief summary of my own approach to therapy of victims of abuse by health professionals. Finally, obstacles to the recovery process will be examined, and it will be noted that this issue overlaps with the previously described secondary-wounding process.

Survivors' Opinions about the Healing Process

'Sarah' was sexually abused by two physicians while she was deeply hypnotized. The after-effects included severe anxiety, depression, paranoia, insomnia, panic attacks, feelings of withdrawal and isolation, sexual disinterest, and extremely low self-esteem. Her 'feelings of faith and hope in both humanity in general and in [her] own life were almost destroyed.' Asked to describe 'healing experiences,' Sarah included the following:

1 Talking to a health care professional who believed me and wanted to help in the best way for my process of healing.
2 My own personal ways of healing myself: being in nature; telling myself healing thoughts; doing some of the things I used to love doing and was good at; staying in a relationship with a loving man, even though many difficulties presented themselves.
3 Telling friends and family about it. Having one close friend with whom I could share details of the abuse and the intense feelings about it. She believed me even when I found it so unbelievable.
4 Knowing that the doctors know that I know what they did. Knowing that my life is good and their lives are pathetic, and that they probably even know this themselves.
5 Looking at the business relationships that intimidate me and [seeing] how this was related to the abuse, and getting help to work through it and do some 'damage control.'
6 Feeling like I'm moving on in my life.

'Lynn,' a social worker who was sexually abused by her therapist, felt that her healing experiences included:

1 Leaving her subsequent therapist when she realized that he did not believe that she had been abused

2 Finding another therapist, who believed her and who arranged for some very practical cognitive and biofeedback treatment for Lynn's severe insomnia
3 Moving to a new community
4 Making an ethics complaint to the abusive therapist's professional organization
5 Getting involved herself in a committee dealing with ethics complaints
6 Addressing conferences about sexual abuse by health professionals and teaching about sexual boundaries
7 Receiving support from colleagues

Charlene had many difficult experiences after the abusive therapy ended. Her marriage broke up and she lost her job, had to sell the house, was drinking heavily, and felt suicidal and hopeless. Suffering from 'toxic shame,' and seeking restitution for her 'sins,' she tried church and Bible study, but neither seemed to help. A crisis centre worker suggested that she should go to Alcoholics Anonymous. There she heard many other men and women describe the use of alcohol and other drugs to drown the pain they felt as a result of earlier traumas, often physical or sexual abuse. There, feeling at last supported, accepted, and understood, she started to talk about her sexual abuse.

At around the same time, she told her family doctor; he believed her and referred to her abuser as 'that bastard.' After this she began to see a woman counsellor. It was, however, a friend who finally helped Charlene to recognize that she had been abused. The friend said, 'Charlene, you're walking down the street and you have your purse in your hand, and some guy grabs your purse and steals it. What would you do? Would you say, "Ooooh, poor thief?" Why not? Then why do you keep saying that about your doctor?' Charlene replied, 'Well, I shouldn't have been in his office,' and her friend responded 'Well, you shouldn't have been on that street either, and you shouldn't have been carrying a purse!' Charlene said, 'That was the first time it kind of dawned on me that it wasn't my fault. Like I was just a victim of circumstances. I was at the wrong place at the wrong time. He was the sexual offender.'

After this Charlene's healing progressed, with the help of several counsellors, long walks, and support from her friends. She joined a support group and talked on the phone with other members.

Asked what helped him feel better, Don, by this time eleven, said rather sarcastically, 'When my parents started to believe me.' Other things that had made Don feel good were getting on the soccer team; starting karate lessons – he felt now that he would be able to defend himself in any situation; thinking about how much he would like to beat up Dr Smith; and making some new friends. He did not mention the weekly sessions he had with a play therapist.

Sylvia felt that she had dealt with her sexual involvement with her general practitioner, Ken, on her own. She felt, 'I had no right to report it … I asked for it and got what I deserved.' After the involvement with Ken ceased, Sylvia went to several counsellors for help with her sexual and relationship problems. She did not mention her involvement with Ken to these counsellors and says that the counsellors were not able to change anything. Eventually she was able to cure herself, by having the courage to talk to her lovers and tell them what she wanted.

Sylvia applies the same philosophy to her relationship with Ken, saying, 'It pushed me to better things with myself and other people. Even though I couldn't change anything with him, it made me determined to change things with myself or others. I feel "lessened" by allowing him to use me as he wanted and not being able to protest or refuse him, but it made me stronger in every other area of my life. By the feeling that he looks at me as something less than "whole," I am forced to make other people see my strength.'

In David's view, the main issue in his healing after the physician fondled his penis, under the guise of 'sex education,' was that he left the office and never went back. Unable to discuss what had happened with his parents or friends, he was left with some feeling of shame and confusion. He felt very suspicious of health professionals, read books of home remedies, and tried to avoid any visits to doctors or hospitals. Years later, he learned of a research study about sexual abuse by health professionals. The researcher was the first person that David told about his experiences, and David said that he felt very relieved to be listened to and taken seriously. He was able to see that he had been abused, that he had done nothing to encourage the doctor, and that, anyway, the doctor was solely and completely responsible for ethical behaviour in the doctor–patient relationship.

These accounts contain many different opinions, varying from Sylvia's grim determination to learn from the experience and find new ways of coping on her own to Sarah, Lynn, and Charlene's descriptions of the multiple dimensions of their healing. Don's response is typical of boys in his age group in our culture. Heavily influenced by 'macho' prescriptions for male behaviour, boys who have been abused concentrate on building power, strength, and, sometimes, popularity. Disclosing to peers and gaining support from them is rarely possible, unless the boy has a group therapy experience. Seeing a therapist is often deemed a sign of weakness in Don's age group; some boys will accept therapy, but want to ensure that their friends do not learn about it.

Self-help: 'I Can't Get Over It'

The first section of Aphrodite Matsakis's handbook for survivors of trauma[2] gives a general overview of PTSD and its biochemistry, and discusses feelings and thoughts arising from trauma, and how to cope with them; the three levels of victimization, with advice about how to overcome secondary wounding and counter victim thinking; triggers that precipitate PTSD symptoms; and various helpful techniques for dealing with those symptoms.

The second part, 'The Healing Process,' takes the survivor through three phases of healing. Remembering the trauma is followed by getting in touch with the feelings, and the final phase is that of empowerment or mastery. The third phase involves discovering a meaning in the trauma and developing a survivor mentality rather than a victim mentality.

Initially and at other points in her book, Matsakis cautions readers that their healing process must be monitored and professional help sought if the person experiences hyperventilation or uncontrollable shaking or irregular heart beat, feels she is losing touch with reality, feels disoriented, develops severe and inexplicable physical symptoms, has memory problems, or develops suicidal, homicidal, self-destructive, or self-mutilating behaviour or urges.

The last section of the book addresses specific traumas, one of which is sexual assault. My experience of recommending this book is that many victims of sexual abuse are not able to read it on their own without becoming extremely distressed and developing some of the symptoms Matsakis mentions in her cautionary list. Before being able to read the book, which can function as an adjunct to other forms of therapy, the victim may need to have some group or individual therapy.

Therapy with Victims of Sexual Abuse by Health Professionals

As a therapist who has worked with many adult and child victims of sexual abuse, and a few victims of sexual abuse by health professionals, I have found most help in the writings of Judith Herman,[3] Kenneth Pope,[4] and Gary Schoener and colleagues.[5] My experience with child victims and adult survivors of incest, and knowledge of the literature in this area have been very helpful, as the health professional–patient relationship is similar to that between parent and child, meaning that sexual abuse in either relationship is incestuous. What follows is a brief and very general overview of my practice.[6]

Over the past ten years, victims who have sought me out or have been referred to me have already learned that I am a survivor too. This reduces, but certainly does not eliminate, the anxiety and distrust that victims feel about starting therapy with another health professional. Some victims are so anxious at first, so scattered and fragmented in their presentation, that it is hard to get a clear idea of their concerns. Therapy is infinitely complicated by the presence of the abuser, almost like a third party in the room. One woman patient, well into the second phase of therapy, became very distressed, anxious, and suspicious when I moved my office to a different location in the hospital. For her, this move brought up feelings about the abusive doctor, who had moved his office just before he molested her. With the abusive health professional, victims have felt controlled, commanded, coerced, brainwashed, used, exploited, humiliated, disregarded, blamed, shamed, and disrespected. So they need an environment where they will feel respected, supported, understood, empowered, and in control of themselves, their feelings, and their decisions.

At first I concentrate on creating a safe environment and making sure that victims know that there are firm boundaries. Some victims, whose abuse happened in a private office, after the secretary left, say they feel very reassured by coming to a children's hospital clinic setting where there are always other people about. One woman came with her husband for many months before she felt secure enough to come on her own. It is important to ensure that patients have support available from friends and relatives and other professionals, such as their family doctor. Self-care is crucial, and encouragement about exercise, diet, sleeping, and general safety may be needed.

In the early sessions, I ask patients to give me as much as they can of their life story, including family background, and I assess symptoms of PTSD, depression, or any other problems. Sometimes medication is useful, particularly in this first phase of therapy, for instance, if the patient is very depressed. Giving information about PTSD or a description of the therapist–patient sex syndrome is important. I always emphasize that therapy is a collaborative endeavour, that patients are the best experts on themselves, and that my role is more like a catalyst than a director.

Herman calls the second phase of therapy 'Remembrance and Mourning.' Pacing is very important, for some devastating memories, insights, and emotions will arise. Patients generally know how much they can deal with, and I try to ensure that devastating new thoughts or feelings do not emerge towards the end of a session. Although adult victims generally remember their abuse in detail, the recollections are often flat, emotionless descriptions. Many patients are very reluctant to confide the details of their abuse, and their stammering, averted eyes, and flushed neck con-

vey the shame and embarrassment that they are feeling.[7] Gradually they realize that they have taken on the shame and self-blame
that should rightly be felt by the abuser.

As survivors tell their story, understand their betrayal, and experience their anger, they begin to grieve for what has been lost as a
result of their abuse and its after-effects. The abusive encounter
may have terminated, or at least hindered, the treatment or therapy they needed when they first went to the health professional.
Perhaps they feel they have lost touch with the person they were
before the abuse started. Other losses may include loss of the feeling of being special and nurtured by the abusive health professional; lost youth, innocence, or years out of a lifetime; lost physical
or mental health; lost marriages or other partnerships; lost jobs or
careers; lost friends and relatives; lost children or potential children; lost lifestyle, activities, and interests; lost faith or spirituality;
lost self-respect, self-control, and self-esteem. At this stage, survivors sometimes feel that 'lakes of tears' will never end.

At this stage, consumed with anger, wanting revenge, some patients decide to make a report to the police or a licensing authority
or to embark on a civil suit. Because of the retraumatizing nature
of many survivors' experiences with these systems, I caution
them about the pros and cons, and often put them in touch with a
survivor who is knowledgable about the legal system.

In addition to recalling the abuse and grieving, patients need to
understand how the abusive experience is affecting their current
behaviour, attitudes, feelings, relationships, occupational and
educational choices, and so on. Previous issues, problems, and
family difficulties that occurred before the abuse may need to be
addressed. Remembering and mourning alone are not enough to
repair the damage that many have sustained. Pointing out that
therapy is expected to be a 'corrective emotional experience' that
has long-lasting positive effects on a person's life, Pope has termed
abusive therapy a 'corrosive emotional experience' that can weaken
and sometimes destroy a person's developmental foundations.[8]
The basic trust, confidence, autonomy, and initiative that a person
gained from his or her parents can be damaged or lost.

Herman calls the third, or final, phase of therapy 'Reconnection.'

Their shame lessened or eliminated, their energy and initiative renewed, their assertiveness regained, their self-esteem, self-respect, and self-control restored, survivors are ready to move out into the world and reconnect with others. This may mean renewing or repairing relationships, increasing intimacy with loved ones, making new friends, or getting involved with other survivors. Survivors look back at their helplessness and powerlessness in the abusive situation and are proud of the courage, strength, and adaptability that enabled them to escape and then transcend their abuse. By this time, patients' intense, often murderous, rage towards their abuser and wish for revenge have often changed into a righteous indignation. Although the quest for justice or compensation may still exist, it is now likely to be accompanied by the wish to help other victims or to embark on educational, preventative, or victim-advocacy programs.

In the final sessions, we discuss the possible resurgence of PTSD symptoms in times of stress or life change and the steps that can be taken to reduce stress and bring the symptoms under control. With the possible exception of the more minor and short-term experiences of exploitation, recovery will never be totally complete. As one survivor told me, 'Never a day goes by without some memory or other.' Instead of focusing on recovery, however, the survivors' energies are now devoted to their everyday lives, jobs, children, relationships, and pleasurable activities.

Obstacles to Healing

Many obstacles to healing are cited by survivors. They involve the survivors' own issues with shame, embarrassment, and self-blame; lack of support by the victims' families; lack of community support for the victims, including unavailability of appropriate therapists; and lack of support, or even silencing, by the health professionals and their organization.

After her abuse, Lynn felt consumed by guilt and shame. She withdrew from relationships and believed that the people she dated viewed her as withdrawn and secretive. She could not confide in friends or colleagues as she felt the information could be used against her. Her subsequent therapist did not believe that she had been abused, and her attempts at lodging complaints were met with resistance and procrastination.

Charlene's 'toxic shame' and the conviction that she was to blame for her own abuse did not allow her to confide in or get support from anyone. Her second therapist had offered only the remark, 'we doctors have our code of ethics,' and she did not know whether he believed her or not. He gave her no support and no indication of her right to make a complaint. Later, she says, he 'French kissed' her once himself. After the therapy ended, she spent many hours with the lawyer working for the licensing body, but for some reason they decided not to pursue the case.

Although Sarah's doctor made a report to the licensing authority on her behalf, Sarah had only vague memories of her abuse and decided that, in the context of the uproar surrounding 'false memory syndrome,'[9] she would be slaughtered by any court or inquiry board. Instead, she wanted to find some way of bringing attention to her abuse and to the abusers, some Gandhi-like form of non-violent protest. Asked about the obstacles or impediments to healing that she had encountered, she listed the following:

1 The extremely difficult task of finding a health care professional who believed me and wanted to help in a way that would be best for me. I saw six (from one to about a dozen visits) before finding one. With one male therapist, I thought I might be victimized again. Two did not seem to believe me. Three did not want to get involved, which varied from mild disinterest to outright rejection.
2 Not remembering
3 Not believing such a thing could happen to me
4 Not believing such a thing did happen to me
5 Minimizing it (at first), knowing that others have suffered worse
6 Letting it live on by putting some sort of retaliatory action in the future as opposed to the present

For me and many other victims, shame plays a special role in maintaining silence, blocking emotions, preventing or slowing the process of healing, and protecting the abusive health professional. Writing eloquently about the power of shame, Jeffery Jay states, 'During 20 years of working with PTSD clients, I have found that, regardless of the victim or the trauma, the response of others will follow a predictable pattern. If reassurance and cheering homilies fail to comfort, if subtle warnings fail to quiet the victim, the ultimate trump card is shame. Only shame is powerful enough to squelch the victim's desperate need to be heard ... Shame causes the private self to retreat into numbness, to repress feelings and dampen personal engagement with others.'[10]

The shame, blame, and lack of support by the community experienced by victims of sexual abuse by health professionals allow some comparisons with soldiers returning from Vietnam. The American public expressed extreme disdain about the Vietnam war, particularly in its final stages. Returning vets were *persona non grata* in the job market, on campuses, and in Veterans Affairs facilities. They met with callous indifference from peers, often of a higher social class, who had managed to avoid the war. The media portrayed vets as unstable, drug-crazed killers. Families were not supportive, and therapists misdiagnosed them, told them they should 'forget' the war, or assumed that their difficulties arose from early family relationships.[11]

Eventually, as a result of efforts by the Vietnam veterans themselves, who held 'rap' groups and invited professionals to join them, this predominant attitude changed, and recent books, media portrayals, and the building of the veterans' memorial wall in Washington have conveyed a greater respect and appreciation for the men who went through those difficult times.

Survivors of sexual abuse by health professionals suffer the same public disbelief, blaming, and lack of support, and are faced by a 'conspiracy of silence' by health professionals, which will be examined in more detail in the next chapter. There are no properly organized and comprehensive treatment or rehabilitation facilities like the ones now available for war veterans. It is very difficult for victims to find appropriate therapy if they are poor and unable to pay for it privately.

Although some progress has recently been made, in that the problem is now more generally recognized and professional bodies are paying more attention to it, there is still a long way to go before victims get the attention and support that they both deserve and need.

Issues for Survivors Who Are Also Health or Mental Health Professionals

In terms of healing, survivors who are health or mental health professionals face special obstacles and benefit from special advantages. Obstacles to disclosure are described in Chapter 7. Before this stage is reached, hurdles to recognition and acknowledgment abound. Loyalty to their chosen profession creates difficulties for those who are abused by a perpetrator in the same profession, for example, a psychologist abused by a psychologist, or a physiotherapist by a physiotherapist. Confronting the abuse could cast doubts on the profession as a whole, its principles and patterns of practice. Several health professionals who were sexually abused by health professionals have told me that they are not able or willing to identify themselves as victims, as this makes them like the other victims, people they view as extremely fragile and emotionally unstable. My own struggle with this is described in Chapter 5, where I recounted my uneasiness with both the professional and the feminist literature on the subject of women who were abused by their therapists.

Those of us who are mental health professionals may be more adept than other health professionals at attributing some responsibility to ourselves or even blaming ourselves totally for the abuse. As revealed in my narrative, I was able to find all sorts of 'reasons' that diminished Dr A's responsibility or absolved him of it altogether. They included the fact that I had problems in the first place, that I was an extremely difficult 'borderline' patient, and that I had a sexualized transference that Dr A 'couldn't help' acting out. Guilt gives one a sense of control and veils other issues such as betrayal and the realization that one was not special or cared for.

When it comes to the healing process and finding a therapist, health professionals have an inside track and are much more likely to find or be referred to an experienced, thoroughly reputable therapist. Henry Grunebaum studied forty-seven mental health professionals who believed that they had been harmed by psychotherapy or psychoanalysis. The harmful therapies were characterized by intense emotional and/or sexual involvement or by therapists who were portrayed as cold, distant, and uninvolved. Eventually, 78 per cent sought further therapy, and 'when they went back into therapy, all of the patients spoke about their fearfulness, their difficulties trusting the new therapist, and their surprise when the experience was both different and helpful.'[12]

Like me, the mental health professionals in Grunebaum's study initially blamed themselves for the failure of their original therapy and continued in the therapy, sometimes for many years, believing that it might eventually turn out to be helpful. Although this was not studied, it seems likely that these 'knowledgeable observers of psychotherapy' made an informed choice when picking their second therapist. In another study, Grunebaum found that experienced therapists chose a therapist who is warm and caring and talks to the patient.[13]

In addition to advantages in the referral process, health professionals are likely to have the financial resources to pay for therapy privately rather than having to rely on publicly financed programs or on funds obtained through victim-compensation sources.

7. Breaking the Silence

'Can You Disclose without Losing Everything?'

The profession historically tended to attribute allegations of sex abuse to a presumably innate female tendency to invent such allegations and hurl them at innocent men.

Kenneth Pope[1]

Breaking the silence is very scary, particularly at first. The memory of telling my ex-husband, the first person I confided in, is still vivid. We were lying in bed. He commented that he was glad I was no longer going to see Dr A, but said to me, 'I know you feel it really helped you a lot.' I felt close to exploding, knew that I couldn't continue to act as if Dr A had helped me, and started to sob, 'No, no, he didn't.' Flooded with pain, remorse, guilt, shame, and embarrassment, I struggled with myself, wanting to tell him, yet fearing that he would be terribly shocked and angry, perhaps even throw me out of the house or tell me our marriage was over. He was, in fact, very supportive, exclaiming that I had been abused and drawing parallels with incest. Admitting that I had been very frightened of telling him and of what his reaction might be, I said that deep down I still partially believed what Dr A had told me: that it was all my fault, that I was seductive.

Making a complaint to Dr A's licensing board or professional association was something I considered carefully. Based on my reading of the psychiatric literature and the outcome of other cases at the time, I felt that I, rather than Dr A, would be the one on trial. Like a rape victim, I would be blamed for having been there in the first place, or for having 'asked for it,' enjoyed it, or deserved it. As a psychiatric patient, I could be written off as 'delusional' or 'borderline,' or, if considered to be a partner in an 'affair,' as a spurned and vindictive woman. So, as described earlier, I eventually decided to confront Dr A myself, in his office.

Telling my women's group was another hurdle. We were sitting in a basement room, the light was fairly dim, but I was aware that my face was flaming, my heart beating wildly, and my voice hoarse and strained as I tried to tell them about my relationship with Dr A: how it started, how it became sexual, and how I kept going, telling myself that it was helping me when it was really very hurtful and reality-bending. They, too, were supportive.

It was at this point that I began an energetic, sometimes even furious, criticism of the way that psychiatry treats women. It was often hard to hold onto this view, particularly when working and teaching in an environment that has little or no awareness that the mental health professions have enormous power in people's lives: power to label, blame, drug, put in hospital, control behaviour, and direct lives. And power to exploit. The recognition of how Dr A had used the power of psychiatry to label, blame, and control me was always there as an underlying driving force and a reminder. In 1973 a study showed that between 5 and 13 per cent of physicians admitted to erotic behaviour, sometimes including intercourse, with patients.[2] Despite this evidence of widespread abuse, no one seemed ready to acknowledge that this was a massive problem, and I, still struggling with shame and fears that my colleagues would write me off as unstable or 'borderline' if they knew my story, was loath to bring up the problem repeatedly.

In 1975, at the annual meeting of the Canadian Psychiatric Association, I co-founded the Task Force on Women's Issues in Psychiatry and served as its coordinator until 1980. There was a good deal of opposition to the formation of this task force. Sadly, some of it came from psychiatrists' wives, who were convinced that we were troublemakers, and probably feared that we would denigrate homemakers. The aims of the task force, which had representatives in each province, were threefold: to introduce new knowledge on women's psychology into psychiatric training and practice, to study the treatment of women psychiatric patients in Canada, and to bring women into positions of influence in the profession.

It was soon clear to me, and to other task force members, that much work needed to be done. Overprescription of medication, especially anti-anxiety medications like Valium, blaming mothers for their children's problems, and victim-blaming approaches to victims of violence were identified as major problems. Although I shared my experiences of sexual abuse by a psychiatrist with a few close female colleagues, I was not yet ready to speak of it openly. In fact, as described in Chapter 5, the demise of my marriage and the experience of being blamed by my ex-husband and his gurus eroded my confidence and certainty about my betrayal and sent me back to a place full of shame and guilt.

At the same time I managed to maintain my overall conviction about the destructive ways in which psychiatry can treat patients and their families, and worked, with a woman colleague, on a book that described, explained, and gave examples of how psychiatry, though seemingly benign and compassionate, can be a source of oppression and social control.[3] We did not include a chapter on sexual exploitation of patients, which is perhaps not surprising in view of the mixed feelings I was experiencing at the time, struggling again with such questions and self-accusations as: Was it my fault? Was I seductive? Was he just acting out my transference? But he must have helped me some of the time! I must have been really crazy to get involved in something like that. How can I trust my perceptions now, as my judgment is obviously so poor?

During and after my therapy with Naida, when the shame and guilt were again diminished, I began to disclose my experiences of childhood sexual abuse, and of doctor/therapist–patient abuse, to friends and colleagues, women's groups, and groups of students when I was doing seminars or workshops on the topic of physician–patient sexual abuse. Around this time there were some well-publicized cases of psychiatrist–patient sexual abuse. These cases allowed a group of women psychiatrists, who like myself belonged to the Section on Women's Issues in Psychiatry of the Canadian Psychiatric Association, to push the association to issue a strong statement that psychiatrist–patient sexual involvement is unethical under any and all circumstances. We also had input into a Canadian Psychiatric Association position paper on sexual exploitation of patients.[4]

While I was at Simon Fraser University I put an advertisement in the newspaper looking for victims of therapist–patient abuse to participate in a research study. Through this, I talked to a number of women, and my understanding grew. Many had had experiences similar to mine, with a period of grooming, a change in roles that put them in the position of hearing about the therapist's problems and difficulties, a feeling that they were special, a conviction that the therapist was the centre of the universe and held the answer to all their problems, and an implicit or explicit agreement about secrecy. Some women who called me were unwilling to give me their names and were obviously suffering from intense shame and self-blame.

Other women, who had not been physically involved with their therapists, described how their therapists had flirted with them, continually emphasized dress and attractiveness, and gave them frequent advice on how to find the right man. These women felt that their therapists had not taken their concerns seriously and had not been intent on promoting their emotional growth. The therapists had, in fact, merely tried to get them to adjust to, or put up with, the stresses and strains of their everyday lives. As a result of this study, I wrote a paper for Canadian Woman Studies *which concluded that 'Sexual issues between therapist and female patient are not merely a matter of the isolation and intimacy of the office setting, of poor training, of personality problems, or of male entitlement. They are of multidimensional origin and are rooted in the power differential between therapist and patient, the mystique of therapy, cultural expectations for men and women, society's proclivity for blaming women, and the mental health professions' self-protective stance. Training and practice must acknowledge all these aspects in order to ensure that therapy does not become superficial flirtation, game playing, exhortations to fulfil cultural prescriptions, or (at worst) sexual abuse of the woman, whose trust is betrayed, old patterns confirmed and new problems created.'[5] But, although I used some case examples which reflected my own experiences, I was not yet ready for a public declaration about my abuse.*

While I toyed with the idea of 'coming out' publicly, and thought that sharing my own experiences of sexual abuse by a therapist would help other victims and make a contribution towards breaking down the 'conspiracy of silence' that muzzles victims and shields abusers, I was still scared. My worst fantasies included my children disowning me, and my colleagues judging me to be unstable, vindictive, seductive, and indiscreet.

In December 1989 a reporter for the Vancouver Sun *called me. She was doing an article on sexual abuse by therapists that would feature a Vancouver woman who would be disclosing her abuse by a local psychiatrist. After the reporter and I had discussed some dimensions of therapist–patient abuse, I mentioned that I was a survivor too. Then, with mounting anxiety, as I still had extremely mixed feelings about making my abuse public knowledge, I tried to backtrack and asked her not to mention my disclosure in the newspaper. She replied, 'Don't you want to back up [the victim]? It will give her much more credibility if you say you were abused too.' How could I refuse?*

In the article, I was quoted as saying, 'For a long time, he blamed me for being seductive and I blamed myself until I went into proper therapy. I had totally put this guy on a pedestal and thought he was going to be the answer to my unhappiness at the time. It was a totally horrible nightmare.'⁶ The article appeared in the 'Life' section of the newspaper, which had earlier replaced the 'Women's pages,' and was consequently read by few of my psychiatric colleagues, but I did receive many calls from women in the community who had been abused by therapists or physicians. Their tragic stories, the abuse and humiliation that they had suffered, made me extremely angry and even more determined that I would do anything I could to break my own and my profession's silence on the topic.

Sharing some details of my abuse with my children was painful and embarrassing, although they accepted it in a supportive and matter-of-fact way. It was much more painful for me than it was for them, as I found myself reliving scenes from their early childhood when I used to travel to see Dr A and spend much time thinking about him. Renewed guilt and shame were hard to avoid.

In October 1990 I was called by Paul Taylor, a reporter with the Globe and Mail, *a newspaper widely read across Canada. He was putting together a story on sexual abuse of patients by therapists. This time I was ready and willing to participate, needing no 'guilt trips' from the reporter. The resulting article started on the front page and included my picture.*

The lengthy passage reporting my experiences includes my comments, 'It sounds crazy in retrospect. How could I, a professional person, get sucked in? I should have known better but he was the psychiatric guru, he was the expert, and I thought maybe I did have a problem ... [it was] a kind of crazy-making, reality-bending experience ... I felt like a puppet in his hands.'⁷ After the telephone interview my resolve quickly evaporated, and I began to worry once more about my colleagues' reception of my disclosure. This time, many read the article, and only one man made a prurient comment. The rest were very supportive and complimented me on my courage.

During this period I was sometimes asked if I had reported Dr A to the state board of health. I replied, at first, that I thought I had done all I could by confronting him in his office. In addition, I suggested, it was such a long time ago that it was too late to take any action. Members of TAAG were not convinced by these statements and urged me to make a formal complaint. A woman colleague who works with victims of sexual abuse by physicians and therapists gently urged me to 'at least write to them … it might help support the claim of another victim.' Gradually I realized that I was hanging on to feelings about being special and unique. I had believed Dr A when he told me that I was the only victim, and that he had learned a painful lesson. How did I know that I wasn't making another mistake? Perhaps I was just protecting myself, and letting some other women down in the process?

In the fall of 1991 I wrote an article for the Canadian Journal of Community Mental Health *entitled 'Sexual abuse by therapists: Maintaining the conspiracy of silence,' which examined why mental health professionals are reluctant to admit, and quick to minimize or deny, therapist sexual abuse. I suggested that the main reasons were an 'us–them' attitude with respect to abusers, a belief that it only happened in the 1960s and 1970s, professional protectionism, denial of sexual attraction to clients, trivialization, idealization of therapist–client sexual contact, victim blaming, and the many fears and feelings that hinder client disclosure.[8] I included a brief paragraph about my own experiences of abuse by a therapist. While writing this article, I became increasingly angry with my profession, and with Dr A. As I mentioned earlier, at one point I momentarily responded to a flash of pure rage by grabbing a carving knife and imagining myself jumping in my car and driving to Dr A's city in order to kill him. Writing this article made it plain to me that I was part of the conspiracy of silence myself if I did not bring Dr A's conduct to the attention of his licensing board.*

In November 1991 I wrote a brief letter of complaint to the State Board of Medical Examiners. An investigator called, in February 1992, to tell me that there were two complainants and that the board was conducting an investigation. When I picked up the phone to talk to her, I was overcome by anxiety and fear, my heart pounded and my hands shook. It brought back memories of Dr A's incredible power over me; like a tiny mouse I was paralyzed with fear while the owl swooped down. After the phone call, my mind reeled. Two victims. He had assured me that I was the only one. What a fool I was! Although I really didn't want to admit it to myself, I had some vague feelings of jealousy and hurt about this 'competitor.'

After responding to a request, in the summer, to send copies of the correspondence between Dr A and myself, and of the notes I had made, I heard nothing. In October 1992 I called the investigator for an update and was referred to the Medical Examining Board's lawyer. He told me that the complaint of the other woman victim referred to the same time period, some twenty years before. An investigation had failed to bring to light any more recent complaints. Because the board's mandate, explained the lawyer, is to focus on current protection of the public, they would be unlikely to pursue such an 'old case.'

Dr A, I was told, had been ordered to undergo a special psychological evaluation by an expert in the area of doctor–patient sexual abuse. This person was so busy that the appointment was set for four months later. Having reviewed the bundle of letters and notes that I'd sent, the lawyer commented that Dr A had a good memory, that his letters of response to the two allegations basically confirmed the details but 'left out all the bad stuff.' Dr A, he said, is contending that the allegations are 'all fantasies' and saying, 'How could they do something like that. I did so much for them.' This, according to the lawyer, was a 'standard response.'

'If the board decides to have a hearing,' asked the lawyer, 'Would you be willing to come to give evidence?' Telling him that I felt really intimidated by the prospect, I nevertheless agreed that I would go. Long after I had put the phone down, I felt anxious and frightened, thinking that facing Dr A across a room and hearing him lie about me would be very painful indeed. He had been so important to me for such a long time. He was the sun, moon, and stars; he was the warm, constant, and supportive father that I had lacked. When I confronted him in his office, I really believed that I was the only patient he had had sex with, that he had realized how destructive this was and resolved never to do it again. Yet, there were two victims, and he was claiming that our allegations were fantasies. How many lies had he told me? How many had I naively swallowed?

After this I heard nothing more for nearly two years. During this time the TAAG group had sporadic meetings. Most members found that all their energy was taken up by the complaints to the College of Physicians and Surgeons, criminal proceedings, or civil suits they'd embarked on. A brief attempt to form a support group was abandoned after lawyers for a defendant in a civil suit threatened to subpoena participants and make them go to court. Although some earlier complaints and criminal proceedings had been successful, it now seemed as though the tide was running fast the other way. Defence lawyers were becoming more and more skilled in strategies to discredit victims, subjecting them to cross-examination for several days; using expert witnesses to suggest that they were mentally ill, were fabricating the allegations, or, at the very least, were unaffected by the sexual involvement; trying to obtain all

possible existing professional reports about the victim, as well as the subse-
quent therapist's notes from therapy sessions (these would be gone through
with a fine-tooth comb to try to find something that could be used against the
victim or the subsequent therapist); bringing hostile ex-spouses, ex-lovers,
and relatives into court; suggesting that the victim was a fortune-hunter, in-
terested only in obtaining money; and insisting that any 'similar fact' witnesses
had colluded to defame the innocent physician. Some survivors reported
being followed and subjected to bizarre phone calls, or to multiple calls dur-
ing which there was heavy breathing or silence. Two victims were accosted
during their court cases by the abusive therapists. One victim was told she was
'a piece of shit,' another that she was 'crazy.' Yet another victim dared not
attend her usual therapist for support during the months-long court process,
after she had been threatened by a defence lawyer that every word she said
would have to be recorded and brought into court.

Hearing of these scenarios, I felt fortunate that my complaint against Dr A
was 'too old' to go ahead. Sometimes I chided myself for being 'chicken,' for
not making a complaint years earlier. It seemed, however, that I had made a
contribution to breaking the silence by participating in workshops and confer-
ences, describing my experiences when teaching medical students and residents,
talking to other survivors in person and on the telephone as well as seeing a
few for therapy, and being interviewed by newspaper and magazine writers.
Surely that was enough? It was enough I told myself, and I was being spared
the ordeal of a hearing, where all kinds of painful secrets would be aired and
I would have to see Dr A.

As described in the Introduction, when Pat, the lawyer with the state
attorney general's department, called me in September 1994, I felt terrified
by the prospect of an inquiry hearing, of being interrogated by hostile lawyers,
and of seeing Dr A once again. For the next few days, it felt as if I were periodi-
cally entering that scary, alien childhood world, the world that had swallowed
me up when I first started to see Dr A and had emerged periodically during
the years that I was travelling to see him. In this world, the light seemed
flatter, different, greyer; the colours were all muted. Here I felt strange, remote,
distant, cut off, not part of the human race. Or, alternatively, I was small,
vulnerable, scared, and helpless.

With a gargantuan effort, I could push this world into the background, so
I could get on with my work. Over the weekend, I arranged to spend some
time with Kate, a long-time friend and colleague, at her island home. I tried

to describe my mental state, which seemed to arise from feeling so frightened and overwhelmed at the prospect of making a deposition and having to participate shortly afterwards in an inquiry hearing. Kate was able to understand how I might feel like a three- or four-year-old in relation to Dr A, and how I might still be petrified by the possibility that his spell over me would reassert itself, that like a helpless fly I would be drawn once again into his sticky spider web.

Kate emphasized that I should stay in the patient role, stress that Dr A was my doctor, and resist being drawn into analysing my behaviour or his. She thought that relying on my ability to function in a kind of feelingless state, on 'automatic pilot,' would be the best way to handle the cross-examination process. Drawing on her wide experience with other survivors who had entered the legal system, Kate suggested that I avoid any chance meetings with Dr A outside the inquiry room. She also suggested that I request a recent photograph or videotape as a way of desensitizing myself and avoiding feeling paralyzed and helpless when I met him. After a lengthy discussion of all the possible strategies that Dr A's lawyer might use to confuse and intimidate me, I found that I was feeling much stronger. Perhaps even looking forward to the hearing as a chance to have my story heard.

A couple of days later I heard from Pat that a settlement had been reached with Dr A and that he had agreed to the specifications of the board, which were (1) that he was to go for therapy for at least a year, with a therapist approved by the commission, and (2) that he was not allowed to see women alone in his office, just men and couples. If he saw a couple in therapy, they had to sign their names on a chart to confirm that they had been seen together.

Pat told me that Dr A had eventually admitted to having sex with me, but continued to deny it with respect to the other woman complainant. I tried to find out a bit more, but Pat would give me little information. She described the other complainant as 'more fragile than you ... she doesn't have the support ... we were really worried about her handling the inquiry ... [Dr A] did some really ugly, emotionally abusive things to her.'

After this conversation, I felt, on the one hand, very relieved that I did not have to face Dr A or submit to a harrowing ordeal of being interrogated about such painful, shameful secrets. On the other hand, I was disappointed: I was missing my day in court. Without this, the resolution did not seem quite real. A few months later, all the copies of my letters and notes were returned, along with a copy of an order from the State Medical Quality Assurance Commission, which confirmed what Pat had told me. Yes, it was real!

Over the course of the next year, I sometimes thought of Dr A. At last, he had to face some consequences. Perhaps now he had some idea of the shame and humiliation that I had experienced? Puzzling over the intensity of my anxiety and fear at the prospect of going to a hearing and seeing him again, I wondered what I was so afraid of. Was it the prospect of being embarrassed, humiliated, and made to look a fool during the hearing? Or was it that I still feared being enslaved by him, or the possibility that I could be reduced to a mere puppet by him, or someone else? Or was it something worse, some deep, dark, destructive part of my personality that could be waiting to wreak havoc?

When I arranged to take a sabbatical, I planned to write some articles and then work on this book. When the time came to start on the book, I found myself procrastinating in every conceivable way. What, I thought, am I afraid of finding out? Am I afraid of confirming that it really was my fault? Or realizing that Dr A had done his best, that I was an impossibly difficult, manipulative, hysterical, borderline patient? Is it that I just can't forgive myself for being such a compliant fool?

Most survivors eventually disclose to people that they trust, including relatives, close friends, family physicians, and therapists. 'Breaking the silence' refers to broader disclosure, encompassing complaints to professional bodies, lawsuits, and public statements – anything that alerts the professions and the public to the common occurrence and tragic consequences of abuse by health professionals. Breaking the silence is not for everyone, and it can be personally disastrous or counter-therapeutic. The old adage 'The best revenge is a good life' must be remembered here.

Breaking the silence is made difficult by a number of factors, including survivors' feelings, community attitudes and lack of support, the self-protective stance of the health professions, and the idiosyncrasies of the legal system.

Survivors' Feelings

Emotions that obstruct survivors' desire to break the silence include shame, self-doubt, and fear. The problems created by the sexual abuse, including pervasive self-doubt about their own judgment, perceptions, and motives, combine with shame and self-blame to make a complaint or public disclosure seem impossible. Who wants to confess publicly that she was duped and used? Quite rightly, survivors fear the consequences of disclosure. They hear tales of husbands divorcing patient-wives, of children being taken away, and of their humiliating sexual secrets being made public.[9] Most survivors are angry with the health professions and reluctant to trust boards of inquiry and committees that consist of other professionals who work in the same field. Still struggling with guilt about their own complicity and lingering positive feelings towards the professional, some survivors hesitate to take the step that may cause the offending health professional pain or even damage his career.

Terrifying to many survivors in the Vancouver area has been the fate of Sian Simmonds, a young woman who was bludgeoned and shot in her basement suite by a man who murdered her at the behest of Dr Josephakis Charalambous, a family doctor. She was slain in January 1993, three months before she was due to testify in a sexual misconduct hearing at the British Columbia College of Physicians and Surgeons.[10]

Barbara Noël quotes Shari Dam, a lawyer who worked for the Professional Education and Registration Board in Illinois, as saying, 'It's the shame, it's being frightened to death and being embarrassed that prevents them from coming forward. I think women's tendencies are to immediately deny what's happened or could have happened. They're reticent because they have self-doubts. Women have been trained to distrust themselves. If something has happened, it's immediately, "That couldn't have happened. He wouldn't do that to me!"'

Noël goes on to describe how women who had been abused by Dr Masserman called her, but were unwilling to come forward. One woman told Noël, 'No, I just couldn't. You're really strong. I'm not.' Noël says that another caller 'didn't have the courage to give me her full name or help me in getting the doctor's licenses revoked. Her husband did not know about her suspicions, and she couldn't risk his finding out.'[11]

Although studies show that most victims are women, and all the published accounts are written by women, it appears that men, too, struggle with shame, fear, and self-doubt. David, fondled as a teenager by his family physician, left the office and refused to return. He felt scared of the physician, was afraid to tell his parents, and said, 'I wanted to make sure nobody would find out because that would cause me great embarrassment.'

After his doctors dismissed his contention that he had been exploited by his physiotherapist, James suffered massive self-doubt. This state of mind was exacerbated by the medication he was given, which made him feel dizzy and unreal. The psychiatrist and nursing staff kept telling him that he was sick and delusional, and that the abuse had not happened. After being discharged from the hospital, James was afraid to mention his experiences to anyone else. He assumed that they would think he was crazy and feared that he would be sent back to the hospital.

Victims who are health professionals themselves may be particularly reluctant to break the silence. Firsten, Wine, and colleagues studied Canadian helping professionals who had been sexually abused by their own therapists, and attribute their difficulties in completing the study to the victim's vulnerable position in their own profession. They note, 'In two instances, women requested withdrawal of their interview transcripts because they are amid proceedings with regulating bodies and feared harmful repercussions. There were three women currently training in psychiatry who ultimately decided against being interviewed out of concern that their careers might somehow be jeopardized as a consequence of any form of disclosure, especially in the light of the prominent status of the offending physicians within the psychiatric community.'[12]

Yet there are indications that a sizable proportion of victims are health professionals. In 1985 a nationwide survey of U.S. psychiatrists showed that 4.4 per cent of female psychiatrists and 0.9 per cent of male psychiatrists had sexual contact with their own therapist.[13] Although an anonymous survey shows this frequency, survivors who are health professionals are loath to make complaints and dare not make their victim status public. Disclosing, they feel, would be harmful to their careers, deter clients from coming to them, and cause their colleagues to treat them with disrespect. Social worker Lynn stated that only her husband and a few trusted colleagues knew of her abuse. She felt that any wider disclosure could harm her career and diminish her in the eyes of her colleagues.

In 1994, hoping to generate more understanding and discussion of the abuse of health professionals by their own therapists, currently veiled in secrecy, I put a notice in the newsletter of the Association of Women Psychiatrists, which has a wide circulation in North America. It included a brief statement describing my own abuse, my long struggle with feelings of shame and self-blame, and the results of the board of inquiry on Dr A, and was followed by a request for participation in a research study. The study would be aimed particularly at how the abuse had affected the survivor's attitude to her profession. I had only two replies, and only one of the women filled out a questionnaire.

As can be seen from my account, my decision to break the silence, by talking about it in public and by making a formal complaint, came in stages and very gradually. My choice was also influenced by my privileged and protected position as a university professor with tenure.

Community Attitudes

On the whole, our society is not particularly sympathetic to victims, and people often assume that the victim causes her own problem in some way. Phrases such as 'she asked for it,' 'she provoked it,' 'she needed it,' 'she deserved it,' 'she was better off for it,' 'she was sexually titillated by it,' 'she liked it,' and so on, are heard in connection with victims of rape, child sexual abuse, and wife battering. Victims of sexual abuse by health professionals attract similar sentiments. Sympathy for child victims is more easily evoked, but adult victims may have little credibility. Why did they choose to go to the abusive professional? Why did they continue going? They are adults, aren't they? What is wrong with them?

Even if the community recognizes that people are being victimized, it tends to distance itself or ignore the problem. Melvin Lerner attributes such attitudes towards victims to what he calls the 'Belief in a Just World' (BJW).[14] In this 'just world,' which guarantees security and success if your behaviour is appropriate and your personal characteristics positive, people are seen to get what they deserve. Even though adults recognize that some people encounter repeated disasters and that justice and deserving have nothing to do with what actually happens to people, adults continue to operate as if they live in a 'just world.'

The BJW is maintained, Lerner believes, by strategies to eliminate threats to its presence. There are rational and irrational tactics. Rational strategies include prevention and restitution by social agencies, taxes, donations, and volunteer work. Non-rational strategies include the following:

1 Denial–withdrawal: removing oneself from any information about, or contact with, victims
2 Reinterpretating the event so that the injustice disappears
3 Reinterpreting the outcome; for example, 'suffering is good for your soul'
4 Reinterpreting the cause, so that the victim's suffering can be blamed on something he or she did or failed to do
5 Reinterpreting the character of the victim, for example, the victim merits the punishment because she is inferior or dangerous

All these irrational strategies are operating and orchestrate community attitudes towards victims of sexual abuse by health professionals. They are reflected and reinforced by the attitudes of the health and legal professions and thus make frequent appearances in boards of inquiry and court cases. Let us go through the above list again, focusing specifically on victims of sexual abuse by health professionals:

1 Denial-withdrawal. A sensational case may be a 'seven-day wonder,' but the general public quickly goes back to its

apparent blindness to violence towards women, children, and vulnerable adults.

2 Reinterpreting the event: The betrayal of trust, of the fiduciary relationship, is seen as an 'affair' between consenting adults.

3 Reinterpreting the outcome: Victims of abuse by health professionals are thought to have benefited from most of the treatment or to have become stronger and more resourceful as a result of the abuse.[15]

4 Reinterpreting the cause: The victim is thought to have seduced the health professional. Or the victim should have said 'no.'

5 Reinterpreting the character of the victim: It is believed that the victim is a dangerous, vindictive, seductive, manipulative person who outwitted and trapped the health professional in a sexual relationship.

The Health Professions' Role in Maintaining the Silence

The health professions rely on a number of rationalizations and assumptions that allow them to maintain certain beliefs: that sexual abuse of patients no longer exists or that it is being greatly exaggerated, causing widespread and unnecessary restrictions on professional practice; that they are able to police themselves; that victims who complain are treated with dignity and respect; and so on. Professionals' beliefs that operate to maintain the silence about sexual abuse of patients are describe below.

'It Only Happened in the Sixties and Seventies'

Those favouring the belief that abuse by professionals is no longer an issue point out that the two publications explicitly recommending sexual intercourse with patients both stemmed from the 1960s and 1970s.[16] At the time, sexual mores were changing, and some mental health professionals got involved in a variety of 'fringe' treatments such as nude marathons and other 'human potential' therapies. There is little evidence for the view that sexual involvement between health professionals and patients was limited to those two decades. Concern about physician–patient sexual relationships dates back to the early days of medicine, as suggested by the Hippocratic Oath.

Historically, most writing is about male physician–female patient erotic relationships. Mesmer, an eighteenth century Viennese physician and magnetist, became permanently estranged from his wife while treating a blind woman patient. Some hundred years later, the erotic attachment of Joseph Breuer, another Viennese physican, to his patient Anna O. caused trouble in his marriage as well. The publication of Sabina Spielrein's papers has demonstrated that Carl Jung seduced one of his first analytic patients, a young girl.[17]

Freud warned that the analyst 'must recognize that the patient's falling in love is induced by the analytic situation and is not to be ascribed to the charms of his person, that he has no reason whatsoever therefore to be proud of such a "conquest" as it would be called outside analysis.' Freud stressed that the analyst's countertransference must never be acted upon, emphasizing, 'If her advances were returned, it would be a great triumph for the patient, but a complete overthrow for the cure … The love relationship actually destroys the influence of analytic treatment on the patient; a combination of the two would be an inconceivable thing.'[18] Despite these warnings, Ferenczi, a disciple of Freud's, believed that emotionally deprived patients needed nurturing, and he began to experiment with hugging and kissing his female patients. Freud warned him, prophetically, that others would use the same rationalization to go even further with their patients.

Karen Horney, famous for her insightful works on women's psychology, rebelled against traditional Freudian psychoanalysis. Her biographer, Susan Quinn, depicts Horney as highly gifted, but somewhat eccentric and impulsive. Towards the end of her career, Horney had a liaison that 'showed the poorest judgement. The partner was a young candidate at her institute who was in treatment with her. Few people knew about it, for obvious reasons. Horney certainly knew that such a relationship was highly unprofessional.'[19]

The disbelief that abuse can still be happening underpins the response that many victims have received from subsequent health professionals – those who ignored or downplayed the abuse or accused the victims of fabricating, imagining, or dreaming it.

Sexual Involvement between Health Professional and Patient Should Be Treated as Sex between Two Consenting Adults

Among the responses to the work of the Independent Task Force on Sexual Abuse of Patients, commissioned by the Ontario College of Physicians and Surgeons, was an article in the *Medical Post* which argued that 'taking money from clinical care to police the behaviour of two competent adults seems a very unethical choice.'[20] A related issue is the belief that a sexual relationship is acceptable if the patient initiates it or gives consent. These views ignore the vast power differential between health professional and patient, the fiduciary relationship, and the parentlike role of the professional. As Freud warned, patients who 'fall in love' with their doctor or other health professional are influenced by childlike incestuous longings towards an idealized parent figure.

The attitude that health professional–patient sexual involvement should be seen as sex between two consenting adults shaped the response that Joyce received from the physician who told her to stop the 'affair' with her family physician, but continue to see him for the treatment of her migraine.

Health Professionals Who Abuse Are 'Bad Apples' That Bear No Relation to the Rest of Us

This convenient belief is fuelled by the few cases of repeated sadistic sexual abuse by professionals whose cruel and often bizarre behaviour seems far removed from that of a caring and compassionate health professional.[21] It is easy to write these people off as sociopaths and espouse an 'us–them' philosophy, but, in fact, problems with sexual and other boundaries are a pervasive difficulty for health professionals, and sometimes the line dividing abuse or impropriety and professional behaviour is not clear.

Almost any sizable community of health professionals has its story of the marriage, elopement, or 'affair' of a health professional with an ex-patient. Professionals and their organizations must stipulate how long a professional must wait after discharging a patient before they may engage in a sexual relationship. This fact gives the lie to the belief that sexually abusive professionals are a rare and alien group.

The conviction that abusive health professionals must be sadists or psychopathic perverts underlies the prevalence of health professionals' scepticism about abuse within their ranks. For instance, many doubt allegations of abuse by the nice doctor next door who has a happy family, and are suspicious of the patient who claims abuse by her dentist who invites her to romantic candlelight dinners and then sleeps with her.

Victim Blaming: The Sexual Involvement Was the Victim's Fault or a Fabrication

Even when the sexual violation is recognized, the professional's fall from grace tends to be seen as a result of the victim's emotional problems or personality traits. Focusing on patient characteristics is a common strategy used by lawyers who defend sexually abusive health professionals. Some descriptions in the literature pathologize patients to such an extent that they appear to exonerate or partially exonerate the professional. Early descriptions of women patients who were sexually involved with their therapists depicted them as 'hysterical,' with 'strong homosexual trends' as well as 'heterosexual promiscuity.' Victims were described as having a 'penchant for seducing professional men.'[22]

In a much more recent victim-blaming article, Gutheil suggests that it is patients with borderline personality disorder who tend to be abused, because therapists are not attracted to psychotic patients, and those suffering from neurosis know better than to become sexually involved with their therapists. Borderline patients, according to Gutheil, induce confusion in their therapists and may 'invite' them to share in a 'narcissistic seduction.' He emphasizes that, although dysfunctional in many areas of life, borderline patients may have 'powerful interpersonal manipulative skills.

They may still be capable of getting even experienced professionals to do what they should know better than do.'[23] 'Fatal Attraction,' the unfortunate title of an otherwise informative paper on therapist–patient involvement,[24] conjures up visions of the predatory, unbalanced, and ultimately murderous woman villain in the movie by the same name who stalks her male victim, a reasonable man who has succumbed to a passing impulse. A woman in the Manitoba study of women who were sexually abused by mental health professionals wrote, 'I have been told that it was all my fault because I projected the image of a lonely, divorced woman. I wore my skirts too short, back-combed my hair and didn't have my boundaries up.'[25]

The old saying 'Hell hath no fury like a woman scorned' seems to underlie findings by ethics committees and courts that women complainants' 'false allegations' were a vindictive retribution for their health professionals' perceived disinterest or rejection. In other cases, the complainant's descriptions have been deemed hysterical fantasies, delusional ideas, or the manifestations of a borderline personality. The issue of false allegations has been fuelled by the backlash against feminism,[26] concerns about false allegations of sexual abuse by adult survivors,[27] and the belief that there has been an 'epidemic' of false allegations in child custody disputes in recent years.[28] In Law, Psychiatry and Morality, Alan Stone states that 'No women who consulted me were fabricating,' and goes on to term this preoccupation with false allegations as the psychiatric profession's 'own wish-fulfilling fantasy.'[29]

Health Professionals Never Feel Attracted to Patients

Health professionals sometimes see themselves as benign, compassionate eunuchs, far removed from the trials and tribulations of ordinary mortals. Conceived of, and indeed viewing themselves as, dedicated and nurturing parent figures, many health professionals are pained at the thought of being sexually attracted to their patients, which they think bears no relation to their everyday functioning. This belief is carried over into training programs, where trainees claim there is little or no instruction pertaining to sexual attraction to patients.[30]

The failure of psychotherapy training systems to acknowledge and examine the issue of sexual attraction to patients has been related to earlier negative views of countertransference. Seen as a manifestation of therapist conflict, countertransference was thought to be an irrational or inappropriate response on the part of the therapist. Analysts strove to be 'blank screens,' and their attitudes to patients were unnatural and stilted. Trainees reporting erotic responses to patients were assumed to have countertransference problems or to have been seductive themselves.[31]

Over the past decade, the once-taboo topic of health professional–patient sex has begun to be discussed. In the last few years, some members of TAAG have volunteered to meet with groups of psychiatric residents to discuss psychiatrist–patient sexual involvement.

Professionals' Bureaucracies and Institutions Are Able to Police Themselves

Health professions, it is believed, are based on an objective and scientific body of knowledge that goes from strength to strength. Training, research, and practice within these professions are thus thought to stand apart from cultural expectations and societal biases such as sexism, racism, and ageism. Similarly, health professionals' inquiry boards and committees are deemed able to be objective and impartial in the handling of patients' complaints.

There is a considerable body of literature demonstrating that the health professions are far from objective and scientific, that they reflect and reinforce cultural biases and stereotypes, and that they represent a force of social control in society.[32] This disjunction between what the health professions think they are and the role they may actually be playing leads to considerable confusion and frustration for the professions and grief, anger, and humiliation for the victims. Peter Rutter reminds us that 'efforts to create a more ethical atmosphere in the male-dominated professions are consistently undermined by the less visible dynamics of masculine sexual psychology ... Asking men in power to prevent their colleagues' sexual exploitation in some way requires them to undermine their own fantasy lives.'[33]

If the members of an inquiry committee are unaware of their biases, victim-blaming tendencies, and 'belief in a just world,' their objectivity will be clouded and they are much more likely to sympathize with, and believe, their fellow professional whose reputation is on trial and whose career is at stake. Another concern, raised by Pope, is that perpetrators may be sitting on inquiry boards and involved in reviewing victims' complaints. In this situation prestigious but abusive health professionals may be extremely influential.[34]

Survivors who have tried to initiate a complaint process with health professionals' licensing organizations describe a very daunting and intimidating process. Some were turned off at the very outset by a negative and critical receptionist. One victim was told, 'He's already in an inquiry, don't add fuel to the fire.' Another victim was informed that he might be sued himself if he registered a complaint.

Almost all the victims I talked to were unaware that the initial complaint letter is crucial, and that a copy of it usually goes to the health professional in question. The next step is often an interview at the professional licensing body's headquarters, where the victim is interviewed by an investigator or a senior member of the bureaucracy. This has been described as an intimidating experience. If the victim survives this far, the next step might be a long wait, punctuated by sessions with a lawyer or investigator, followed eventually by an inquiry hearing. During inquiry hearings, survivors are usually subjected to a lengthy and hostile cross-examination. One woman said that the inquiry process of the College of Physicians and Surgeons of British Columbia was 'like another abuse.'

One survivor, a Vancouver lawyer, complained to reporters that 'doctors left her in legal and emotional limbo for four years,' until the doctor's licence was suspended. During this time private investigators snooped around her life. She described the hearing at the College of Physicians and Surgeons of British Columbia as a brutal and gruelling process, noting that 'as a lawyer, she was prepared to face down hostile questions that would not be allowed in an ordinary court of law.'[35]

Technically, the survivor is appearing as a key witness for the professional body and is playing a crucial role in helping the profession to discipline its members. In fact, however, survivors typically describe their sense that the professional process is carefully designed to make the complainants look like criminals and to protect the professional wherever possible. Even if they were not made to feel unwelcome, witnesses described feeling ignored, unsupported, and trivialized. One woman took time off from her demanding career, was on the witness stand for four days, and was offered only twenty dollars to defray the costs of parking. Expert witnesses were making hundreds of dollars per day.

Similarly, health professionals who report their colleagues or support the victims are made to seem like traitors. The documentary film *My Doctor, My Lover*, recounts how the victim's second psychiatrist, Dr Martha Gay, who provided treatment subsequent to the original abuse, was fired from the local ethics committee, and eventually, because of dwindling referrals, had to give up her practice in Denver and move to another city.[36]

The beliefs described here about the questionable existence of sexual abuse, about the presumed characteristics of abusers, about professional objectivity, and about the culpability of victims explain why health professions have been extremely slow in responding to clear evidence of widespread sexual abuse of patients, and in recognizing the need to develop services, support, and compensation for the people who have been damaged. In my case against Dr A, I had fortunately kept many incriminating letters and notes, and was lucky enough to write in a complaint at the same time as the only other complainant. And because I am a professor of psychiatry with a successful career, investigators and board members would be less likely to assume that I was disturbed, vindictive, or fabricating.

The Legal System

Lawyers, judges, and their institutions bring to bear the same kinds of biases and assumptions about professional objectivity and about victims that are seen in the health professions and in the community. In some cases there is an 'unholy alliance' between the defence lawyer and an expert witness health professional (usually a psychiatrist or a psychologist) that exploits to the maximum one or more of the myths and stereotypes about victimization and victims. Occasionally these expert witnesses for the defence in abuse cases are later discovered to be abusers themselves. Lawyer Shari Dam told Barbara Noël, 'The defense lawyer's tactics can make a woman who testifies look immoral to the point that she's the one on trial, not the doctor.'[37] In the face of a lawyer's attack, Noël found, 'It didn't take long for me to feel like a shamed little girl again.'[38] Survivors of abuse by mental health professionals may have a particularly difficult time, as lawyers are quick to point out that they had emotional problems in the first place; hence, the lawyers contend, they must be 'delusional' or fabricating. As can be seen in their accounts, Barbara Noël, Ellen Plasil, and Julie Roy all had to contend with disbelief and lack of credibility until other victims started to come forward.

In some areas, courts have lagged behind professional organizations and dismissed cases where it was believed that the patient gave consent to the sex with the health professional. Apparent mutual consent for sexual involvement was an issue in the precedent-setting *Norberg v Wynrib* case. Between 1983 and 1985 Dr Wynrib, then in his seventies, exchanged prescriptions for Fiorinal, to which Laura Norberg, then in her twenties, became addicted, for sex. Between 1986 and 1990 several courts in British Columbia denied Norberg's original suit on the grounds that she had consented to the sex and contributed to the situation by her own illegal conduct. It was not until the case reached the Supreme Court of Canada, in 1992, that the inequality between the parties and the special 'power-dependency' relationship between physician and patient were recognized and damages awarded to Norberg.[39]

Some judges appear ready to believe that women are colluding and fabricating allegations of sexual abuse against innocent physicians. In Prince George, British Columbia, a judge did not believe the complaints of twelve women against a local doctor, and in Vancouver a judge decided that four women had colluded to give 'similar fact' evidence against a psychiatrist.[40] This alleged 'collusion' took place despite the fact that one of them had never met the other three!

In Canada, further hurdles and possible damage for sexual abuse victims are being produced by a growing trend towards court-ordered production of the complainant's medical records, therapy records, school and employment records, personal diaries, and even computer hard drives. Defence lawyers can demand the detailed therapy notes made on a victim of abuse by a health professional and can go through them to try to find ammunition to discredit the complainant or her subsequent therapist. Lawyer Marilou McPhedran argues that 'discrediting witnesses is an important trial technique. A vigorous defence is a defendant's right in our legal system. However, a line is crossed when our courts allow evidence about the key witness that, by feeding unsubstantiated prejudices, heightens the chance of acquittal.'[41]

In the United States, psychiatrist Martha Gay Rhoades cautions, 'It remains unsafe to treat patients who are pursuing malpractice suits against other physicians. This is because there is no commercially available insurance that insures against the possibility of being pulled into a malpractice suit as a named non-party.' She goes on to say that even if the subsequent psychiatrist handles the assessment and therapy perfectly, 'It is still possible for the attorneys for the defense to allege that 100 per cent of the damages are the result of the subsequent treatment ... Defense attorneys pursuing such tactics may pursue the personal sexual history of the subsequent treating psychiatrist rather than his or her professional expertise and reputation, in attempts to get the case dismissed or at least muddy the waters enough to decrease the award arrived at by the jury.'[42]

Thus, if a survivor decides to go to the police and lay a criminal charge, or to mount a civil suit against an abusive health professional, there are many obstacles and pitfalls. With a civil suit, in which the victim hopes to get some compensation, finding a lawyer to take the case is a major challenge. Most women survivors have incurred multiple losses, have no money, and need to find a lawyer who will work on a contingency basis. Even with funds available, Noël had lawyers that backed out and was unable to find a psychiatrist to testify as an expert witness. One lawyer advised her, 'Give up. That man is going to cream you.'[43]

A major drawback in any legal or health professional advisory board case or hearing is that it takes a great deal of time, at least two years, and energy. In the meantime, the person becomes once again immersed in feelings and memories about the abusive professional. Therapeutic work, and indeed one's general emotional, social, and occupational functioning, may be stalled. Herman states that, 'During the process of mourning, the survivor must come to terms with the impossibility of getting even. As she vents her rage in safety, her helpless fury gradually changes to a more powerful and satisfying form of anger: righteous indignation. This transformation allows the survivor to free herself from the prison of the revenge fantasy, in which she is alone with the perpetrator ... Giving up the fantasy of revenge does not mean giving up the quest for justice; on the contrary, it begins the process of joining with others to hold the perpetrator accountable for his crimes.'[44]

Addressing this dilemma, Bates comments, 'In a sense, my decision to confront Dr X publicly was countertherapeutic.' During the case, her therapy had to focus on maintaining her coping skills. On the other hand, she points to a number of positive consequences. She had to give up her helplessness and 'victim stance' and become assertive and determined. In the process, she gained unexpected support from peers and relatives. During the trial, she writes, 'I saw my illusions disintegrate as he engaged in muckraking tactics ... Because his defense felt like a smear campaign against my character and behaviour outside his office, and because he continually denied the truth, my idealisations of him were undone and replaced with a more realistic assessment.'[45]

Another dilemma that some survivors voice is that of being offered a settlement during the course of a civil dispute. A financial settlement may enable the survivor to go back to school, take time off, secure housing, or obtain therapy. The stress of a court appearance, including seeing the abusive professional and being subjected to intense hostile cross-examination, is avoided. But there is a price to pay, as the complainant is expected to sign a 'gag order,' in which she agrees never to write, speak, or in any way communicate to others about her allegations or the settlement. This allows the abusive professional to resume practice, with no threat to licence or reputation. For some survivors this represents letting the abusive professional 'get away with it' and means that the survivor's actions in bringing the case to court have not resulted in making the abuse public and have not prevented the professional from wreaking further abuse on other victims.

Some survivors have asked me why health professionals' insurance companies are covering sexual abusers, thinking that if the companies did not cover this type of malpractice some potential perpetrators might be deterred. This issue is not what it seems. In the United States, many insurance companies have eliminated or capped insurance coverage for suits involving sexual violations. In Canada, the Canadian Medical Protective Association, which provides coverage to most physicians, pays for a doctor's legal defence in criminal, civil, and licensing disputes. The CMPA's usual policy is not to pay a financial settlement or damage award in civil suits about physician sexual misconduct.[46] This practice of eliminating or capping coverage or payment of settlements effectively discriminates against victims of sexual abuse who bring a civil suit against the offending professional.[47] If the health professional cannot pay the award, then the survivor gets no payment and ends up doubly harmed – by the abuse, and then by the lack of compensation. These policies also deter legal firms from getting involved on a contingency basis. Noting that the victims of sexual abuse by psychiatrists are typically women, Alan Stone, professor of psychiatry and law at Harvard, and a former president of the American Psychiatric Association, termed the changes in coverage unfair gender discrimination and argued that they also undermine patient welfare.[48]

The idiosyncrasies of the legal system, and the danger for survivors who venture into it expecting to get justice, are a huge topic. Suffice it to say that survivors need to consider this option very carefully, as there is a definite risk of revictimization. Women survivors, I have found, are particularly naive about the legal system and do not realize that they are venturing into a vastly un-equal playing field, where hostile lawyers may use any and all strategies to discredit, humiliate, and confuse them. After her devastating experience in court, where she was totally demoralized by the lawyer's tactics and made out to be sick and vindictive, one woman told me plaintively, 'But I expected the judge to realize the truth.'

8. Towards Less Abuse and More Healing

'Why Don't the Professionals Themselves Do More and Care More about It?'

When, when will they stop believing that we're all lying, crazy, or just want to get back at the doctor? It took all the courage I have, and more besides, to be on that witness stand for four days.

Survivor

In this final chapter my two voices seem very close, begin to merge. In writing my account, and reflecting on its meaning, I feel that I have moved even further from that deep, dark pit of shame and self-blame. There seem to be so many complicated memories, imprints, and patterns that coalesced to influence my enslavement by Dr A and my capitulation to his labelling of me as angry, difficult, needy, and 'borderline,' and his deeming my anger pathological. From the vantage point of having reread all my notes, letters, and journals, and reflected on how they might fit together, there seem to be some major factors that influenced or determined what happened to me with Dr A. They are as follows:

1 *Sexual abuse by Umpi, and lesser molestation by a number of other men. Because of this I was loath to trust men and thought that men were interested in me for my sexuality alone. Although Umpi induced terror in me, there are also some indications, from memories and photos, that he could be warm and caring. Like Umpi, Dr A displayed both of these dimensions, moving from being warm and caring to having sexual expectations.*
2 *Subjugation by Auntie. She exacted my compliance by periodically threat-*

ening to reject me or send me home, and expected me to minister to her needs exclusively. In the same way, Dr A was repeatedly rejecting and expected me to fit in with his needs.

3 *Repeated separations from my biological parents. This left me with a profound anxiety about being separated from parent figures. When Dr A, as my doctor, was in the role of a parent figure I became frantic about being parted from him and convinced that I could not manage without him.*

4 *Partial identification with Umpi. The psychoanalysts have a term 'identification with the lost object,' which means that you take on some of the characteristics of the person who has died or gone away. When I refused to go to stay with Auntie, I removed myself also from the sphere of Umpi's influence. But it was at that time that I decided that I wanted to go to medical school, transformed myself at school, and began to get very good grades. I was being like Umpi. This led to fears, however, that I might be like the 'bad Umpi' as well – drunken, seductive, maniacal, and evil. When Dr A blamed me for being seductive, angry, vindictive, or demanding, my negative self-image (or Umpi-image) agreed with him.*

5 *The secrecy and double life that I had as a young child and a teenager were replicated in my relationship with Dr A.*

6 *My family had boundary problems with physicians. As a child it was not clear what the relationship was between my mother and Umpi. Was he a doctor, a friend, a co-parent?*

7 *Umpi had sex with a patient, Helen, then left his marriage and lived with her. Did I think that Dr A would repeat this with me?*

8 *Dr A convinced me that my mother was the villain, that I suffered from enormous rage and terrible insecurity because she had repeatedly abandoned me. It was my conflicts with my mother, according to Dr A, that repeatedly surfaced during therapy and made me angry with him. This blaming of my mother obscured the role of the two perpetrators, the two abusers, Umpi and Dr A. Although my mother did leave me (she herself admits as much), she thought she was leaving me in a familiar environment with a couple who were doting co-parents. She was, in fact, leaving me in a dangerous, even terrifying, situation.*

While Dr A's mother blaming was in line with the psychiatric ideology of the time, which blamed mothers for practically all mental illness, it seems likely that his was particularly virulent and fuelled by his unresolved anger towards his own mother.

9   *The intensity of the relationship between Dr A and myself was not just a
result of my transference, of my childhood traumas revisited. As Naida
divined, it seems likely that Dr A reframed the supervisor–trainee relationship to increase the intensity of our involvement and heighten his power
over me. As my friend and colleague Kate has pointed out, it was the very
last thing that I needed at that point. Pregnant, soon to move, about to fin-
ish my training, what I needed was his blessing to leave the program and
focus on the new life I would be starting. If indeed he felt I needed some
therapy, he could have suggested it as a future endeavour, to be undertaken
after all the other changes had been made and my life had settled down.*

Perhaps, on a superficial level, Dr A was attracted by my looks, warmth,
and spontaneity. At a less conscious level, I may have represented a woman
he could dominate and control, thus enabling him to act on some of his angry
impulses towards women. While I will never know the exact nature of Dr A's
issues and how much his background shaped the relationship, the fact re-
mained that his difficulties and inability to set boundaries created an intense
and sometimes tempestuous interaction that was totally absent in my therapy
with Naida.

For a long time, I have wondered how I could have maintained a kind of
'doublethink' about what went on with Dr A. Telling myself that he helped
me, convincing myself that some of the relationship was positive, deluding
myself that it was really my fault, that I was seductive and lured him into acting out my transference. But I realize that my profession, psychiatry, spent
many years engaged in that selfsame 'doublethink.' Even though as far back
as 1970 Masters and Johnson spoke out about patients who were being
sexually abused in the name of treatment[1] and were supported in this position
by Kardener and colleagues in 1973,[2] psychiatrists totally ignored the finding.
No attention was given to it, no teaching done about it, no research imple-
mented. As far as the psychiatric establishment was concerned, it did not
exist. Not until the late 1980s and early 1990s did psychiatry, and medicine
as a whole, start to pay attention to the problem in its midst. This attention
was largely generated from without by consumers, the media, the survivors,
who wrote books and initiated lawsuits, and the women's groups that supported
them. The profession, at last, was forced to give up its 'doublethink.'

Although writing this account and researching its meaning has led to some *personal growth for me, it has deepened my anger and frustration about the self-protecting stance of the professions, the blaming of victims, and the general apathy of society about abuse of weaker and more vulnerable members by those in positions of power. Professional organizations sometimes seem to operate like incestuous families, turning a blind eye to the abuse, colluding with and protecting the perpetrator, blaming the victim, and in some cases acknowledging the problem briefly and then hurriedly sweeping everything under the rug. Barbara Noël's account shows how her complaint to the Ethics Committee of the Illinois Psychiatric Society, a district branch of the American Psychiatric Association, was not heard until three and a half years later. The outcome, almost five years after she had registered the complaint, was a suspension of Dr Masserman for five years. At first jubilant, Noël later wondered why he had not been expelled, learning much later that 'by suspending Dr Masserman rather than expelling him, the American Psychiatric Association avoided any publicity that might have stemmed from public notification about their decision. The name of any member who is expelled must be reported in* Psychiatric News, *the APA's newspaper, to warn the public, [but] the same is not true for someone who has been suspended.'*[3]

Recent surveys seem to indicate that there is less sexual exploitation of patients by health professionals. Is this real, or is the problem just going underground?[4] *Are abusing professionals less likely to acknowledge their guilt in anonymous surveys because they are afraid that their identity could be revealed in some way? Studies have shown that most sexually exploited patients never make a formal complaint,*[5] *and the numbers are certainly not likely to rise as people learn of survivors' ordeals in court or of the murder of a woman who made a complaint about sexual misconduct by her family doctor.*

Survivors of sexual abuse by health professionals are not getting the help they need in order to heal. They are unable to find therapists, and self-help manoeuvres such as forming a support group are sabotaged by fears of being accused of collusion in court. Their stigmatized identity and sense of difference are reinforced by these alienating experiences, even after the abuse has stopped. I have a fantasy of winning the lottery and setting up an advocacy and therapy centre for victims of sexual abuse by health professionals. It would make available individual and group counselling, an information and education program for consumers and professionals, and a legal arm to dispense legal advice and finance some legal actions.

What does the merging of the two voices at the end of my journey towards healing and understanding suggest? The first voice represents the part of myself that is more spontaneous and emotional and has largely taken the role of describing the various events of my life, my reactions and feelings. The second voice, embodying the part of me that is the woman psychiatrist struggling to understand how a complex jigsaw fits together, is more analytical, dispassionate, objective, reflective, and intellectual. In years past, as the reader can readily determine from the early chapters, I tended to perceive the emotional part of myself as a wild, dangerous, secret element that had to be firmly suppressed. This conviction gained momentum as I struggled to escape from my enslavement by Dr A. At times I felt as if I was cut off at the neck, unaware of my body and my feelings, able to operate only on a detached and intellectual basis.

This reaction, as well as representing the numbness and distancing of a person trying to avoid reminders of trauma, represents an attempt to maintain or regain control. Blaming myself – feeling that I had been seductive and rationalizing that Dr A had been driven to re-enact my childhood abuse – was another way in which I tried to take control of the situation and ensure that it could never happen again. But both these forms of gaining control were emotionally crippling. My journey towards meaning and healing has involved hearing and recording both voices, dissolving any remaining partition between the two parts of myself, challenging, in a sense, that dark, wild, shameful monster to come to the light of day and be examined.

Given full voice, and under close scrutiny, the so-called monster turns out to be an eloquent and discerning inner voice that expresses the pain and displays the coping reactions that are shared by many others in similar predicaments. It is my journey, then, that allows me to embrace both aspects of myself, to stop viewing myself as an impostor hiding a dreadful secret and see instead a well-rounded person who has survived and grown through a variety of difficult life experiences.

Although I am depicting myself as largely recovered from my childhood traumas and the abuse by Dr A, this is not a black-and-white issue. Like the proverbial castle built in the sand, my foundations are not rock-hard. Although I have long wanted to write this book and have been collecting material for years, my lingering feelings of shame and embarrassment about having been so thoroughly duped and used presented an obstacle. Added to this was my fear that such a massive disclosure could only lead to negative feedback, even ridicule. Even now, I have no illusions about some of the feedback I will receive. As described in the previous chapter, attitudes characterized by the 'belief in a just world'⁶ will lend themselves to criticism and invalidation of my work, in the same way that they are used to ignore, label, blame, and trivialize victims. People who have already made up their minds about this issue or have no interest in it, will not be touched by it, and their victim blaming and blindness about violence towards the vulnerable will go unchecked. Some may decide that Dr A and I were merely having an affair. Others might postulate that I was having 'false memories,' or made most of it up, or was doing it for attention or for money. Yet others, possibly my psychiatric colleagues, may suggest that Dr A had little to do with my difficulties and lay all the blame at the door of my mother and my early separation experiences. Or, even worse, I could be thoroughly blamed for being a seductive, unstable, dangerous, angry, manhater.

Because my fears, shame, and embarrassment competed with my wish to do something to defeat the conspiracy of silence and the enormous powers of shame that surround this topic, my plans for the book sometimes revolved around using the literature, published accounts, and information collected from other survivors more than my own story. I had thought of presenting the issues without mentioning my own abuse, or perhaps alluding to it only briefly. When Dr A was held accountable by the state authority, however, some more shame leaked away, and I was finally able to contemplate making public my account and my attempts to understand what had happened to me.

Additionally, knowing that all the confidential information that I had collected over the years would have to be presented in a disguised form or in composites and that it would be almost impossible to construct a detailed narrative out of it about the various stages that a victim or survivor goes through, I realized that I would have to tell my own story. A form of research could be done, I argued, by making myself both the subject and the researcher. The ideas generated by a dialogue between the two parts of myself, as both subject and researcher, could then be explored and buttressed by information from other survivors and the literature.

Towards Greater Understanding

My belief is that understanding is the key to healing. My hopes about who might be touched, who could be helped, and who could stand to learn more about this complex and emotionally loaded topic include victim–survivors of abuse by health professionals, victims of other types of abusive relationships, health and legal professionals and their students, family and friends of victims, and people who have a general interest in understanding the abuse of power by those in positions of authority.

In the Introduction to this book the 'first voice' describes the utter panic generated by the phone call from a state lawyer informing me that Dr A's lawyers were expecting me to make a deposition, and goes on to give a brief overview of my experiences as Dr A's patient. The 'second voice' gives the reader some historical background about the recognition of the psychological effects of trauma, and how public and professional interest has waxed and waned over the years. Statistics demonstrating the magnitude of the problem of sexual abuse by health professionals and a description of how a sexually exploitative process typically unfolds are followed by a description of some of the questions that I have been asked since I started to disclose my abuse some twelve years ago.

In Chapter 1, the first voice describes events and experiences in my life as a child, adolescent, and young adult that may have made me more susceptible to exploitation. Using examples from other victims and examining relevant literature, the second voice attempts to explore and explain the three factors, often interwoven, that operate to transform the relationship between health professional and patient in such a way that the professional's needs come first, and the patient is exploited or abused. These three dimensions are patient vulnerability, health professional risk factors, and the special status and role accorded to health professionals. The reader can see that, given the right combination of circumstances, it could happen to practically anyone.

Building on the risk factors outlined in Chapter 1, the second chapter, 'Initiation,' describes the often subtle process by which the health professional reframes the relationship, begins a gradual departure from accepted practice, and starts to groom the patient for sex. This process is illustrated by my subjective account and details from other victims. The analytical portion of the chapter includes a discussion of the literature on boundary violations, the 'slippery slope' concept for errant therapists, and psychologist Kenneth Pope's portrayal of the ten common scenarios leading to therapist abuse. Special issues faced by people who are already victims of childhood sexual abuse or other trauma are delineated.

Chapter 3, 'Entrapment,' tackles the most important, and most misunderstood, issue in health professional–patient abuse. Here, I address the relationship that is long standing and entails the possibility of some kind of romantic attachment. Largely ignored in the professional literature, the crucial dimensions of a victim's dependency, subjugation, isolation, idealization of the professional, emotional paralysis, and suspension of critical judgment are illustrated by the first voice and other victims' stories. The second voice culls relevant concepts from the trauma and therapy literature, including soul murder, traumatic transference, and physical and psychological addiction to painful experiences in order to enable the reader to understand, and hopefully gain compassion for, people who get caught up in abusive relationships and are unable to leave them.

The object of Chapter 4, 'Escape,' is to show the reader that escape is not likely to be a one-time occurrence, but is rather a gradual process of escape from the bondage described in the previous chapter. The subjective account spans some five or six years, beginning with initially dismissed questions that surfaced during the last two or three years of therapy with Dr A, and ending with the confrontation in his office. Seeking understanding, the second voice draws again on the trauma literature and other victims' accounts to challenge the common perception of an everlastingly helpless victim. The reader learns that the survivor's motivation and ability to terminate or begin to terminate a relationship with an abusive health professional stems from a variety of experiences, and that most survivors eventually do resist, fight back, and start to reclaim their identity.

In Chapter 5, 'After-effects,' sexual abuse is likened to a rock thrown into a calm pond, resulting in ever-widening concentric circles of ripples. Any lingering notions that health professional–patient sexual involvement can be viewed as merely a romantic and mutually beneficial interlude are dispelled. The account by the first voice, reflected and reinforced by other victims' stories, shows that damage is often profound, far-reaching, and long-lasting. Investigating the pervasive effects of trauma on mind and body, and the particular effects of sexual abuse by a parentlike authority figure, the second voice examines three overlapping frameworks. These are the diagnostic concept of post-traumatic stress disorder, the three levels of victimization described by self-help writer Aphrodite Matsakis, and the 'therapist–patient sex syndrome,' outlined by Kenneth Pope. Finally, the powerful and crippling effects of shame, a common thread in the next two chapters, are brought forward.

Healing, as explained in Chapter 6, is a gradual process that may proceed in fits and starts. Many areas of life and relationships have the potential to aid healing. This is illustrated by my subjective account of a second, constructive experience of therapy, rewarding family relationships, meeting other victims, and beginning to disclose. Further exploration includes other survivors' opinions about their own healing processes, the principles of Matsakis's self-help approach, Judith Herman's description of the three phases of therapy with a trauma victim, and my own therapeutic techniques with victims of abuse. The central issue of shame emerges repeatedly in this chapter, where it is shown to be a major obstacle to healing. The chapter ends by laying out special issues in the healing process for victims who are themselves health professionals.

Building on the obstacles to healing presented in the previous chapter, Chapter 7, 'Breaking the Silence,' emphasizes the enormity of the barriers created by the survivors' feelings, their isolation and lack of support, community victim-blaming attitudes, the self-protective stance of health professions, and the idiosyncrasies of the legal system. The story narrated by the first voice, the survivors' accounts, and an examination of the role of health professionals and their organizations in maintaining a 'conspiracy of silence' are used to emphasize the obstacles and to counter beliefs that victims are spurned lovers; emotionally disturbed, vindictive man-haters; or lying fortune-hunters. The use of these beliefs, in legal settings, to discredit complainants, is examined. The daunting nature of numerous obstacles and barriers and the risk of revictimization by a court or inquiry board make it clear that confronting these obstacles and making a public statement are formidable tasks, and certainly not for everyone.

To understand more fully the whole process of sexual abuse of patients by health professionals we need more information about the abusive professionals, their vulnerabilities, motivation, and role in the development of the exploitative process, and whether they can be successfully treated and rehabilitated. Psychoanalyst H.S. Strean makes a plea for the compassionate study of clinicians who have sex with their patients, saying that they are 'for the most part, demeaned, detested and derided by their colleagues.' In his book he presents four detailed case studies: 'Ron' and 'Roslyn' are psychiatrists, 'Bob' is a psychologist, and 'Al' is a social worker. Ron, Roslyn, and Bob ask for therapy; Al comes involuntarily. Ron, Bob, and Al exploit women patients, and Bob has had multiple victims. Roslyn becomes sexually involved with a man she is treating. Strean depicts these clinicians as 'childishly narcissistic people who could not relate to their patients with sustained empathy, objectivity or appropriate restraint.' Although he makes a telling case for a sympathetic approach, his contention that clinicians who act out sexually are no more hurtful than those who squelch a patient's spontaneity is worrying.[7]

Towards More Healing

If they do not realize it already, after reading this book victims will know that they are not alone in their struggle with shame, self-blame, lack of self-esteem, loss of confidence, mistrust, depression, anxiety, and the myriad ripple effects on their lives, jobs, careers, relationships, children, financial resources, and physical and mental health that can follow being exploited and trapped in an abusive relationship. While staying mired in a perpetual victimhood is to be avoided, if at all possible, there is no single blueprint for healing. As shown by various survivors' accounts, many experiences can be helpful, including meeting other victims; reading survivors' stories; having individual or group counselling; disclosing one's story to trusted relatives or friends; being believed by friends, relatives, or professionals; learning to nurture and care for oneself; writing one's own story; belonging to a consumer action group; confronting the abuser, with the help of a third party; initiating a formal complaint or legal action against the abuser; helping other victims; writing briefs or making representations to professional organizations or government; and, most importantly, regaining control of the direction of one's life, job, career, and relationships.

Having ongoing support is of crucial importance, as is vigilance about resisting revictimization or those who seek to explain victimization in terms of individual emotional fragilities or inadequacies. Women, who are socialized to view themselves as emotional mediators and nurturers, are probably more vulnerable to the latter interpretation. (Although I explore other factors later, the first voice for this chapter illustrates this very phenomenon by identifying seven determinants in my own background and emotional make-up and only two related to Dr A as major factors determining or influencing what happened to me with him!)

What are health professionals and their organizations doing to help victims transcend the damage they have suffered and rebuild their shattered lives? Very little, I am afraid. What is needed, in my opinion, is some kind of collective professional responsibility for the healing of patients who are sexually abused by members of the given profession.

Where are the crisis lines, free legal advice, free counselling, financial compensation, employment, and educational counselling that these victims need and deserve? Licensing boards appear to think that their responsibility ends when some kind of sanctions are applied to the professional. For instance, in my case, Dr A's practice was limited, he had to go for therapy, and he had to pay a $2,000 fine to the licensing board. Compensating me for all those painful and damaging years, plus the thousands of dollars it cost me for private therapy, does not enter into the equation. I could afford therapy, but what about victims who lack financial resources? In the United States, if they are uninsured or underinsured, they cannot access therapy; here in Canada, under medical plans, they are eligible for psychiatric care. But some psychiatrists resist seeing victims of abuse by health professionals because they view them as difficult patients who might involve the subsequent therapist in a messy court case. In addition, health professionals may struggle with mixed feelings and loyalty issues towards fellow professionals. As a result they may tend to collude with offenders, minimize or deny their misconduct, and enable them, inappropriately, to stay in practice or return to it. This tendency may be particularly pronounced if the health professional is prestigious.[8]

In British Columbia, if the patient who was sexually abused by a health professional has reported the abuse to the police, she may be eligible for non-medical therapy under the Victim's Compensation Program. If this type of funding was more available, it would meet the need of some survivors for accessible therapy. The women participating in the CMHA study felt that their healing process would be assisted by education about the process of health provider–patient abuse and explanations as to why it was not their fault. They felt that affordable, competent, accessible, long-term counselling was essential, and they recommended support groups, literature resources, and self-help groups as well. Some women 'suggested that counselling paid for by the offender would aid in the healing process as well as demonstrate that the offender had taken some responsibility for his actions.'[9]

As professionals and their organizations are so extraordinarily slow in facing up to their responsibilities, consumers may need to develop their own strategies for dealing with or discrediting abusive health professionals. One group of consumers paraded outside a health professional's office with placards advising passers-by to look elsewhere for the type of service he offered. Others have grown sophisticated in their understanding and use of the media. The organization Out of Patients in Toronto is an aptly named consumer advocacy group that disseminates information, prints pamphlets, organizes workshops, researches issues, and supports victims of abuse by health professionals. There are similar organizations in other major cities.

Towards Less Abuse

During this decade, education of health professionals and trainees about sexual abuse of patients has begun. For example, articles for physicians recognize that sexual feelings towards patients are normal, but that patients can be damaged if these feelings are acted upon. It is acknowledged that all physicians are at risk of exploiting patients, particularly in times of personal crisis, and doctors are informed about the special nature of the physician–patient relationship, the vulnerability of patients, and the need for professional boundaries. Extreme caution is advised when physicians find themselves considering exceptions to their usual practices, even around lesser boundaries, as this can be a signal of the start of a descent along the 'slippery slope' towards a serious boundary violation. Consultation with colleagues about any doubts is suggested, along with an emphasis on having a satisfying personal life outside one's professional work.[10]

Similarly, nurses are advised to seek help and supervision if they feel sexually attracted to a patient and want to act on that feeling. They should not tell the patient about their sexual feelings, and they must recognize that 'transferring care to another nurse is not sufficient justification to maintain the relationship ... Nursing is practised within a construct of beneficence: the nurse is there for the patient's needs.'[11]

Addressing the issue of female–female abuse has been difficult for lesbian communities and lesbian health professionals, as beliefs that feminists do not need boundaries, that men alone abuse, and that women patients and health professionals are equally oppressed and lack power have sometimes led to misuse of power and to exploitation of women patients. Educational articles have stressed the need for recognition of the power differential and the creation of firm boundaries.[12] In her article on boundaries in lesbian therapy relationships, psychiatrist Nanette Gartrell lays out strategies for managing gifts from patients, physical contact with patients, self-disclosure, and requests for special treatment, as well as the recommendations about maintaining personal privacy in the lesbian community.[13]

Educating trainees about these issues is crucial. In 1992 the Canadian Psychiatric Association endorsed and published guidelines under the title 'The Prevention of Sexual Exploitation of Patients: Educational Issues' in the *Canadian Journal of Psychiatry*. The guidelines address the need for residency training to include basic information on ethical prohibitions; some key literature about sexual exploitation of patients; exposure to gender-related issues in identity formation, self-esteem, and restriction of options for both sexes; reminders that psychiatrists in training have not escaped gender-role socialization, so need to be alert to how it affects their work with patients; encouragement of awareness of power imbalances in physician–patient relationships; and supervision that facilitates the discussion of sexual attraction to patients and proper management of countertransference feelings.[14]

While educational and preventative measures should decrease the number of exploitative health professionals in the future, what is to be done about present offenders? Can professional organizations effectively police their members, or will they subtly or perhaps not so subtly organize their efforts in a way that continues to deter complainants and protect professionals? Many feel that individual professions should not be left with this responsibility, but should be subject to some kind of overall health professional quality assurance organization that investigates complaints and disciplines abusers. This organization would have input from both professionals and consumers.

Addressing therapists who sexually abuse patients, Kenneth Pope has concerns about the present tendency of licensing boards and bodies to assume that perpetrators can be rehabilitated. He suggests that this 'may support a deep and chronic sense of special entitlement among therapists.' In other professions, Pope maintains, sexual offenders would not be allowed to return to their job in contact with the population that they had abused. Allowing a perpetrator to resume a limited therapy practice, he points out, such as seeing only male patients, ignores the more fundamental issue of abusing a position of power and trust.[15]

Pope draws attention to an article that addresses a case where a psychiatrist was prohibited from treating females, and stresses that such interventions 'do little to address the underlying failures of self and clinical management that characterize patient–clinician sexual contact .... In our forensic psychiatric experience ... cases where such contact has occurred are also characterized by other serious breeches of the standard of care, such as the failure to focus on the development of a therapeutic alliance essential for treatment to proceed ... We are concerned that a clinician who cannot be considered competent to treat women should be considered as competent to treat men.'[16]

It seems that licensing boards, like students and trainees, need a great deal of education to make them aware that sexual abuse of patients, like other varieties of sexual assault, is not just about sex. Other dimensions such as the power differential between health professional and patient; the mystique and special entitlement accorded to health professionals; the breech of trust and fiduciary duty; the lack of caring, empathy, and concern; as well as other personality and situational factors, are all involved. If health professionals who sexually abuse patients are allowed to return to practice, they should have a lengthy period of monitoring and supervision as there is little evidence that rehabilitation plans are effective, and the recidivism rate is high.[17]

At the same time, judges, juries, lawyers, other legal professionals, and their students must become aware of how difficult it is for victims to obtain redress in the court system and how often they are revictimized. It has been suggested that about 4 per cent of allegations of sexual abuse by health professionals are false,[18] and that 'It is not inherently unreasonable for a juror to presume that if a female claimant is willing to take the emotionally painful step of not only making a formal charge but pursuing it [for] the entire course of civil litigation, then it must have some truth in it.'[19] But in the vastly unequal playing field created by high-powered lawyers financed by defendants' insurance companies; the adversarial system; the burden of proof expected;[20] and the biases and stereotypes described in the previous chapter, every victim faces an arduous uphill struggle.

In some areas, groups of professionals have devoted special time and attention to sexual abuse by health professionals. For instance, in Toronto, a group of mental health practitioners came together to found CHASTEN, the Canadian Health Alliance to Stop Therapist Exploitation Now. This group has organized a crisis line and one-day workshops for victims, participated in the activities of the Independent Task Force on Sexual Abuse of Patients of the College of Physicians and Surgeons of Ontario, and hosted the Third International Conference on Sexual Exploitation by Therapists and Clergy that was held in Toronto in October 1994.

Speaking from the perspective of the consumer, the CMHA Women and Mental Health Committee report stressed the need for a safe reporting procedure to a complaints or advocacy committee operating independently of the various professional bodies. Such a committee would also give information, legal advice, and initial counselling. Women suggested that professional bodies should have very clear ethical policies and severe consequences for members who violate these codes. Specific training on boundary issues and screening procedures for applicants for professional training were recommended. Public education was deemed vital, and this included spreading awareness that professionals had the responsibility for maintaining boundaries, and that it was never the victim's fault.[21]

Health Professionals and Consumers Working Together

Given the strength of forces operating to deny or minimize the problem of sexual exploitation of patients by health professionals, it is obvious that professionals and consumers need to work both separately and together on a number of different levels to ensure that abuse does not continue. A concerted effort needs to be made to put the shame and responsibility back where they belong – with the professionals, not the victims. Only then, I believe, will professions put enough time, energy, and resources into stopping the abuse and promoting healing of victims.

What happens in abusive health professional–patient relationships is a microcosm, a miniature representation of what is happening in society as a whole. Despite some changes, there are still dominant–subordinate relationships between men and women, and between the strong and the weak. The dominant parties are entitled to have their needs met; the subordinates are expected to defer and cater to the dominants. Victims are ignored, trivialized, or despised and considered to have caused, needed, wanted, enjoyed, or deserved their fate. These sentiments underpin much of the violence in society towards women, children, and vulnerable adults.

Present conservative trends in society, with an increased tendency to attribute all responsibility to the individual and blame victims for incurring their own abuse, make the task of increasing understanding of, and compassion for, abuse victims even more difficult. Added to this is the backlash against the women's movement, and the furious debate about the veracity of new memories of abuse.[22] The conviction that some therapists, mostly women and largely feminists, are inducing false memories of childhood incest in gullible patients, primarily women, has added fuel to cultural stereotypes about women as lying, vindictive, and destructive. It seems likely that the perception that complaints about sexual abuse tend to be false and that the complainants tend to be vindictive and unstable is also influencing reactions to allegations of sexual abuse in general, including abuse that has never been forgotten. How far will this go? Will the incidence of sexual abuse apparently disappear? Are we about to go through one of those periods of denial, as described in the Introduction, when the psychological effects of trauma are largely forgotten?

Unfortunately, it is naively idealistic to hope to change societal attitudes, but we can hope to decrease the amount of abuse in health professional–patient relationships. We can do this by talking about it openly; by embracing educational approaches that lay bare cultural determinants and gender and power issues; by reaffirming the sacred trust in the professional–patient relationship; by refusing to protect professionals who abuse; and by refraining from blaming victims.

Epilogue

September 1997

Recently I learned that, as a result of several more complaints, Dr A has finally lost his licence to practise. Because of the barriers of secrecy and confidentiality imposed by the inquiry process, I have no idea who the other ex-patients are. Sometimes I imagine what it might be like to meet them. From my involvement with the Therapist Abuse Action Group I know that some survivors have gained validation and support by meeting and talking with other victims of the same abusive health professional.

By I am left to wonder about Dr A's other victims. Were they all referred to him as patients? Or did anyone else start off like me, as a student who was told by Dr A that I needed therapy. How long were they in therapy with him? When did they start to realize that they had been exploited? How did they escape? What effects has the abuse had on their lives? Without blaming themselves, what personal issues did they have which left them open to Dr A's manipulations and reframing of the relationship? Have they come to some kind of understanding of what happened to them? How much have they been able to share with friends and relatives? What has helped them heal?

My hope is that these victims of Dr A, along with all other victims of abusive health professionals, will be accorded the understanding and support that they need by friends, relatives, community, and other professionals. My fervent wish is that this book will make a contribution to this understanding and to survivors' healing.

Notes

Introduction

1 P.S. Penfold, 'Sexual abuse by therapists: Maintaining the conspiracy of silence,' *Canadian Journal of Community Mental Health* 11, 1 (1992): 5–15.

2 S.H. Kardener, M. Fuller, and I.N. Mensch, 'A survey of physicians' attitudes and practices regarding erotic and non-erotic contact with patients,' *American Journal of Psychiatry* 130 (1973): 1077–81.

3 J.A. Perry, 'Physicians' erotic and non-erotic physical involvement with patients,' *American Journal of Psychiatry* 133 (1976): 838–40.

4 J.C. Holroyd and A.M. Brodsky, 'Psychologists' attitudes and practices regarding erotic and non-erotic physical contact with patients,' *American Psychologist* 32 (1977): 843–9.

5 W.H. Masters and V.E. Johnson, 'Principles of the new sex therapy,' *American Journal of Psychiatry* 133 (1976): 548–54.

6 N. Gartrell, J. Herman, S. Olarte, M. Feldstein, and R. Localio, 'Psychiatrist–patient sexual contact: Results of a national survey. I: Prevalence,' *American Journal of Psychiatry* 143 (1986): 1126–31.

7 N. Gartrell, J. Herman, S. Olarte, M. Feldstein, and R. Localio, 'Reporting practices of psychiatrists who knew of sexual misconduct by colleagues,' *American Journal of Orthopsychiatry* 57, 2 (1987): 287–95.

8 K.S. Pope, P.C. Keith-Spiegel, and B.G. Tabachnick, 'Sexual attraction to clients: The human therapist and the (sometimes) inhuman training system,' *American Psychologist* 41 (1986): 147–58.

9 L. Gechtman, 'Sexual contact between social workers and their clients,' in Gabbard ed., *Sexual Exploitation in Professional Relationships* (Washington, DC: American Psychiatric Press, 1989), pp. 27–38.

10 D.T. Collins, 'Sexual involvement between psychiatric hospital staff and

their patients,' in Gabbard, ed., *Sexual Exploitation in Professional Relationships*, 151–62; M.H. Stone, 'Boundary violations between therapist and patient,' *Psychiatric Annals* 6 (1976): 670–77.

11 E. Berger and N. Staisey, 'Initial analysis of a survey of Ontario women regarding sexual harassment and abuse by Ontario physicians,' *Canada Health Monitor Report*, 27 Oct. 1991.

12 British Columbia College of Physicians and Surgeons, Committee on Physician Sexual Misconduct, *Crossing the Boundaries: Executive Summary* (Vancouver, BC, 1992), pp. 1–2.

13 J.A. Lamont and C. Woodward, 'Patient–physician sexual involvement: A Canadian survey of obstetrician-gynecologists,' *Canadian Medical Association Journal* 150 (1994): 1433–39.

14 R. Gallop, 'Sexual contact between nurses and patients,' *Canadian Nurse* (Feb. 1993): 28–31; E.M. Munsat and J.J. Riordan, 'Prevalence of staff–patient sexual interactions on inpatient units,' *Journal of Psychosocial Nursing* 28 (1990): 23–6; L. Jorgenson and A. Hirsch, 'Sexual contact between dentist and patient: Is dating ethical?' *CDS Review* (Aug. 1994): 24–7.

15 T. Garrett and J. Davis, 'Epidemiology in the U.K.,' in D. Jehu, ed., *Patients as Victims* (Chichester, England: John Wiley & Sons, 1994), pp. 37–57; C. Quadrio, 'Sexual abuse in therapy: Gender issues,' *Australian and New Zealand Journal of Psychiatry* 30 (1996): 124–33.

16 Gartrell et al., 'Psychiatrist–patient sexual contact'; Gechtman, 'Sexual contact between social workers and their clients.'

17 K.S. Pope, *Sexual Involvement with Therapists: Patient Assessment, Subsequent Therapy, Forensics* (Washington, DC: American Psychological Association, 1994), p. 87.

18 BC College of Physicians and Surgeons, Committee on Physician Sexual Misconduct, *Crossing the Boundaries*, pp. 3, 11.

19 Gary Schoener, personal communication, 15 Feb. 1997; G.R. Schoener and E.T. Luepker, 'Boundaries in group therapy: Ethical and practice issues,' in B. DeChant, ed., Women and Group Psychotherapy (New York: Guilford Press, 1996).

20 L.S. Brown, 'Beyond thou shalt not: Thinking about ethics in the lesbian community,' Women and Therapy 8, nos. 1, 2 (1989): 13–25; N.K. Gartrell, 'Boundaries in lesbian therapy relationships,' *Women and Therapy* 12, 3 (1992): 29–50; N.K. Gartrell and B.E. Sanderson, 'Sexual abuse of women in psychotherapy: Counseling and advocacy,' *Women and Therapy* 15, 1 (1994): 39–54.

21 C.M. Bates and A.M. Brodsky, *Sex in the Therapy Hour: A Case of Professional Incest* (New York: Guilford Press, 1989).

22 J.L. Herman, *Trauma and Recovery* (New York: Basic Books, 1992), pp. 1, 9.

23 P. Briquet, *Traite de l'hystérie* (Paris: J.B. Baillière, 1859).

24 Herman, *Trauma and Recovery*, pp. 10–11.

25 J. Breuer and S. Freud, *Studies on Hysteria (1893–1895)*, in *Standard Edition of the Works of Sigmund Freud*, vol. 2, trans. J. Strachey (London: Hogarth Press, 1955), pp. 1–319.

26 P. Janet, *L'Automatisme psychologique: Essai de psychologie experimentale sur les formes inférieures de l'activité humaine* (Paris: Felix Alcan, 1989; Paris: Société Pierre Janet/Payot, 1973).

27 J.M. Masson, *The Assault on Truth: Freud's Suppression of the Seduction Theory* (New York: Farrar, Straus and Giroux, 1984).

28 A. Leri, *Shellshock: Commotional and Emotional Aspects* (London: University of London Press, 1919), p. 118.

29 J.W. Appel and G.W. Beebe, 'Preventive psychiatry: An epidemiological approach,' *Journal of American Medical Association* 131 (1946): 1468–71.

30 A. Kardiner, 'Traumatic neurosis of war,' in S. Arieti, ed., *American Handbook of Psychiatry* (New York: Basic Books, 1959), pp. 245–57.

31 American Psychiatric Association, *Diagnostic and Statistical Manual of Mental Disorders*, 3rd ed (Washington, DC: APA, 1980), pp. 236–8.

32 C.A. Ross, 'Errors of logic in biological psychiatry,' in C.A. Ross and A. Pam, eds., *Pseudoscience in Biological Psychiatry: Blaming the Body* (New York: John Wiley and Sons, 1995).

33 J.B. Murray, 'Relationship of childhood sexual abuse to borderline personality disorder, posttraumatic stress disorder, and multiple personality disorder,' *Journal of Psychology* 127, 6 (1993): 657–76; D. Speigel, 'Dissociative disorders,' in R.E. Hales, S.C. Yudofsky and J.A. Talbott, *The American Psychiatric Press Textbook of Psychiatry* (Washington, DC: American Psychiatric Press, 1994), pp. 633–52.

34 Herman, *Trauma and Recovery*, p. 123.

35 For a review of this literature, see P.S. Penfold, 'The repressed memory controversy: Is there middle ground?' *Canadian Medical Association Journal* 1996; 155, 6 (1996): 647–53.

36 R. Ofshe and E. Watters, *Making Monsters: False Memories, Psychotherapy, and Sexual Hysteria* (New York: Charles Scribner's Sons, 1994), p. 5.

37 J.F. Borus and W.H. Sledge, 'Psychiatric education,' in Hale et al., *The American Psychiatric Press Textbook of Psychiatry*, p. 1469.

38 British Columbia Psychological Association, Referral Service, brochure, 1997.

39 British Columbia Association of Social Workers, Information pamphlet: 'Considering a career in social work,' 1997.

40 S.B. Bisbing, L.M. Jorgenson, and P.K. Sutherland, *Sexual Abuse by Professionals: A Legal Guide* (Charlottesville, Va.: The Michie Company, 1995), pp. 4–8.

41 Ibid., pp. 403–45.
42 T.G. Gutheil and G.O. Gabbard, 'The concept of boundaries in clinical practice: Theoretical and risk-management dimensions,' *American Journal of Psychiatry* 150, 2 (1993): 188–96.
43 Bisbing et al., *Sexual Abuse by Professionals*, pp. 447–83.
44 For instance, see Canadian Medical Association Policy Summary, 'The patient–physician relationship and the sexual abuse of patients,' *Canadian Medical Association Journal* 150, 1 (1994): 1884A–C.
45 Independent Task Force commissioned by the College of Physicians and Surgeons of Ontario, *Final Report: Task Force on Sexual Abuse of Patients* (Toronto: College of Physicians and Surgeons of Ontario, 1991), pp. 23–4.
46 R.J. Ursano and E.K. Silverman, 'Psychoanalysis, psychoanalytic psychotherapy, and supportive psychotherapy,' in Hale et al., *American Psychiatric Press Textbook of Psychiatry*, pp. 1035–60; psychotherapy defined on pp. 1035–7; see also Bisbing et al., *Sexual Abuse*, pp. 160–1.
47 S. Freud, *An Outline of Psychoanalysis* (New York: Norton, 1949), p. 194.
48 C.K. Mann and J.D. Winer, *Psychotherapists' Sexual Contact with Clients*, American Jurisprudence Proof of Facts, 3rd series, vol. 14 (Rochester, NY: Lawyers Cooperative Publishing, 1991), pp. 319–431.
49 For a full description of PTSD, see *Diagnostic and Statistical Manual of Mental Disorders*, 4th ed. (*DSM IV*) (Washington, DC: American Psychiatric Association, 1994), pp. 424–9.
50 *DSM IV*, pp. 645–50.
51 *DSM IV*, pp. 658–61.
52 *DSM IV*, pp. 650–4.
53 D. Simmons, 'Gender issues and borderline personality disorder: Why do females dominate the diagnosis?' *Archives of Psychiatric Nursing* 6 (1992): 219–23; see also D.E. Reiser and H. Levenson, 'Abuses of the borderline diagnosis: A clinical problem with teaching opportunities,' *American Journal of Psychiatry* 141 (1984): 1528–32.
54 S. Arieti, *Interpretation of Schizophrenia* (New York: Brunner, 1955).

1: Vulnerability and Risk Factors

1 B. Noël, with K. Watterson, *You Must Be Dreaming* (New York: Poseidon Press, 1992), p. 17.
2 M. Atwood, *The Handmaid's Tale* (Toronto: Seal Books, 1985), pp. 221–2.
3 E. Plasil, *Therapist* (New York: St Martin's Press, 1985); see pp. 11–23 for a description of Plasil's family background, and pp. 217–18 for a depiction of the similarities between Dr Leonard and her parents; quotes on p. 218.

4 Noël, with Watterson, *You Must Be Dreaming*, p. 265.
5 C.M., Bates and A.M. Brodsky, *Sex in the Therapy Hour: A Case of Professional Incest* (New York: Guilford Press, 1989), pp. 7–16.
6 G.R. Schoener, J.H. Milgrom, J.C. Gonsoriek, E.T. Luepker, and R.M. Conroe, *Psychotherapists' Sexual Involvement with Clients: Intervention and Prevention* (Minneapolis: Walk-in-Counselling Center, 1989), pp. 227–32.
7 M. Stone, 'Boundary violations between therapist and patient,' *Psychiatric Annals* 6, 12 (1976): 670–82.
8 R.P. Kluft, 'Incest and subsequent revictimisation: The case of therapist–patient sexual exploitation, with a description of the sitting duck syndrome,' in R.P. Kluft, ed., *Incest-related Syndromes of Adult Psychopathology* (Washington, DC: American Psychiatric Press, 1990), pp. 263–87.
9 M.W. Armsworth, 'Therapy of incest survivors: Abuse or support?' *Child Abuse and Neglect* 13 (1989): 549–62.
10 J.L. Herman, *Trauma and Recovery* (New York: Basic Books, 1992), p. 111.
11 J.B. Miller, *Toward a New Psychology of Women*, 2nd ed. (Boston: Beacon Press, 1986).
12 A. Horwitz, 'The pathways into psychiatric treatment: Some differences between men and women,' *Journal of Health and Social Behaviour* (June 1977): 169–78.
13 R.P. Greenberg, S. Fisher, and J. Shapiro, 'Sex role development and response to medication by psychiatric inpatients,' *Psychological Reports* 33 (1973): 675–7.
14 P. Chesler, *Women and Madness* (New York: Avon Books, 1972), p. 156.
15 C. Hyde, *Abuse of Trust: The Career of Dr James Tyhurst* (Vancouver: Douglas and McIntyre, 1991).
16 S. Smith, 'The sexually abused patient and the abusing therapist: A study in sadomasochistic relationships,' *Psychoanalytic Psychology* 1, 2 (1984): 89–98.
17 S. Butler and S.L. Zelen, 'Sexual intimacies between therapists and patients,' *Psychotherapy:Theory, Research, and Practice* 14, 2 (1977): 139–45.
18 A. Stone, *Law, Psychiatry and Morality* (Washington, DC: American Psychiatric Press, 1984), pp. 211–12.
19 G.R. Schoener and J. Gonsoriek, 'Assessment and development of rehabilitation plans for counsellors who have sexually exploited their clients,' *Journal of Counselling and Development* 67 (1988): 227–32.
20 P. Rutter, *Sex in the Forbidden Zone* (Los Angeles: Jeremy P. Tarcher, 1989), pp. 91–111.
21 K.S. Pope, P.C. Keith-Speigel, and B.G. Tabachnick, 'Sexual attraction to clients: The human therapist and the (sometimes) inhuman training system,' *American Psychologist* 41 (1986): 147–58.

22 K.S. Pope, H. Levenson, and L. Schover, 'Sexual intimacy in psychology training programs: Results and implications of a national survey,' *American Psychologist* 34 (1979): 682–9.

23 M.L. Carr, G. Erlick Robinson, D.E. Stewart, and D. Kussin, 'A survey of Canadian psychiatric residents regarding resident–educator sexual contact,' *American Journal of Psychiatry* 148 (1991): 216–20.

24 K.J. Margittai, R. Moscarello, and M.F. Rossi, 'Medical students' experiences of abuse: A Canadian perspective,' *Annals of the Royal College of Physicians and Surgeons of Canada* 27 (1994): 199–204; see also, C.P. McKegney, 'Medical education: A neglectful and abusive family system,' *Family Medicine* 21 (1989): 452–7.

25 For a description of struggles shared by lesbian health professional and patient, see S.F. Pearlman, 'Lesbian clients / lesbian therapists: Necessary conversations,' in N.D. Davis, E. Cole, and E.D. Rothblum, eds., *Lesbian Therapists and Their Therapy* (New York: Harrington Park Press, 1996), p. 77.

26 L.S. Brown, 'Beyond thou shalt not: Thinking about ethics in the lesbian therapy community,' *Women and Therapy* 8, nos. 1, 2 (1988): 15.

27 Ibid., p. 22.

28 C. Heyward, *When Boundaries Betray Us* (San Francisco: Harper, 1993).

29 Noël, with Watterson, *You Must Be Dreaming*, p. 50.

30 Atwood, *Handmaid's Tale*, pp. 221–2.

31 E. Cole, 'When a straight psychologist works with lesbian clients,' in Davis, Cole, and Rothblum, eds., *Lesbian Therapists and Their Therapy*, p. xvii.

32 N.K. Gartrell and B.E. Sanderson, 'Sexual abuse by women in psychotherapy counseling and advocacy,' *Women and Therapy* 15, 1 (1994): 41.

33 E. Plasil, *Therapist*, pp. 36, 52.

34 M.R. Peterson, *At Personal Risk: Boundary Violations in Professional–Client Relationships* (New York: W.W. Norton, 1992), pp. 13–14.

35 Ibid., p. 24.

36 Ibid., p. 33.

2: Initiation

1 C.M. Bates and A.M. Brodsky, *Sex in the Therapy Hour: A Case of Professional Incest* (New York: Guilford Press, 1989), p. 26.

2 Ibid., pp. 26, 27.

3 E. Plasil, *Therapist* (New York: St Martin's Press, 1985), pp. 51–66.

4 L. Freeman and J. Roy, *Betrayal* (New York: Pocket Books, 1976).

5 G.O. Gabbard, ed., *Sexual Exploitation in Professional Relationships* (Washington, DC: American Psychiatric Press, 1989).

6 S. Butler and S.L. Zelen, 'Sexual intimacies between therapists and patients,' *Psychotherapy: Theory, Research, and Practice* 14, 2 (1977): 139–45.

7 J. Marmor, 'Some psychodynamic aspects of the seduction of patients in psychotherapy,' *American Journal of Psychoanalysis* 36 (1976): 319–23; see also S.H. Kardener, 'Sex and the physician–patient relationship,' *American Journal of Psychiatry* 131, 10 (1974): 1134–6; J.C. Holroyd and A.M. Brodsky, 'Psychologists' attitudes and practices regarding erotic and non-erotic physical contact with patients,' *American Psychologist* 32 (1977): 843–9.

8 N. Gartrell, J. Herman, S. Olarte, M. Feldstein, and R. Localio, 'Psychiatrist–patient sexual contact: Results of a national survey. I: Prevalence,' *American Journal of Psychiatry* 143 (1986): 1126–31.

9 Marmor, 'Some psychodynamic aspects,' p. 323.

10 M.R. Peterson, *At Personal Risk: Boundary Violations in Professional–Client Relationships* (New York: W.W. Norton, 1992).

11 B. Noël, with K. Watterson, *You Must Be Dreaming* (New York: Poseidon Press, 1992), p. 15.

12 R.S. Epstein and R.I. Simon, 'The exploitation index: An early warning indicator of boundary violations in psychotherapy,' *Bulletin of the Menninger Clinic* 54 (1990): 450–65.

13 See also B.W. Dziech and L. Weiner, *The Lecherous Professor: Sexual Harassment on Campus* (Boston: Beacon Press, 1984).

14 K.S. Pope and J.C. Bouhoutsos, *Sexual Intimacy between Therapists and Patients* (New York: Praeger, 1986), p. 4.

15 L. Gechtman, 'Sexual contact between social workers and their clients,' in G.O. Gabbard, ed., *Sexual Exploitation in Professional Relationships* (Washington, DC: American Psychiatric Press, 1989), pp. 27–38.

16 M. DeYoung, 'Case reports: The sexual exploitation of incest victims by health professionals,' *Victimology* 6 (1981): 92–101.

17 R.C. Summit and J.A. Kryso, 'Sexual abuse of children: a clinical spectrum,' *American Journal of Orthopsychiatry* 48 (1978): 237–51.

18 J.L. Herman, *Trauma and Recovery* (New York: Basic Books, 1992), p. 139.

19 R.P. Kluft, 'Incest and subsequent revictimisation: The case of therapist–patient sexual exploitation, with a description of the sitting duck syndrome,' in R.P. Kluft, ed., *Incest-related Syndromes of Adult Psychopathology* (Washington, DC: American Psychiatric Press, 1990), pp. 263–87.

20 See the section entitled 'Some Basic Definitions' in the Introduction to this book. An excellent self-help book on PTSD is A. Matsakis, *I Can't Get Over It: A Handbook for Trauma Survivors* (Oakland, Calif.: New Harbinger Publications, 1992).

21 Herman, *Trauma and Recovery*, pp. 136–40.

22 M. Carr and G. Erlick Robinson, 'Fatal attraction: The ethical and clinical dilemma of patient–therapist sex,' *Canadian Journal of Psychiatry* 35 (1990): 122–7.
23 R.P. Kluft, 'Incest and subsequent revictimisation.' Also see M.W. Armsworth, 'Therapy of incest survivors: Abuse or support?' *Child Abuse and Neglect* 13 (1989): 549–62.

3: Entrapment

1 G. Orwell, *Nineteen Eighty-four* (New York: Harcourt, Brace, 1949), p. 36.
2 P. Conroy, *The Prince of Tides* (New York: Bantam Books, 1987). On p. 69, Tom's sister Savannah's psychiatrist, Dr Susan Lowenstein, thanks Tom for wanting to help Savannah, but he replies 'Help *me*. Help *me*.' But, despite long sessions in her office, both later emphatically insist that she is not his psychiatrist, he is not her patient. See pp. 163–5.
3 E. Plasil, *Therapist* (New York: St Martin's Press, l985), pp. 81, 97, 98, 100.
4 B. Noël, with K. Watterson, *You Must Be Dreaming* (New York: Poseidon Press, 1992), pp. 87, 92, 195, 210.
5 C.M. Bates and A.M. Brodsky, *Sex in the Professional Hour: A Case of Professional Incest* (New York: Guilford Press, 1989), pp. 21–39.
6 M.S. Rapp, 'Sexual misconduct,' *Canadian Medical Association Journal* 137 (1987): 193–4; J. Marmor, 'Some psychodynamic aspects of the seduction of patients in psychotherapy,' *American Journal of Psychoanalysis* 36 (1976): 319–23.
7 L. Shengold, *Soul Murder: The Effects of Childhood Abuse and Deprivation* (New Haven and London: Yale University Press, 1989), pp. 2, 39, 40.
8 D. Dutton and S.L. Painter, 'Traumatic bonding: The development of emotional attachment in battered women and other relationships of intermittent abuse,' *Victimology* 6 (1981): 139–55.
9 L. Walker, *The Battered Woman* (New York: Harper and Row, 1979).
10 J.L. Herman, *Trauma and Recovery* (New York: Basic Books, 1992), pp. 79, 92.
11 R.C. Summit, 'The child sexual abuse accommodation syndrome,' *Journal of Child Abuse and Neglect* 7 (1983): 177–93.
12 H. Krystal, 'Trauma and affects,' *Psychoanalytic Study of the Child* 33 (1978): 81–116; A. Miller, *Thou Shalt Not Be Aware: Society's Betrayal of the Child* (New York: Farrar, Straus and Giroux, 1984).
13 B.A. Van der Kolk, 'Compulsion to repeat the trauma,' in R.P. Kluft, ed., *Treatment of Victims of Sexual Abuse. Psychiatric Clinics of North America* 12, 2 (1989): 389–411.
14 P. Rutter, *Sex in the Forbidden Zone* (Los Angeles: Jeremy P. Tarcher, 1989), pp. 65–7, 133, 134.

15 E. Kaschak, *Engendered Lives* (New York: Basic Books, 1992).

16 C. Gilligan, *In a Different Voice* (Cambridge, Mass.: Harvard University Press, 1982).

17 M.R. Peterson, *At Personal Risk: Boundary Violations in Professional–Client Relationships* (New York: W.W. Norton, 1992), pp. 72–104.

18 S. Krugman, 'Trauma in the family: Perspectives on intergenerational transmission of violence,' in B. Van der Kolk, ed., *Psychological Trauma* (Washington, DC: American Psychiatric Press, 1987), p. 135.

19 J.L. Herman, *Trauma and Recovery*, pp. 138, 139.

20 M.W. Armsworth, 'Therapy of incest survivors: Abuse or support?' *Child Abuse and Neglect* 13 (1989): 549–62.

4: Escape

1 This term is used to describe a relationship between two people where there is a shared delusion, or false belief. Rosie Alexander's book, *Folie à Deux: An Experience of One-to-One Therapy* (London: Free Association Books, 1995), is a disturbing account of her damaging, destructive, and totally engrossing relationship with a French psychoanalyst.

2 E. Plasil, *Therapist* (New York: St Martin's Press, 1985), p. 145. This quote is a telling example of the traumatic bonding described in Chapter 3, showing how Plasil had no compassion for herself and how she judged herself much more harshly than she did others.

3 B. Noël, with K. Watterson, *You Must Be Dreaming* (New York: Poseidon Press, 1992), pp. 108–22.

4 C.M. Bates and A.M. Brodsky, *Sex in the Therapy Hour: A Case of Professional Incest* (New York: Guilford Press, 1989), pp. 37–9.

5 J. Roy and L. Freeman, *Betrayal* (New York: Pocket Books, 1976), p. 91.

6 Noël, with Watterson, *You Must Be Dreaming*, p. 143.

7 Bates and Brodsky, *Sex in the Therapy Hour*, pp. 42–3, 85, 92–3.

8 Plasil, *Therapist*, pp. 152–3, 159.

9 M.E.P. Seligman, *Helplessness: On Depression, Development and Death* (San Francisco: W.H. Freeman, 1975).

10 R.P. Kluft, 'Incest and subsequent revictimisation: The case of therapist–patient sexual exploitation, with a description of the sitting duck syndrome,' in R.P. Kluft, ed., *Incest-related Syndromes of Adult Psychopathology* (Washington, DC: American Psychiatric Press, 1990), pp. 263–87.

11 L.H. Bowker, *Beating Wife-beating* (Lexington, Mass.: Lexington Books, 1983); A.L. Horton and B. Johnson, 'Profiles and strategies of women who have ended abuse,' *Families in Society* 74 (1993): 481–92.

12 K. Lecovin and P.S. Penfold, 'The emotionally abused woman: An existential–phenomenological exploration,' *Canadian Journal of Community Mental Health* 15, 1 (1996): 39–48.

13 J.L. Herman, *Trauma and Recovery* (New York: Basic Books, 1992), p. 91.

14 Ibid., p. 84.

15 L. Lovelace and M. McGrady, *Ordeal* (Secaucus, NJ: Citadel, 1980), p. 70.

16 P. Levi, *Survival in Auschwitz: The Nazi Assault on Humanity* (New York: Collier, 1961); H. Krystal, 'Trauma and affects,' *Psychoanalytic Study of the Child* 33 (1978): 81–116; E. Wiesel, *Night* (New York: Hill and Wang, 1960).

17 P.C. Hearst and A. Moscow, *Every Secret Thing* (New York: Doubleday, 1982), pp. 75–6.

18 Plasil, *Therapist*, pp. 144–54.

19 G. Greer, *The Female Eunuch* (St Albans, England: Paladin, 1971).

5: After-effects

1 R.W. Medlicott, 'Erotic professional indiscretions, actual or assumed, and alleged,' *Australian and New Zealand Journal of Psychiatry* 2 (1968): 17–23; M.H. Stone, 'Boundary violations between therapist and patient,' *Psychiatric Annals* 6, 12 (1976): 670–7.

2 P. Chesler, *Women and Madness* (New York: Avon Books, 1972), p. 149.

3 J. Sonne, B. Meyer, D. Borys, and V. Marshall, 'Clients' reactions to sexual intimacy in therapy,' *American Journal of Orthopsychiatry* 55 (1985): 183–9; J. Pennebaker and J.R. Susman, 'Disclosure of traumas and psychosomatic processes,' *Social Sciences and Medicine* 26 (1988): 327–32.

4 G.R. Schoener, J.H. Milgrom, J.C. Gonsoriek, E.T. Luepker, and R.M. Conroe, *Psychotherapist's Sexual Involvement with Clients: Intervention and Prevention* (Minneapolis: Walk-In Counselling Center, 1989), p. 235. A fictionalized account of a psychiatrist's disastrous marriage to a patient can be found in F. Scott Fitzgerald, *Tender Is the Night* (New York: Charles Scribner's Sons, 1933).

5 S. Feldman-Summers and G. Jones, 'Psychological impacts of sexual contact between therapists or other health care practitioners and their clients,' *Journal of Consulting and Clinical Psychology* 52, 6 (1984): 1054–61.

6 J.W. Appel and G.W. Bebe, 'Preventive psychiatry: An epidemiological approach.' *Journal of the American Medical Association* 131 (1946): 1468–71.

7 A. Matsakis, *I Can't Get Over It: A Handbook for Trauma Survivors* (Oakland, Calif.: New Harbinger Publications, 1992), pp. 75–102.

8 Women and Mental Health Committee of the Canadian Mental Health Association, Manitoba Division. *Women's Voices Shall Be Heard: Report on*

the *Sexual Abuse of Women by Mental Health Service Providers* (Winnipeg: CMHA, 1993).

9 D. Simmons, 'Gender issues and borderline personality disorder: Why do females dominate the diagnosis?' *Archives of Psychiatric Nursing* 6, 4 (1992): 219–23.

10 Matsakis, *I Can't Get Over It*, pp. 95–102.

11 K.S. Pope, *Sexual Involvement with Therapists* (Washington, DC: American Psychological Association, 1994), pp. 117–56.

12 Women and Mental Health Committee of CMHA, *Women's Voices*, p. 22.

13 B. Noël, with K. Watterson, *You Must Be Dreaming* (New York: Poseidon Press, 1992), p. 211.

14 L. Freeman and J. Roy, *Betrayal* (New York: Pocket Books, 1976), p. 112.

15 R. Moscarello, 'Victims of violence: Aspects of the "victim-to-patient" process in women,' *Canadian Journal of Psychiatry* 37 (1992): 497–502.

16 Freeman and Roy, *Betrayal*, pp. 115, 117.

17 J.C. Bouhoutsos, J. Holdroyd, H. Lerman, B. Forer, and M. Greenberg, 'Sexual intimacy between psychotherapists and patients,' *Professional Psychology: Research and Practice* 14 (1983): 185–96; K.S. Pope and V.A. Vetter, 'Prior therapist–patient sexual involvement among patients seen by psychologists,' *Psychotherapy* 28 (1991): 429–38.

18 E. Walker and T.D. Young, *A Killing Cure* (New York: Holt, Rinehart and Winston, 1986), pp. 51–2.

19 M.R. Peterson, *At Personal Risk: Boundary Violations in Professional–Client Relationships* (New York: W.W. Norton, 1992), pp. 76–80.

20 Noël, with Watterson, *You Must Be Dreaming*, p. 132.

21 Ibid., p. 132.

22 C.M. Bates and A.M. Brodsky, *Sex in the Therapy Hour: A Case of Professional Incest* (New York: Guilford Press, 1989), p. 96.

6: Healing

1 G.R. Schoener and J.H. Milgrom, 'Helping clients who have been sexually abused by therapists,' in P.A. Keller and S.R. Heyman, eds., *Innovations in Clinical Practice: A Source Book*, vol. 6 (1987), p. 407. Available from Professional Resources Exchange, PO Box 15560, Sarasota, Fl. 34277–1560.

2 A. Matsakis, *I Can't Get Over It: A Handbook for Trauma Survivors* (Oakland, Calif.: New Harbinger, 1992).

3 J.L. Herman, *Trauma and Recovery* (New York: Basic Books, 1992).

4 K.S. Pope, *Sexual Involvement with Therapists: Patient Assessment, Subsequent Therapy, Forensics* (Washington, DC: American Psychological Association, 1994).

5 G.R. Schoener, J.H. Milgrom, J.C. Gonsoriek, E.T. Luepker, and R.M. Conroe, *Psychotherapists' Sexual Involvement with Clients* (Minneapolis: Walk-In Counselling Center, 1989).
6 Foundations for treatment, specific treatment approaches to common problems, and some modalities for intervention are also described in D. Jehu, *Patients as Victims* (Chichester, England: John Wiley and Sons, 1994), pp. 117–45.
7 D.L. Nathanson, 'Understanding what is hidden: Shame in sexual abuse,' in R.P. Kluft, ed., *Treatment of Victims of Sexual Abuse. Psychiatric Clinics of North America* 12, 2 (1989): 381–8; R. Karen, 'Shame,' *Atlantic Monthly* (Feb. 1992): 40–70.
8 Pope, *Sexual Involvement with Therapists*, p. 101.
9 R. Ofshe and E. Watters, *Making Monsters: False Memory, Psychotherapy and Sexual Hysteria* (New York: Charles Scribner's Sons, 1994); E.F. Loftus, 'The reality of repressed memories,' *American Psychologist* 48, 5 (1993): 518–37; E. Loftus and K. Ketcham, *The Myth of Repressed Memory* (New York: St Martin's Press, 1994).
10 J. Jay, 'Terrible knowledge,' *Family Therapy Networker* (Nov/Dec 1991): 24–5.
11 W.E. Kelly, ed., *Post-traumatic Stress Disorder and the War Veteran Patient* (New York: Brunner/Mazel, 1985); J.P. Wilson, Z. Harel, and B. Kahana, eds., *Human Adaptation to Extreme Stress: From the Holocaust to Vietnam* (New York: Plenum, 1988).
12 H. Grunebaum, 'Harmful psychotherapy experience,' *American Journal of Psychotherapy* 40 (1986): 165–76.
13 H. Grunebaum, 'A study of therapists' choice of a therapist,' *American Journal of Psychiatry* 140 (1983): 1336–9.

7: Breaking the Silence

1 K.S. Pope, *Sexual Involvement with Therapists: Patient Assessment, Subsequent Therapy, Forensics* (Washington, DC: American Psychological Association, 1994), p. 25.
2 S.H. Kardener, M. Fuller, and I.N. Mensh, 'A survey of physicians' attitudes and practices regarding erotic and nonerotic contact with patients,' *American Journal of Psychiatry* 130 (1973): 1077–81.
3 P.S. Penfold and G.A. Walker, *Women and the Psychiatric Paradox* (Montreal: Eden Press, 1983). For a summary of the ideas in this book, see P.S. Penfold and G.A. Walker, 'The psychiatric paradox and women,' *Canadian Journal of Community Mental Health* 5, 2 (1986): 9–15.
4 U. Sreenivasen, 'Sexual exploitation of patients: The position of the Canadian Psychiatric Association,' *Canadian Journal of Psychiatry* 34 (1988): 234–5.

5 S. Penfold, 'Sexual abuse between therapist and woman patient,' *Canadian Woman Studies* 8, 4 (1987): 29–31.

6 M. Stainsby, 'Betrayal of trust: When the therapist wants sex,' *Vancouver Sun*, 16 Dec. 1989, pp. D16, D18.

7 P. Taylor, 'When seeking help brings additional grief,' *Globe and Mail*, 8 Oct. 1990, pp. A1, A4.

8 P.S. Penfold, 'Sexual abuse by therapists: Maintaining the conspiracy of silence,' *Canadian Journal of Community Mental Health* 11, 1 (1992): 5–15.

9 J.C. Bouhoutsos, 'Therapist–client sexual involvement: A challenge for mental health professionals and educators,' *American Journal of Orthopsychiatry* 55 (1985): 177–182.

10 J. Griffiths, *Fatal Prescription: A Doctor without Remorse* (Surrey, BC: Hancock House, 1995).

11 Noël, with Watterson, *You Must Be Dreaming* (New York: Poseidon Press, 1992), pp. 234, 238, 240.

12 T. Firsten and J. Wine, 'Sex exploitation of clients: Breaking the silence and exploding the myths,' *Canadian Woman Studies* 12, 1 (1990): 94–7.

13 N. Gartrell, J. Herman, S. Olarte, M. Feldstein, and R. Localio, 'Psychiatrist–patient sexual contact: Results of a national survey. I: Prevalence,' *American Journal of Psychiatry* 143, 9 (1986): 1126–31.

14 M.J. Lerner, *The Belief in a Just World: A Fundamental Delusion* (New York: Plenum Press, 1980), pp. 9–30.

15 An amazing example of this sleight of hand, of reinterpreting the outcome, is seen in the psychiatric literature where Clements states, 'Even if we accept the imaginary numbers of 5% to 13% [of psychiatrists sexually exploiting patients], that was quite a low incidence that the profession did not need to feel ashamed about, but rather proud of.' C.D. Clements, 'The transference: What's love got to do with it?' *Psychiatric Annals* 17 (1987): 556–63.

16 J.L. McCartney, 'Overt transference,' *Journal of Sex Research* 2, 3 (1966): 227–37; M. Shepard, *The Love Treatment: Sexual Intimacy between Patients and Psychotherapists* (New York: Wyden, 1971).

17 A. Carotenuto, *A Secret Symmetry: Sabina Spielrein between Jung and Freud*, trans. A. Pomerans, J. Shepley, and K. Winston (New York: Pantheon, 1982).

18 S. Freud, 'Further recommendations in the technique of psychoanalysis: Observations on transference-love,' in P. Reiff, ed., *Freud, Therapy and Technique* (New York: Collier Books, 1963), p. 169. Originally published in 1915.

19 S. Quinn, *A Mind of Her Own: The Life of Karen Horney*. Radcliffe Biography Series (Reading, Mass.: Addison-Wesley, 1988), p. 377.

20 C. Clements, 'Doctor's dilemma: Task force on sex is taking "hanging judge" approach,' *Medical Post*, 24 Sept. 1991, p. 18.

21 L. Freeman and J. Roy, *Betrayal* (New York: Stein and Day, 1976); S. Smith, 'The sexually abused patient and the abusing therapist: A study in sadomasochistic relationships,' *Psychoanalytic Psychology* 1, 2 (1984): 89–98; E. Plasil, *Therapist* (New York: St Martin's Press, 1985); E. LeBourdais, 'Case involving prominent B.C. psychiatrist puts the medical profession on trial,' *Canadian Medical Association Journal* 145, 5 (1991): 501–5.

22 R.W. Medlicott, 'Erotic professional indiscretions, actual or assumed, and alleged,' *Australian and New Zealand Journal of Psychiatry* 2 (1968): 17–23.

23 T.S. Gutheil, 'Borderline personality disorder, boundary violations, and patient–therapist sex: Medico-legal pitfalls,' *American Journal of Psychiatry* 146, 5 (1989): 597–602.

24 M. Carr and G.E. Robinson, 'Fatal attraction: The ethical and clinical dilemma of patient–therapist sex,' *Canadian Journal of Psychiatry* 35 (1990): 122–7.

25 Women and Mental Health Committee of the Canadian Mental Health Association, *Women's Voices Shall Be Heard: Report on the Sexual Abuse of Women* (Winnipeg: CMHA, June 1993), p. 22.

26 S. Faludi, *Backlash: The Undeclared War against American Women* (New York: Crown, 1991).

27 M.D. Yapko, *Suggestions of Abuse: True and False Memories of Childhood Sexual Trauma* (New York: Simon and Schuster, 1994); R. Ofshe and E. Watters, *Making Monsters: False Memories, Psychotherapy and Sexual Hysteria* (New York: Charles Scribner's Sons, 1994).

28 P.S. Penfold, 'Mendacious moms or devious dads? Some perplexing issues in child custody/sexual abuse allegation disputes,' *Canadian Journal of Psychiatry* 40 (1995): 337–41.

29 A. Stone, 'Sexual exploitation of patients in psychotherapy,' in A. Stone, ed., *Law, Psychiatry and Morality* (Washington, DC: American Psychiatric Press, 1984), pp. 191–216.

30 M.L. Carr, G. Erlick Robinson, D.E. Stewart, and D. Kussin, 'A survey of Canadian psychiatric residents regarding resident–educator sexual contact,' *American Journal of Psychiatry* 148, 2 (1991): 216–20; N. Gartrell, J. Herman, S. Olarte, R. Localio, and M. Feldstein, 'Psychiatric residents' sexual contact with educators and patients: Results of a national survey,' *American Journal of Psychiatry* 145, 6 (1988): 690–4; K.S. Pope, P.C. Keith-Speigel, and B.G. Tabachnick, 'Sexual attraction to clients: The human therapist and the (sometimes) inhuman training system,' *American Psychologist* 41 (1986): 147–58.

31 Pope et al., 'Sexual attraction to clients.'

32 R.T. Walsh, 'The dark side of our moon: The iatrogenic aspects of professional psychology,' *Journal of Community Psychology* 16 (1988): 244–8; P.S. Penfold and G.A. Walker, *Women and the Psychiatric Paradox* (Montreal:

Eden Press, 1983), pp. 35–56; M. Foucault, *Madness and Civilisation: A History of Insanity in the Age of Reason* (New York: Pantheon Books, 1965); I. Illich, *Limits to Medicine–Medical Nemesis: The Expropriation of Health* (Harmondsworth, England: Pelican Books, 1977).

33 P. Rutter, *Sex in the Forbidden Zone* (Los Angeles: Jeremy P. Tarcher, 1989), p. 63.

34 Pope, *Sexual Involvement with Therapists*, p. 87.

35 R. Ouston, 'Sexual abuse victim says doctors left her in legal and emotional limbo for 4 years,' *Vancouver Sun*, 19 March, 1994, p. A4.

36 U.S. Public Broadcasting Service, *My Doctor, My Lover*, 12 Nov. 1991.

37 Noël, with Watterson, *You Must Be Dreaming* (New York: Poseidon Press, 1992), p. 271.

38 Ibid., p. 174.

39 West Coast Women's Legal Education and Action Fund, *Leaflet* 5, 2 (1992): 1–2.

40 L. Still, 'Unscarred psychiatrist cleared in sexual abuse case,' *Vancouver Sun*, 15 Feb. 1995, p. B2.

41 M. McPhedran, 'The legal assault on physician–patient privilege,' *Canadian Medical Association Journal* 153 (1995): 1502–6.

42 M.G. Rhoades, 'Therapist–patient impropriety: Issues seldom discussed,' *News for Women in Psychiatry* (Dec. 1993): 5–6.

43 Noël, with Watterson, *You Must Be Dreaming*, p. 145.

44 J.L. Herman, *Trauma and Recovery* (New York: Basic Books, 1992), p. 189.

45 C.M. Battes and A.M. Brodsky, *Sex in the Therapy Hour: A Case of Professional Incest* (New York: Guilford Press, 1989), pp. 101–2.

46 W.L. Maurice, 'Physician sexual misconduct: Questions and answers,' *BC Medical Journal* 37 (1995): 630–3.

47 Pope, *Sexual Involvement with Therapists*, pp. 29–34.

48 A.A. Stone, 'No good deed goes unpunished,' *Psychiatric Times* (March 1990): 24–7.

8: Towards Less Abuse and More Healing

1 W.H. Masters and V.E. Johnson, *Human Sexual Inadequacy* (Boston: Little, Brown, 1970), p. 390.

2 S.H. Kardener, M. Fuller, and I.N. Mensh, 'A survey of physicians' attitudes and practices regarding erotic and non-erotic contact with patients,' *American Journal of Psychiatry* 130 (1973): 1077–81.

3 B. Noël, with K. Watterson, *You Must Be Dreaming* (New York: Poseidon Press, 1992), pp. 267–82; quote on p. 281.

4 W.L. Maurice, 'Physician sexual misconduct: Questions and answers,' *BC Medical Journal* 37 (1995): 630–3.

5 K.S. Pope and V.A. Vetter, 'Prior therapist–patient sexual involvement among patients seen by psychologists,' *Psychotherapy* 28 (1991): 429–38; J.S. Vinson, 'Use of complaint procedures in cases of therapist–patient sexual contact,' *Professional Psychology: Research and Practice* 18 (1987): 159–64.

6 M.J. Lerner, *The Belief in a Just World: A Fundamental Delusion* (New York: Plenum Press, 1980), pp. 9–30.

7 H.S. Strean, *Therapists Who Have Sex with Their Patients: Treatment and Recovery* (New York: Brunner/Mazel, 1993), pp. xii, 161. See also S.B. Levine, C.B. Risen, and S.E. Althof, 'Professionals who sexually offend: Evaluation procedures and preliminary findings,' *Journal of Sex and Marital Therapy* 20, 4 (1994): 288–302.

8 K.S. Pope, *Sexual Involvement with Therapists: Patient Assessment, Subsequent Therapy, Forensics* (Washington, DC: American Psychological Association, 1994), pp. 22–4, 40–1.

9 Women and Mental Health Committee of the Canadian Mental Health Association, *Women's Voices Shall Be Heard: Report on the Sexual Abuse of Women by Mental Health Service Providers* (Winnipeg: CMHA, June 1993), p. 26.

10 P.G.R. Patterson and S. Blackshaw, 'Abuse of patients by physicians,' *Medicine North America* (Oct. 1993): 721–4; G.A. Golden and M. Brennan, 'Managing erotic feelings in the physician–patient relationship,' *Canadian Medical Association Journal* 153 (1995): 1241–5.

11 G. Gallop, 'Sexual contact between patients and nurses,' *Canadian Nurse* (Feb. 1993): 28–31.

12 L.S. Brown, 'Beyond thou shalt not: Thinking about ethics in the lesbian therapy community,' *Women and Therapy* 8, nos. 1, 2 (1988): 13–25: N.K. Gartrell and B.E. Sanderson, 'Sexual abuse by women in psychotherapy: Counseling and advocacy,' *Women and Therapy* 15, 1 (1994): 39–54.

13 N.K. Gartrel, 'Boundaries in lesbian therapy relationships,' *Women and Therapy* 12, 3 (1992): 29–50.

14 S.L. Blackshaw and P.G.R. Patterson, 'The prevention of sexual exploitation of patients: Educational issues,' *Canadian Journal of Psychiatry* 37 (1992): 350–3.

15 Pope, *Sexual Involvement with Therapists*, pp. 35–6.

16 H.J. Bursztajn and T.G. Gutheil, 'Protecting patients from clinician–patient sexual contact,' *American Journal of Psychiatry* 149 (1992): 1276–81.

17 Pope, *Sexual Involvement with Therapists*, p. 43.

18 K.S. Pope and V.A. Vetter, 'Prior therapist–patient sexual involvement among patients seen by psychologists,' *Psychotherapy* 28 (1991): 429–38.

19 S.B. Bisbing, L.M. Jorgenson, and P.K. Sutherland, *Sexual abuse by professionals: A legal guide* (Charlottesville, Va.: The Michie Company, 1995), p. 451, n16.
20 Ibid., pp. 447–83.
21 Women and Mental Health Committee of CMHA, *Women's Voices*, pp. 25–6.
22 P.S. Penfold, 'The repressed memory controversy: Is there middle ground?' *Canadian Medical Association Journal* 155 (1996): 647–53. Some interesting new ideas are provided by J. Freyd in *Betrayal Trauma* (Cambridge: Harvard University Press, 1996). She postulates that victims of incestuous child sexual abuse may lose memories of the abuse because they have to maintain their attachment to, and reliance on, the abuser.

References

Alexander, R. *Folie à Deux: An Experience of One-to-One Therapy*. London: Free Association Books, 1995.

Appel, J.W., and G.W. Bebe. 'Preventive psychiatry: an epidemiological approach.' *Journal of the American Medical Association* 131 (1946): 1468–71.

American Psychiatric Association. *Diagnostic and Statistical Manual of Mental Disorders*. 3rd ed. Washington, DC: American Psychiatric Association, 1980.

– *Diagnostic and Statistical Manual of Mental Disorders*. 4th ed. Washington, DC: American Psychiatric Association, 1994.

Arieti, S. *Interpretation of Schizophrenia*. New York: Brunner, 1955.

Armsworth, M.W. 'Therapy of incest survivors: Abuse or support?' *Child Abuse and Neglect* 13 (1989): 549–62.

Atwood, M. *The Handmaid's Tale*. Toronto: Seal Books, 1985.

Bates, C.M., and A.M. Brodsky. *Sex in the Therapy Hour: A Case of Professional Incest*. New York: Guilford Press, 1989.

Berger, E., and N. Staisey. 'Initial analysis of a survey of Ontario women regarding sexual harassment and abuse by Ontario physicians.' *Canada Health Monitor Report*, 27 Oct. 1991.

Bisbing, S.B., L.M. Jorgenson, and P.K. Sutherland. *Sexual Abuse by Professionals: A Legal Guide*. Charlottesville, Va.: The Michie Company, 1995.

Blackshaw, S.L., and Paul G.R. Patterson. 'The prevention of sexual exploitation of patients: Educational issues.' *Canadian Journal of Psychiatry* 37 (1992): 350–3.

Bouhoutsos, J.C. 'Therapist-client sexual involvement: A challenge for mental health professionals and educators.' *American Journal of Orthopsychiatry* 55 (1985): 177–82.

Bouhoutsos J.C., J. Holdroyd, H. Lerman, B. Forer, and M. Greenberg. 'Sexual intimacy between psychotherapists and patients.' *Professional Psychology: Research and Practice* 14 (1983): 185–96.

Bowker L.H. *Beating Wife-Beating*. Lexington, Mass.: Lexington Books, 1983.
Breuer, J., and S. Freud. *Studies on Hysteria (1893–1895)*. In *Standard Edition of the Works of Sigmund Freud*. Vol. 2, pp. 1–319. Trans. by J. Strachey. London: Hogarth Press, 1955.
Briquet, P. *Traite de l'hystérie*. Paris: J.B. Bailliere, 1859.
British Columbia College of Physicians and Surgeons. Committee on Physician Sexual Misconduct. *Crossing the Boundaries: Executive Summary*. Vancouver, BC, November 1992.
Brown, L.S. 'Beyond thou shalt not: Thinking about ethics in the lesbian community.' *Women and Therapy* 8, nos. 1, 2 (1989): 13–25.
Bursztajn, H.J., and T.G. Gutheil. 'Protecting patients from clinician–patient sexual contact.' *American Journal of Psychiatry* 149 (1992): 1276–81.
Butler, S., and S.L. Zelen. 'Sexual intimacies between therapists and patients.' *Psychotherapy: Theory, Research and Practice* 14, 2 (1977): 139–45.
Canadian Medical Association. 'Policy Summary: The patient–physician relationship and the sexual abuse of patients.' *Canadian Medical Association Journal* 150, 1 (1994): 1884A–C.
Carotenuto, A. *A secret symmetry: Sabina Spielrein between Jung and Freud*. Trans. A. Pomerans, J. Shepley, and K. Winston. New York: Pantheon, 1982.
Carr, M.L., and G. Erlick Robinson. 'Fatal attraction: The ethical and clinical dilemma of patient–therapist sex.' *Canadian Journal of Psychiatry* 35 (1990): 122–7.
Carr M.L., G. Erlick Robinson, D.E. Stewart, and D. Kussin. 'A survey of Canadian psychiatric residents regarding resident–educator sexual contact.' *American Journal of Psychiatry* 148 (1991): 216–20.
Chesler, P. *Women and Madness*. New York: Avon Books, 1972.
Clements, C.D. 'The transference: What's love got to do with it?' *Psychiatric Annals* 17 (1987): 556–63.
– 'Doctor's dilemma: Task force on sex is taking "hanging judge" approach.' *Medical Post*, 24 Sept. 1991, p 18.
College of Physicians and Surgeons of Ontario. *Final Report: Task Force on Sexual Abuse of Patients*. Toronto: College of Physicians and Surgeons of Ontario, 1991.
Collins, D.T. 'Sexual involvement between psychiatric hospital staff and their patients.' In G.O. Gabbard, ed., *Sexual Exploitation in Professional Relationships*, pp. 151–62. Washington, DC: American Psychiatric Press, 1989.
Conroy, P. *The Prince of Tides*. New York: Bantam Books, 1987.
DeYoung, M. 'Case reports: The sexual exploitation of incest victims by health professionals.' *Victimology* 6 (1981): 92–101.
Dutton, D., and S.L. Painter. 'Traumatic bonding: The development of emotional

attachment in battered women and other relationships of intermittent abuse.' *Victimology* 6 (1981): 139–55.

Dziech, B.W., and L. Weiner. *The Lecherous Professor: Sexual Harassment on Campus.* Boston: Beacon Press, 1984.

Edelstein, L. *The Hippocratic Oath: Text, Translation and Interpretation.* Baltimore: Johns Hopkins University Press, 1943.

Epstein, R.S., and R.I. Simon. 'The exploitation index: An early warning indicator of boundary violations in psychotherapy.' *Bulletin of the Menninger Clinic* 54 (1990): 450–65.

Faludi, S. *Backlash: The Undeclared War against American Women.* New York: Crown, 1991.

Feldman-Summers, S., and G. Jones. 'Psychological impacts of sexual contact between therapists or other health care practitioners and their clients.' *Journal of Consulting and Clinical Psychology* 52, 6 (1984): 1054–61.

Firsten, T. and J. Wine. 'Sex exploitation of clients: Breaking the silence and exploding the myths.' *Canadian Woman Studies* 12, 1 (1990): 94–7.

Fitzgerald, F.S. *Tender Is the Night.* New York: Charles Scribner's Sons, 1933.

Foucault, M. *Madness and Civilisation: A History of Insanity in the Age of Reason.* New York: Pantheon Books, 1965.

Freeman, L., and J. Roy. *Betrayal.* New York: Stein and Day, 1976.

Freud, S. *An Outline of Psychoanalysis.* New York: Norton, 1949.

– 'Further recommendations in the technique of psychoanalysis: Observations on transference-love.' In P. Reiff, ed., *Freud, Therapy and Technique*, p. 169. New York: Collier Books, 1963.

Gabbard, G.O., ed. *Sexual Exploitation in Professional Relationships.* Washington, DC: American Psychiatric Press, 1989.

Gallop, G. 'Sexual contact between patients and nurses.' *Canadian Nurse* (Feb. 1993): 28–31.

Gartrell, N. 'Boundaries in lesbian therapy relationships.' *Women and Therapy* 12, 3 (1992): 29–50.

Gartrell, N., J. Herman, S. Olarte, M. Feldstein, and R. Localio. 'Psychiatrist–patient sexual contact: Results of a national survey. I: Prevalence.' *American Journal of Psychiatry* 143 (1986): 1126–31.

– 'Reporting practices of psychiatrists who knew of sexual misconduct by colleagues.' *American Journal of Orthopsychiatry* 57, 2 (1987): 287–95.

– 'Psychiatric residents' sexual contact with educators and patients: Results of a national survey.' *American Journal of Psychiatry* 145, 6 (1988): 690–4.

Gartrell, N.K., and B.E. Sanderson. 'Sexual abuse of women by women in psychotherapy: Counseling and advocacy.' *Women and Therapy* 15, 1 (1994): 39–54.

Garrett, T., and J. Davis. 'Epidemiology in the UK.' In D. Jehu, ed., *Patients as Victims*, pp. 37–57. Chichester, England: John Wiley & Sons, 1994.

Gechtman, L. 'Sexual contact between social workers and their clients.' In G.O. Gabbard, ed., *Sexual Exploitation in Professional Relationships*, pp. 27–38. Washington, DC: American Psychiatric Press, 1989.

Gilligan, C. *In a Different Voice*. Cambridge, Mass.: Harvard University Press, 1982.

Golden, G.A., and M. Brennan. 'Managing erotic feelings in the physician–patient relationship.' *Canadian Medical Association Journal* 153 (1995): 1241–5.

Greenberg, R.P., S. Fisher, and J. Shapiro. 'Sex role development and response to medication by psychiatric inpatients.' *Psychological Reports* 33 (1973): 675–7.

Greer, G. *The Female Eunuch*. St Albans, England: Paladin, 1971.

Griffiths, J. *Fatal Prescription: A Doctor without Remorse*. Surrey, B.C.: Hancock House, 1995.

Grunebaum, H. 'A study of therapists' choice of a therapist.' *American Journal of Psychiatry* 140 (1983): 1336–9.

– 'Harmful psychotherapy experience.' *American Journal of Psychotherapy* 40 (1986): 165–76.

Gutheil, T.S., 'Borderline personality disorder, boundary violations, and patient–therapist sex: Medico-legal pitfalls.' *American Journal of Psychiatry* 146, 5 (1989): 597–602.

Gutheil, T.S., and G.O. Gabbard. 'The concept of boundaries in clinical practice: theoretical and risk-management dimensions.' *American Journal of Psychiatry* 150, 2 (1993): 188–96.

Hearst, P.C. and A. Moscow *Every Secret Thing*. New York: Doubleday, 1982.

Herman, J.L. *Trauma and Recovery*. New York: Basic Books, 1992.

Heyward, C. *When Boundaries Betray Us*. San Francisco: Harper, 1993.

Horton, A.L., and B. Johnson. 'Profiles and strategies of women who have ended abuse.' *Families in Society* 74 (1993): 481–92.

Horwitz, A. 'The pathways into psychiatric treatment: Some differences between men and women.' *Journal of Health and Social Behaviour* (June 1977): 169–78.

Hyde, C. *Abuse of Trust: The Career of Dr James Tyhurst*. Vancouver: Douglas and McIntyre, 1991.

Illich, I. *Limits to Medicine – Medical Nemesis: The Expropriation of Health*. Harmondsworth, England: Pelican Books, 1977.

Janet, P. *L'Automatisme psychologique: Essai de psychologie experimentale sur les formes inférieures de l'activité humaine*. Paris: Felix Alcan, 1989; Paris: Société Pierre Janet/Payot, 1973.

Jay, J. 'Terrible knowledge.' *Family Therapy Networker* (Nov/Dec 1991): 18–29.

Jehu, D. *Patients as Victims*. Chichester, England: John Wiley and Sons, 1994.

Jorgenson, L., and A. Hirsch. 'Sexual contact between dentist and patient: Is dating ethical?' *CDS Review* (August 1994): 24–7.

Kardener, S.H. 'Sex and the physician–patient relationship.' *American Journal of Psychiatry* 131, 10 (1974): 1134–6.

Kardener, S.H., M. Fuller, and I.N. Mensh. 'A survey of physicians' attitudes and practices regarding erotic and non-erotic contact with patients.' *American Journal of Psychiatry* 130 (1973): 1077–81.

Kardiner, A. 'Traumatic neurosis of war.' In S. Arieti, ed., *American Handbook of Psychiatry*, pp. 245–57. New York: Basic Books, 1959.

Karen, R. 'Shame.' *Atlantic Monthly* (Feb. 1992): 40–70.

Kaschak, E. *Engendered Lives*. New York: Basic Books, 1992.

Kelly, W.E., ed. *Post-Traumatic Stress Disorder and the War Veteran Patient*. New York: Brunner/Mazel, 1985.

Kluft, R.P. 'Therapy of incest survivors: Abuse or support?' *Child Abuse and Neglect* 13 (1989): 549–62.

– 'Incest and subsequent revictimisation: The case of therapist–patient sexual exploitation, with a description of the sitting-duck syndrome.' In R.P. Kluft, ed., *Incest-Related Syndromes of Adult Psychopathology*, pp. 263–87. Washington, DC: American Psychiatric Press, 1990.

Krugman, S. 'Trauma in the family: Perspectives on intergenerational transmission of violence.' In B. Van der Kolk, ed. *Psychological Trauma*, p. 135. Washington, DC: American Psychiatric Press, 1987.

Krystal H. 'Trauma and affects.' *Psychoanalytic Study of the Child* 33 (1978): 81–116.

Lamont, J.A., and C. Woodward. 'Patient–physician sexual involvement: A Canadian survey of obstetrician-gynecologists.' *Canadian Medical Association Journal* 150 (1994): 1433–9.

LeBourdais, E. 'Case involving prominent B.C. psychiatrist puts the medical profession on trial.' *Canadian Medical Association Journal* 145, 5 (1991): 501–5.

Lecovin, K., and P.S. Penfold. 'The emotionally abused woman: An existential-phenomenological exploration.' *Canadian Journal of Community Mental Health* 15, 1 (1996): 39–48.

Leri, A. *Shellshock: Commotional and Emotional Aspects*. London: University of London Press, 1919.

Lerner, M.J. *The Belief in a Just World: A Fundamental Delusion*. New York: Plenum Press, 1980.

Levi, P. *Survival in Auschwitz: The Nazi Assault on Humanity*. New York: Collier, 1961.

Levine, S.B., C.B. Risen, and S.E. Althof. 'Professionals who sexually offend:

Evaluation procedures and preliminary findings.' *Journal of Sex and Marital Therapy* 20, 4 (1994): 288–302.

Loftus, E.F. 'The reality of repressed memories.' *American Psychologist* 48, 5 (1993): 518–53.

Loftus, E., and K. Ketcham. *The Myth of Repressed Memory*. New York: St Martin's Press, 1994.

Lovelace, L., and M. McGrady. *Ordeal*. Secaucus, NJ: Citadel, 1980.

Mann, C.K., and J.D. Winer. 'Psychotherapists' sexual contact with clients.' *American Jurisprudence Proof of Facts*. 3rd series, vol. 14, pp. 319–431. Rochester, NY: Lawyers Cooperative Publishing, 1991.

Margittai, K.J., R. Moscarello, and M.F. Rossi. 'Medical students' experiences of abuse: A Canadian perspective.' *Annals of the Royal College of Physicians and Surgeons of Canada* 27 (1994): 199–204.

Marmor, J. 'Some psychodynamic aspects of the seduction of patients in psychotherapy.' *American Journal of Psychoanalysis* 36 (1976): 319–23.

Masson, J.M. *The Assault on Truth: Freud's Suppression of the Seduction Theory*. New York: Farrar, Straus and Giroux, 1984.

Masters, W.H., and V.E. Johnson. *Human Sexual Inadequacy*. Boston: Little, Brown, 1970.

– 'Principles of the new sex therapy.' *American Journal of Psychiatry* 133 (1976): 548–54.

Matsakis, A. *I Can't Get Over It: A Handbook for Trauma Survivors*. Oakland, Calif.: New Harbinger, 1992.

Maurice, W.L. 'Physician sexual misconduct: Questions and answers.' *BC Medical Journal* 37 (1995): 630–3.

McCartney, J.L. 'Overt transference.' *Journal of Sex Research* 2, 3 (1966): 227–37.

McKegney, C.P. 'Medical education: A neglectful and abusive family system.' *Family Medicine* 21 (1989) : 452–7.

McPhedran, M. 'The legal assault on physician–patient privilege.' *Canadian Medical Association Journal* 153 (1995): 1502–6.

Medlicott, R.W. 'Erotic professional indiscretions, actual or assumed, and alleged.' *Australian and New Zealand Journal of Psychiatry* 2 (1968): 17–23.

Miller, A. *Thou Shalt Not Be Aware: Society's Betrayal of the Child*. New York: Farrar, Straus and Giroux, 1984.

Miller, J.B. *Toward a New Psychology of Women*, 2nd ed. Boston, Mass.: Beacon Press, 1986.

Moscarello, R. 'Victims of violence: Aspects of the "victim-to-patient" process in women.' *Canadian Journal of Psychiatry* 37 (1992): 497–502.

Munsat, E.M., and J.J. Riordan. 'Prevalence of staff–patient sexual interactions on inpatient units.' *Journal of Psychosocial Nursing* 28 (1990): 23–6.

Murray, J.B. 'Relationship of childhood sexual abuse to borderline personality disorder.' *Journal of Psychology* 127, 6 (1993): 657–76.

Nathanson, D.L. 'Understanding what is hidden: Shame in sexual abuse.' In R.P. Kluft, ed., *Treatment of Victims of Sexual Abuse. Psychiatric Clinics of North America* 12, 2 (1989): 381–8.

Noël, B., and K. Watterson. *You Must Be Dreaming*. New York: Poseidon Press, 1992.

Ofshe, R., and E. Watters. *Making Monsters: False Memories, Psychotherapy and Sexual Hysteria*. New York: Charles Scribner's Sons, 1994.

Orwell, G. *Nineteen Eighty-four*. New York: Harcourt, Brace, 1949.

Ouston, R. 'Sexual abuse victim says doctors left her in legal and emotional limbo for 4 years.' *Vancouver Sun*, 19 March 1994, p. A4.

Patterson, P.G.R., and S. Blackshaw. 'Abuse of patients by physicians.' *Medicine North America* (Oct. 1993): 721–4.

Pearlman, S.F. 'Lesbian clients/lesbian therapists: Necessary conversations.' In N.D. Davis, E. Cole, and E.D. Rothblum, eds., *Lesbian Therapists and Their Therapy*, p. 77. New York: Harrington Park Press, 1996.

Penfold, P.S. 'Sexual abuse between therapist and woman patient.' *Canadian Woman Studies* 8, 4 (1987): 29–31.

– 'Sexual abuse by therapists: maintaining the conspiracy of silence.' *Canadian Journal of Community Mental Health* 11, 1 (1992): 5–15.

– 'Mendacious moms or devious dads? Some perplexing issues in child custody/ sexual abuse allegation disputes.' *Canadian Journal of Psychiatry* 40 (1995): 337–41.

– 'The repressed memory controversy: Is there middle ground?' *Canadian Medical Association Journal* 155, 6 (1996): 647–53.

Penfold, P.S., and G.A. Walker. *Women and the Psychiatric Paradox*. Montreal: Eden Press, 1983.

– 'The psychiatric paradox and women.' *Canadian Journal of Community Mental Health* 5, 2 (1986): 9–15.

Pennebaker, J., and J.R. Susman. 'Disclosure of traumas and psychosomatic processes.' *Social Sciences and Medicine* 26 (1988): 327–32.

Perry, J.A. 'Physicians' erotic and nonerotic physical involvement with patients.' *American Journal of Psychiatry* 133 (1976): 838–40.

Peterson, M.R. *At Personal Risk: Boundary Violations in Professional–Client Relationships*. New York: W.W. Norton, 1992.

Plasil, E. *Therapist*. New York: St Martin's Press, 1985.

Pope, K.S., *Sexual Involvement with Therapists: Patient Assessment, Subsequent Therapy, Forensics*. Washington, DC: American Psychological Association, 1994.

Pope, K.S., and J.C. Bouhoutsos. *Sexual Intimacy between Therapists and Patients.* New York: Praeger, 1986.

Pope, K.S., P.C. Keith-Speigel, and B.G. Tabachnick. 'Sexual attraction to clients: The human therapist and the (sometimes) inhuman training system.' *American Psychologist* 41 (1986): 147–58.

Pope, K.S., H. Levenson, and L. Schover. 'Sexual intimacy in psychology training programs: Results and implications of a national survey.' *American Psychologist* 34 (1979): 682–9.

Pope, K.S., and V.A. Vetter. 'Prior therapist–patient sexual involvement among patients seen by psychologists.' *Psychotherapy* 28 (1991): 429–38.

Quadrio, C. 'Sexual abuse in therapy: Gender issues.' *Australian and New Zealand Journal of Psychiatry* 30 (1996): 124–33.

Quinn, S. *A Mind of Her Own: The Life of Karen Horney.* Radcliffe Biography Series. Reading, Mass.: Addison-Wesley, 1988.

Rapp, M.S. 'Sexual misconduct.' *Canadian Medical Association Journal* 137 (1987): 193–4.

Reiser, D.E., and H. Levenson. 'Abuses of the borderline diagnosis: A clinical problem with teaching opportunities.' *American Journal of Psychiatry* 141 (1984): 1528–32.

Rhoades, M.G. 'Therapist–patient impropriety: Issues seldom discussed.' *News for Women in Psychiatry* (Dec. 1993): 5–6.

Ross, C.A. 'Errors of logic in biological psychiatry.' In C.A. Rose and A. Pam, eds., *Pseudoscience in Biological Psychiatry: Blaming the Body.* New York: John Wiley and Sons, 1995.

Roy, J., and L. Freeman. *Betrayal.* New York: Pocket Books, 1976.

Rutter, P. *Sex in the Forbidden Zone.* Los Angeles: Jeremy P. Tarcher, 1989.

Schoener, G.R., and J.H. Milgrom. 'Helping clients who have been sexually abused by therapists.' In P.A. Keller and S.R. Heyman, eds., *Innovations in Clinical Practice: A Source Book,* vol. 6, pp. 407–16. N.p.: 1987.

Schoener, G.R., and J. Gonsoriek. 'Assessment and development of rehabilitation plans for counsellors who have sexually exploited their clients.' *Journal of Counselling and Development* 67 (Dec. 1988): 227–32.

Schoener, G.R., and E.T. Luepker. 'Boundaries in group therapy: Ethical and practice issues.' In B. Dechant, ed., *Women and Group Psychotherapy.* New York: Guilford Press, 1996.

Schoener, G.R., Milgrom, J.H., Gonsoriek, J.C., Luepker E.T., and R.M. Conroe. *Psychotherapists' Sexual Involvement with Clients: Intervention and Prevention.* Minneapolis: Walk-In Counselling Center, 1989.

Seligman, M.E.P. *Helplessness: On Depression, Development and Death.* San Francisco: W.H. Freeman, 1975.

Shengold, L. *Soul Murder: The Effects of Childhood Abuse and Deprivation.* New Haven: Yale University Press, 1989.

Shepard, M. *The Love Treatment: Sexual Intimacy between Patients and Psychotherapists.* New York: Wyden, 1971.

Simmons, D. 'Gender issues and borderline personality disorder: Why do females dominate the diagnosis?' *Archives of Psychiatric Nursing* 6, 4 (1992): 219–23.

Smith, S. 'The sexually abused patient and the abusing therapist: A study in sadomasochistic relationships.' *Psychoanalytic Psychology* 1, 2 (1984): 89–98.

Sonne, J., B. Meyer, D. Borys, and V. Marshall. 'Clients' reactions to sexual intimacy in therapy.' *American Journal of Orthopsychiatry* 55 (1985): 183–9.

Speigel, D. 'Dissociative disorders.' In R.E. Hales, S.C. Yodofsky, and J.A. Talbott, eds., *The American Psychiatric Press Textbook of Psychiatry*, pp. 633–52. Washington, DC: American Psychiatric Press, 1994.

Sreenivasen, U. 'Sexual exploitation of patients: The position of the Canadian Psychiatric Association.' *Canadian Journal of Psychiatry* 34 (1988): 234–5.

Stainsby, M. 'Betrayal of trust: When the therapist wants sex.' *Vancouver Sun*, 16 Dec. 1989, pp. D16, D18.

Still, L. 'Unscarred psychiatrist cleared in sexual abuse case.' *Vancouver Sun*, 15 February 1995, p. B2.

Stone, A.A. 'No good deed goes unpunished.' *Psychiatric Times* (Mar. 1990): 24–7.

Stone, A. *Law, Psychiatry and Morality: Essays and Analysis.* Washington, DC: American Psychiatric Press, 1984.

– 'Sexual exploitation of patients in psychotherapy.' In A. Stone, ed., *Law, Psychiatry and Morality: Essays and Analysis*, pp. 191–216. Washington, DC: American Psychiatric Press, 1984.

Stone, M. 'Boundary violations between therapist and patient.' *Psychiatric Annals* 6, 12 (1976): 670–7.

Strean, H.S. *Therapists Who Have Sex with Their Patients: Treatment and Recovery.* New York: Brunner/Mazel, 1993.

Summit, R.C. 'The child sexual abuse accommodation syndrome.' *Journal of Child Abuse and Neglect* 7 (1983): 177–93.

Summit, R.C., and J.A. Kryso. 'Sexual abuse of children: A clinical spectrum.' *American Journal of Orthopsychiatry* 48 (1978): 237–51.

Taylor, P. 'When seeking help brings additional grief.' *Globe and Mail*, 8 Oct. 1990, pp. A1, A4.

U.S. Public Broadcasting Service. *My Doctor, My Lover.* 12 November 1991.

Van der Kolk, B.A. 'Compulsion to repeat the trauma.' In R.P. Kluft, ed., *Treatment of Victims of Sexual Abuse. Psychiatric Clinics of North America* 12, 2 (1989): 389–411.

Vinson, J.S. 'Use of complaint procedures in cases of therapist–patient sexual contact.' *Professional Psychology: Research and Practice* 18 (1987): 159–64.

Walker, E., and T.D. Young. *A Killing Cure*. New York: Holt, Rinehart and Winston, 1986.

Walker, L. *The Battered Woman*. New York: Harper and Row, 1979.

Walsh, R.T. 'The dark side of our moon: The iatrogenic aspects of professional psychology.' *Journal of Community Psychology* 16 (1988): 244–8.

West Coast Women's Legal Education and Action Fund. *Leaflet* 5, 2 (1992): 1–2.

Wiesel, E. *Night*. New York: Hill and Wang, 1960.

Wilson, J.P., Z. Harel, and B. Kahana, eds., *Human Adaptation to Extreme Stress: From the Holocaust to Vietnam*. New York: Plenum, 1988.

Women and Mental Health Committee of the Canadian Mental Health Association, Manitoba Division. *Women's Voices Shall Be Heard: Report on the Sexual Abuse of Women by Mental Health Service Providers*. Winnipeg: CMHA, 1993.

Yapko, M.D. *Suggestions of Abuse: True and False Memories of Childhood Sexual Trauma*. New York: Simon and Schuster, 1994.

Index

ambivalence about abuser, 123–4
American Psychiatric Association Diag-
nostic and Statistical Manual III, 22
American Psychiatric Association Diag-
nostic and Statistical Manual IV, 22–4
anger, 126
anti-social personality disorder, 23,
  39
archetypes, 82
Armsworth, Mary, 34, 86–7
attachment theory, 85–6

Bates, Carolyn, 33, 50, 76, 96, 99, 103,
  130–1, 177
battered women, 80, 102
borderline personality disorder: diagnostic criteria, 24; earlier usage,
  25; inviting abuse, 170–1; misuse
  of diagnosis, 24, 119
boundaries in health professional–
  patient relationships, 19
boundary disturbance following
  abuse, 128–9
boundary violations, 84–5; characteristics of, 19, 55–6; double-binds in,
  85; and indulgence of professional
  privilege, 84; non-sexual, 54; role

reversal in, 84; scenarios leading
  to abuse, 57–8; secrecy in, 84–5
Breuer, Joseph, 15, 168
Butler, Sandra, 140

Canada Health Monitor Study, 9–10
Canadian Health Alliance to Stop
  Therapists Exploitation Now
  (CHASTEN), 195
Canadian Medical Protective Association, 178
captivity: extreme stress in, 102–3;
  psychological equivalent of, 103
Charalambous, Josephakis, 163
childhood sexual abuse: as a risk factor, 34, 59–63; traumatic bonding
  in survivors of, 80
cognitive dysfunction, 129–30; attention difficulties, 129; poor concentration, 129
College of Physicians and Surgeons
  of Ontario: *Canada Health Monitor*
  Study, 9–10; levels of impropriety,
  20
Committee on Physician Sexual Misconduct of the B.C. College of
  Physicians and Surgeons, 10, 11

compensation, lack of, 190–1
complaints: obstacles to making, 173; victim-blaming in, 174
confusion, sexual, 126–7
consent, mutual, 53, 169, 175
consumer expectations, 195
countertransference, 21–2
courts. *See* legal system, malpractice suits
cycle of violence, 80

decompensation: of childhood trauma victims, 62: and emergence of post-traumatic stress disorder symptoms, 62
denial by health professionals: of abuse, 8–9, 166–73; allegations of mutual consent in, 53, 169; 'bad apple' theory in, 169–70; and effectiveness of self-policing, 172; of sexual feelings, 171; victim-blaming in, 170–1
disclosure: consequences of, 163–4; by victims who are health professionals, 164
double-bind in boundary violations, 85
DSM III and *DSM IV*, 22–4

education of health professionals, 192–4
education, public, 195
emptiness, 124–5
enslavement. *See* trapped in abusive relationships
entitlement: in boundary violations, 84; to exploit patients, 42
escape from abusive relationships, 102–3; inner struggle in, 102; phases of, 102

ethical codes of health professional organizations, 17. *See also* licensing bodies
exploitation index for therapists, 57

false allegations, 171, 195
false memories of childhood abuse, 17, 196
fiduciary relationship, 19
Freud, Sigmund, 15, 168

gag order, 178
grief, 147
grooming for sex, 50–4; and increased risk for childhood abuse victims, 59–63; manifestations of, 55–6; ten common scenarios of, 57–8
guilt: definition of, 130; resulting from sexual abuse, 121–2, 151

Herman, Judith, 15, 34, 62–3, 86, 102, 146–8, 177
Horney, Karen, 168
hyperarousal in chronic trauma, 81
hysteria, 15, 17; new diagnostic concepts of, 17; pejorative use of, 119

incest victim: reliving abuse by, 63; revictimization of, 63; seen as publicly deflowered, 61. *See also* childhood sexual abuse
inquiry committees: biases of, 173; composition of, 193–4; process of, 173–4
insurance, malpractice, 178
isolation, 124–5

Jung, Carl, 168

Kluft, Richard, 34, 63

legal system, 174–9; consent, 175; defence strategies, 175–6; education of
practitioners in, 194–5; revictimization by, 178–9, 195; victim-blaming
in, 174–6
Lerner, Melvin, 166–7
lesbian health professionals: boundary
problems in, 40–1; education of,
193; reluctance to confront abusers,
43
licensing bodies, 17–18; assumptions
about rehabilitation, 194; education
of, 194
losses suffered by victims, 12–13, 113,
147

malpractice insurance, 178
malpractice suits: defence strategies
in, 176; obstacles in, 176–7. *See also*
legal system
Masserman, Jules. *See* Noël, Barbara
Matsakis, Aphrodite, 116, 120, 144–5
men's socialization, 39–40, 74
Mesmer, Anton, 168
Minneapolis Walk-In Counselling
Center, 11, 38, 140
mood swings, 125–6
mourning of losses, 146–7

narcissistic personality disorder, 23–4,
39
Noël, Barbara, 33, 42, 54, 75–6, 96, 99,
103, 129, 130, 163, 177, 183
Norberg v *Wynrib*, 175
numbness, 124–5

objectivity of health professionals,
172, 175
obstacles to healing, 148–51; conspiracy of silence creating, 150; shame,

149; for survivors who are health
professionals, 151

personality disorder: anti-social personality, 23, 39; borderline personality disorder, 24; definition, 23;
narcissistic personality disorder,
23–4, 39
Peterson, Marilyn, 43, 84–5
physician–patient sexual relationships,
historical aspects, 168
Plasil, Ellen, 32–3, 43, 50, 59, 74–5,
95–6, 99–100, 103–4
Pope, Kenneth, 40, 121–9, 147
post-traumatic stress disorder (PTSD),
22–3, 115–16; characteristics of, 16,
22, 115; controversies about, 17;
delayed onset of, 115; diagnosis
aids understanding of survivors,
115; diagnostic criteria of, 22; recur-
rence of symptoms of, 140, 148;
self-help for, 144–5; in wartime, 115
power: in abusive relationships, 39;
conferred by status, 44; differen-
tials in society, 196
prohibitions, may be unfair in some
circumstances, 11
prominent health professionals: abusing patients, 10–11; reluctance to
confront, 43; viewed with reverence, 42
psychotherapy, definition, 20. *See also*
therapy

reconnection, 147–8
rehabilitation of offenders, 194
reporting sexual abuse, by health professionals, 8
research studies, 7–11; case studies of
abusive professionals, 189; claim-

ing positive benefits of erotic
practices, 7, 8, 53; consumer survey,
9–10; educator–student sexual
involvement, 40; false allegations,
195; female–female sexual contact,
11; gender differences, 7–10; hospital staff, 9; motivation of offender,
8; obstetrician–gynaecologists, 10;
offenders' referral practices, 8;
physicians, 7, 10; psychiatrists, 8,
37; psychologists, 7, 9, 37; social
workers, 9; victims who are health
professionals, 164; victim's suicide,
128
revictimization: by the legal system,
178–9, 195; role of childhood abuse
in, 34
risk factors, health professional, 36–41;
deficiencies in training, 40; life
crises, 36; male socialization, 39–40;
masculine woundedness, 39
risk factors, patient, 32–6; family background, 32; gender issues, 34; illness, 33–4; life crises, 33; minority
group membership, 40; rationalization of, 34; women's socialization, 82–3
role of health professionals. See status
of health professionals
role reversal: following abuse, 128–9;
in boundary violations, 84
Roy, Julie, 51, 96–7, 117, 126, 127
Rutter, Peter, 39, 81–2

sadism, by therapist, 37–8
Schoener, Gary, 11, 34, 38, 113–14
secondary victims of abusive professionals, 113–14
secondary wounding, 116–17
secrecy, 84–5

self-help, 144–5, 190
services provided by mental health
professionals, 18
settlement, 177
sexual confusion, 126–7
shame: as a silencer, 150; definition
of, 130; as an obstacle to healing,
13, 149
Shengold, Leonard, 79
slippery slope for professionals, 53
socialization: men's, 39–40, 74;
women's, 42–3, 82–3, 126
soul murder, 79
status of health professionals, 41–4;
and compliance, 12, 44; and entitlement, 42; power associated with,
12, 42, 44; spiritual dimensions of,
43; trust generated by, 41–2
Stone, Alan, 171, 178
suicide, 13, 128
survivors who are health professionals, 151; benefits for, 152; obstacles
to disclosure for, 164; obstacles to
healing for, 151
symbiosis, 86

Therapist Abuse Action Group (TAAG),
139, 157, 159, 172
therapist–patient sex syndrome, 121–9
therapy, 145–8; assessment, 146;
boundaries in, 146; choice by mental health professional, 152; definition of, 20; grief in, 147; mourning
in, 147; phases of, 145–8; self-help,
144–5; shame in, 147; understanding current relationships in, 147
training: and abuse of patients, 10; of
health professionals, 17–18; program deficiencies, 40; of psychiatrists, 18; of psychologists, 18;

sexual exploitation of students in, 40; of social workers, 18

training programs: instruction re sexual attraction to patients in, 171–2; more education in, 193

transference: and malpractice charges, 20–1; causing re-enactment of past relationships, 20–1; characteristics of, 20–1; traumatic, 62–3, 86–7

trapped in abusive relationships, 12, 78–87

trauma, recognition of the psychological effects of, 15–17; combat neurosis, 16; hysteria, 15; post-traumatic stress disorder, 16; shell shock, 15

traumatic bonding, 79–81; abused children, 80; abusive marriages, 80; childhood abuse survivors, 80; hostages, 80; neurochemical theories, 80

traumatic transference, 62–3, 86–7

trust, decreased ability, 122–3

typologies: of abusers, 37–9

victim-blaming, 165–7; belief in a just world causing, 166–7; by community, 165–7; by inquiry boards, 173–4; by the legal system, 174–6; by pathologizing the victim, 170–1

victimization, three levels of, 116–20

Vietnam war, soldiers returning from, 150

Walker, Evelyn, 128

warning signs, of possible sexual exploitation, 55–6

women's socialization, 42–3, 82–3, 126

Women and Mental Health Committee of Canadian Mental Health Association, Manitoba Division, 117, 171, 191–2, 195

women's movement, 16, 196